Y0-BIU-746

ELEMENTS OF BIBLIOGRAPHY:

a simplified approach

Revised Edition

by

ROBERT B. HARMON

The Scarecrow Press, Inc.
Metuchen, N.J., & London
1989

British Library Cataloguing-in-Publication data available

Library of Congress Cataloging-in-Publication Data

Harmon, Robert B. (Robert Bartlett), 1932–
Elements of bibliography : a simplified approach / by Robert B. Harmon. — Rev. ed.
p. cm.
Bibliography: p.
Includes indexes.
ISBN 0-8108-2218-0 (alk. paper)
1. Bibliography—Methodology. 2. Bibliography—Bibliography. I. Title.
Z1001.H29 1989
010'.44—dc20 89-35367

Manufactured in the United States of America

Printed on acid-free paper

Dedicated to the Memory of

RALPH R. SHAW

and

RICHARD H. SHOEMAKER

No one has yet discovered why people become bibliographers—all that is known is that it is an instinctive impulse and that it starts imperceptibly at a very young age. The results are extraordinary: there are examples of bibliographers who have literally given up everything they possess to this task and even cases of bibliographers who have ruined themselves, their families, and driven themselves to an early grave in the vain hope of completing their bibliography. Why this should be so no one knows, but it is as much a phenomenon of life as the migrations of lemmings in Scandinavia.

ROBERT COLLISON

CONTENTS

PREFACE

When the first edition of *Elements of Bibliography* was published, there were few books available giving students and librarians a thorough guide to the literature. The response to the first edition seems to justify an updated edition, supplying new information and clarifications.

By design, this work is primarily a guide to the literature of bibliography; it is accompanied by basic standards for compiling various kinds of bibliographic instruments. The intended audience is, first, the prospective librarian and second, anyone who is compiling a bibliography. As a practicing reference librarian for over twenty-five years, I have found that librarians and others tend to create bibliographies that fail to provide enough accurate information for users to locate materials. Therefore, suggested standards and readings are cited that will assist in the compiling process.

For this edition, all entries were reviewed. Most were revised, some were deleted, and many new titles were added. The method of presentation is expository at the introductory level. While differing points of view are noted frequently, the book is not intended to provide definitive critical evaluation. Research is reviewed to indicate current thinking and activities in this wide-ranging field.

The chapters are arranged in a systematic sequence to provide the reader with a broad overview of bibliography and its numerous applications.

Chapter One outlines the dimensions and structure of the field followed by a historical survey in Chapter Two. The main objects or kinds of materials studied by bibliographers are covered in Chapter Three, and the specific branches of the field explored in greater detail in Chapters Four and Five.

The practical aspects of bibliographic compilation and evaluation are presented in Chapters Six and Seven. A new chapter exploring the dimensions of online bibliographic searching is given in Chapter Eight. Chapter Nine gives direction on possible areas of specialized training available to librarians and others in bibliographically related fields and Chapter Ten suggests future trends in the study of bibliography.

The final chapters, Eleven and Twelve, are annotated guides to reference sources and periodicals in the field. Five appendixes provide additional information for aspiring bibliographers followed by an extensive annotated bibliography arranged alphabetically by author or title entry. Detailed access to the entire work is provided by separate name, title, and subject indexes.

It is not a simple matter to conduct a search for subject materials, but it can be interesting, enlightening, and rewarding. I hope this guide will help prospective librarians and others become more effective and productive bibliographers.

ACKNOWLEDGMENTS

The material for this revised edition was drawn from a wide variety of sources with the help of many to whom I am deeply indebted. First, to San Jose State University I am grateful for granting me a sabbatical leave during the spring of 1988 that allowed me time to complete most of the work on the final manuscript.

Most particularly I wish to thank Roy Stokes and Jennifer McDowell for their careful, critical scrutiny of the entire manuscript, and their editorial suggestions. Much appreciation is also due Terry Crowley of the Division of Librarianship at San Jose State University for his review of the overall structure of the project and careful editing of the first four chapters. To my colleagues Sandra Belanger and Tina Brundage I owe thanks for their assistance with Chapter Eight which deals with online searching; their expertise was invaluable. Two other colleagues were also very helpful. Jeff Paul and his expertise with the camera and Bob McDermand and his special talent with the Macintosh were of great assistance in providing most of the illustrations. To them I am very appreciative. Gaining access to many materials not available locally was made possible through the assistance of the Interlibrary Loan staff at San Jose State under the direction of Jean Meyer. I appreciate their willingness to go the extra mile.

I owe a special debt of gratitude to several noted bibliographers for their assistance in locating specific materials and in answering particular queries. They include Dean Lawrence J. McCrank, Ferris State University, G. Thomas Tanselle, Vice President, John Simon Guggenheim Memorial Foundation, Fredson T. Bowers, University of Virginia, and Terry Belanger of Columbia University.

To the Grolier Club I express thanks for permission to use the title pages from Tritheim's *Liber de Scriptoribus Ecclesiasticis* and Gesner's *Bibliotheca Universalis* appearing on pages 29 and 38 respectively of their catalogue, *Bibliography, Its History and Development* (1984), as illustrations. Also I thank Elizabeth K. Lieberman for permission to use as an illustration, the piece of type appearing on page 10 of *Type and Typefaces*

(1978) by the late J. Ben Lieberman, published by The Myriade Press, Inc.

I am grateful to my wife, Merlynn, and my children who endured much during the time I have worked on this project. Their patience and understanding is much appreciated. As always, full responsibility for the entire work, mistakes and all, is of course mine alone.

Robert B. Harmon
Clark Library
San Jose State University

ABBREVIATIONS USED IN THE TEXT

AACR2	Anglo-American Cataloging Rules [Second edition]
BIP	Books in Print
BRS	Bibliographic Retrieval Service, Inc. [Search system]
CBI	Cumulative Book Index
CD-ROM	Compact Disk—Read Only Memory
CIS	Congressional Information Service
DIALOG	On-Line Search Service [Knight-Ridder]
ERIC	Educational Research Information Center
ISSN	International Standard Serial Number
LC	Library of Congress
LISA	Library and Information Science Abstracts [both hard-copy abstracts and database]
MEDLARS	Medical Literature Analysis and Retrieval System
OCLC	Online Computer Library Center, Inc.
ORBIT	On-Line Retrieval of Bibliographic Text [Search system]
PRECIS	PREserved Context Index System
RLIN	Research Libraries Information Network

Chapter One

THE DIMENSIONS OF BIBLIOGRAPHY

Introduction

What is bibliography? What areas or branches constitute its structure, and what roles and functions does it perform with respect to the dissemination of information and the advancement of knowledge. This task is not always easy because dozens of definitions exist reflecting various forms and emphases.

To some scholars, bibliography is a humanistic science: *humanistic* in the sense that it is devoted to the record of the minds of men and women; *scientific* in the sense that it is exceedingly rigorous, systematic, and analytical to the end of discovering the place of a work among all the works of one person; of that person among all others who ever lived and wrote; and of his or her works among those in all fields of concern to humankind.[1]

Bibliography also takes on both a general and comprehensive meaning. Like a large umbrella it covers a wide variety of functions and activities. Beneath its protective shield can be found amateurs and professionals, scholars and mechanics, dilettantes and the gainfully employed. Also within its confines one can find textual critics, indexers, and compilers; historians, scientists, and researchers; catalogers, reference librarians, and administrators.[2]

In the development of knowledge, bibliography is a secondary and contributing force, not a principal one, supporting and encouraging creative activity but not producing new knowledge. To sustain the sciences, humanities, and social sciences, bibliography must serve many masters, but not aimlessly.[3] However, attempting to know and understand more about bibliography in a modern context is beset with some difficulty.

The term, first of all, is much misunderstood, signifying both the art and craft as well as the artifact. Most of us fail to make the distinction between "a bibliography" and bibliography. In practice, the word has become pervasively associated with some kind of listing of books and other forms of published writings, or with enumerating materials in other recorded formats.[4] Since the beginning of the current century, bibliography has branched out into many areas that once were only the province of textual critics, printing historians, and several branches of applied science. Indeed in the information age bibliography has assumed a much broader role than that of a mere enumerative process.

As an independent field of study, bibliography is vast and dynamic, affecting almost every other area of knowledge. Especially in this era of rapid technological change and development along with increasing specialization, bibliography has reaped all the advantages and disadvantages inherent in this trend. Once practiced and understood by only a few, the field now incorporates hundreds of specialists with degrees of sophistication and maturity not anticipated a few short years ago. Of course, this specialization and diversity has created problems such that specialists have difficulty communicating with one another.[5] Despite this condition, however, bibliographic applications and techniques continue to expand to meet human information needs and to advance scholarship in many fields.

In the remainder of this chapter we will examine the meaning of the term *bibliography* both as to origin and current meaning. The main aspects or branches that make up the field currently will be identified and related to the entire structure. Bibliography in its practical and intellectual applications will be discussed, as will the role of the bibliographer within the bibliographic process.

Bibliography Defined

The word *bibliography* originated in post-classical Greece. It is derived from the Greek words *biblion* (meaning book) and *graphein* (meaning to write). The word originally meant "the writing of books."[6] The Greek *bibliographos* was a copyist of manuscripts, and bibliography was originally defined as "the mechanical writing and transcription of books, but not their construction." Later on bibliography included composition as well. This meaning persisted as late as the eighteenth century when in France its meaning changed from "the writing of books" to "writing about books." This new meaning did not take long to gain acceptance throughout France and later on in such countries as Germany and England.[7]

In attempting to ascertain current usage of the term, we find a great diversity of opinion among practitioners. As G. Thomas Tanselle has pointed out "everything in bibliography—including the meaning of the word itself—seems to give rise to controversy."[8] Bibliography, "suffers from its name."[9] The problem is not, however, that the word can no longer be precisely defined on the basis of its etymologically derived parts.[10] The problem today in English lies rather in the multiplicity of meanings assigned to the term "bibliography," as well as in the relationship between them, for bibliography is not a subject but a related group of subjects that happen to be commonly referred to by the same term.[11] This multiplicity of meanings is well documented by Percy Freer in a study published in 1954, where he cites fifty definitions given since 1678, most of them appearing after 1900.[12] Few of these definitions agree completely; many differ widely. Even statements at different times by the same author do not always agree.[13]

Looking at the term from a somewhat different perspective, Terry Belanger indicates that to the book collector, the word *bibliography* properly means *the study of books;* a *bibliographer* is one who studies them. But the word is shopworn. *Bibliography* has many common definitions, and because collectors, scholars, and librarians too often use the word indiscriminately, it lacks precision. For this reason, *bibliography* is often qualified by adjectives like enumerative, systematic, analytical, critical, descriptive, historical, or textual.[14]

Others believe that *bibliography* is an ambiguous and much abused term and that it is difficult to characterize because it is shared by all humanities, the humanistic components of all subject areas, and librarianship.[15]

An obvious conclusion from the foregoing is that in attempting to define the meaning of bibliography one has to contend with the problems of controversy, a multiplicity of meanings, indiscriminate usage, and some confusion between techniques of compilation and end product, i.e., bibliographies. Out of this mess, however, we can detect some elements of commonality. Most prominent of these is the book and its development from ancient times to the present in all of its physical aspects. There is also the recording and description of all types of graphic materials to provide identification of ideal copies and to achieve some semblance of bibliographic order or control over published and unpublished documents of various kinds.

Organization and Structure

Over the past few decades the organization and structure of bibliography has changed little except for the addition of new areas of emphasis. Essentially there are two broad classes that serve to differentiate the main branches of the subject. *Analytical* or *critical bibliography* is the study of books as physical objects, the details of their production, the effects of the method of manufacture on the text, and the like. As the science of the transmission of literary documents, analytical bibliography may deal with the history of printers and booksellers; with the description of paper, bindings, or with textual matters arising during the progression from writer's manuscript to published book.[16] By contrast *enumerative* or *systematic bibliography* involves the listing of books or other materials in an orderly arrangement.[17] In the past, bibliography has mostly concentrated on book materials. However, today both branches are concerned with other vehicles of ideas as well as books. Microforms of all kinds, databases, CD-ROMs, motion pictures, recording of various kinds, video tapes, and other graphic objects can be studied bibliographically.[18]

Three major subdivisions or specialized functions constitute *analytical* or *critical bibliography:* textual, historical, and descriptive. *Textual bibliography* is the study of the relationship between the printed text and the text as conceived by the author. In essence it deals with the study and comparison of texts and their transmission through different printings and editions. It is synonymous with textual criticism. *Historical* or *material bibliography* deals mainly with the history of books and of the persons, institutions, and machines producing them. This may range from technological history to the history of art in its concern with the evidence books provide about culture and society in specific eras of time. This type of bibliographic study may also include along with book production, binding, paper making, illustrating, and publishing. Closely associated with these two branches of the field is *descriptive bibliography* which is the detailed physical study and description of books, including details about the author, exact title, date, place, and circumstances of format, pagination, illustrations, binding and other physical details. A book or other material which is the object of such a study is subjected to a full physical description of the books and other works it includes, and normally deals with the output of a particular author, illustrator, publisher, period or place. [19]

As the more common and practical branch of the field, enumerative or systematic bibliography seeks to identify and describe in a systematic arrangement the books, other materials, or both that may be suitable for a particular purpose or that have other common characteristics.[20] There are many types of enumerative bibliographies,[21] but certain characteristics can be associated with most of them. Timeliness is one, and many bibliographies are issued regularly and limit their listings to publications of recent date. For example, the *Cumulative Book Index* and *American Book Publishing Record* are both periodical lists of new books. A second kind of listing, the retrospective list, includes whatever fits within its scope. Joseph Sabin's *Bibliotheca Americana: A Dictionary of Books Relating to America* is an example. Bibliographies may also be comprehensive or narrow or anywhere in between. The *Cumulative Book Index*, again, attempts to include all publications in English no matter where published, while *Booklist*, a review periodical published by the American Library Association (Chicago) since 1905, reviews only titles of probable interest to libraries. Bibliographies may or may not be annotated, but annotations, usually enhance the usefulness of any bibliography.

Uses and Functions of Bibliography

Both major sectors of bibliography have similar as well as differing functions and purposes. No discussion of bibliography, especially in its modern context, can neglect to mention its relation to the increasing demand for rapid and accurate methods of communicating information; and similarly its relation to the requirement for the rapid and accurate retrieval of information from the enormous accumulations of records on which contemporary civilization depends.[23]

Analytical bibliography serves as the vehicle of the textual critic in the continual quest to document any changes that occur in a manuscript from its creation to its printed or published form. A basic historical function is also provided by analytical bibliography in relating the mechanisms and tools of the printing trade to a particular historical period. In its descriptive function analytical bibliography assists in the identification process of specific documents. The tools and procedures of analytical bibliography have been useful in the exposure of literary forgeries such as the work by John Carter and Graham Pollard, published in 1934, uncovering the Thomas J. Wise forgeries. Also in recent times these methods were applied in exposing the Mark Hofmann forgeries of Mormon historical documents.[24] Booksellers and collectors depend on descriptive bibliographies to identify first editions and important literary works.

I. Study of graphic materials as physical entities or material objects:

		textural Bibliography: Study and comparison of texts and their transmission through editions and printings.
PURPOSE: Accurate, precise identification and description	Analytical or Critical Bibliography	Historical Bibliography: Placing and dating of individual books or other graphic materials.
		Descriptive Bibliography: Identification of the "ideal copy" and all its variants.

II. Study of graphic materials as intellectual entities:

PURPOSE: Assembling of information about individual books or other graphic materials into a logical and useful arrangement	Enumerative or Systematic Bibliography	Compilation of lists of books or other graphic materials: Author Bibliographies Lists of works by and about an author Bibliographies of Bibliographies Lists of bibliographies on any subject. Catalogs Lists of institutional holdings. Guides to the Literature Lists and "how to" information on any subject. National Bibliography Lists of works produced in one particular nation. Selective or Elective Bibliography Lists of "best books" in any subject Subject Bibliography Lists of materials on any subject. Trade Bibliography Lists of materials for the book trade. Universal Bibliography Lists of materials published in any country.

Figure No. 1. The Study of Bibliography

Enumerative or systematic bibliography attempts to bring order out of chaos. Given the enormous number of printed records extant, it seems almost impossible that enumerative or systematic bibliography can accomplish this ordering function. William A. Katz, the author of a widely used text in schools of library and information science, has indicated that regardless of form, a bibliography is used primarily for three basic purposes: (1) to identify and verify, (2) to locate, and (3) to select.

Identification and Verification

Most bibliographers provide standard information such as author, title, edition, place of publication, publisher, date of publication, a collation (i.e., number of pages, presence of illustrations, size), and sometimes price. Other information may also be added depending upon the purposes of the bibliography. In seeking to identify or verify any of these elements, a trained searcher will turn to an appropriate bibliography, usually beginning with one of the general titles, such as the *Cumulative Book Index* or *American Book Publishing Record*, and moving to the particular, such as a bibliography in a narrow subject area.[25]

Location

Location may refer to where a book is published, where it can be found in a library, or where it can be purchased. Just knowing that something exists is usually not enough. One needs to lay hands on a specific item in order to be able to use it.[26] Thus locating material is extremely important.

Selection

Whether it is your own personal library or that of a particular public, private, or academic institution, useful collecting according to some predetermined plan is of prime importance. In order to assist the selector, certain bibliographies indicate what is available in a given subject area, by a given author, in a given form, or for given groups of readers. A bibliography may give an estimate of the value of the particular work for a certain type of reader.[27] A selector needs to be familiar with a wide variety of bibliographies in order to be effective in the selection process.

On Bibliographers

Bibliography may be among the oldest professions, for there have been librarians, archivists, and bibliographers since there have been written records.[28] Relatively speaking, those who engage in only bibliographic pursuits are few. Practicing bibliographers are normally members of larger professional groups such as librarians, university professors, booksellers, collectors, etc.

Librarians as Bibliographers

Many librarians, whether in public, school, academic, or special libraries, are expected to participate in collection development. Such a task, if it is to be done well, demands that one become familiar with the collection. To do this the librarian can check comprehensive and critical bibliographies against the card catalog to reveal the strengths and weaknesses of the collection. One needs as well to check the shelf list and abstracting and indexing services. To carry out these activities, one must have a knowledge of trade bibliographies and other sources of authoritative bibliographic information. Many librarians have received much of the preliminary training in the use of such tools in schools of library and information science, but expertise in using them is gained on the job.[29] As a consequence one must keep abreast of new sources as they become available and be able to utilize them effectively. This includes new bibliographic databases that are now available on CD-ROM such as *Books In Print*.

The term "bibliographer" can also be applied to librarians verifying bibliographic information for acquisitions purposes or to catalogers, who must be able to use highly specialized bibliographic tools and mechanized information-retrieval systems, such as the Research Libraries Network (RLIN) and the Online Computer Library Center, Inc. (OCLC).

Another major bibliographic activity that librarians perform is helping patrons obtain information. This may be done in several ways: by answering reference questions of varying degrees of difficulty, by teaching their bibliographic specialties to others in the classroom, by preparing ready reference lists, or by compiling different types of bibliographic lists on specific subjects.

Booksellers as Bibliographers

Knowledge of and expertise in the use of bibliographic tools are essential for the bookseller. Here the divisions of the field to consider are trade bibliography, author bibliography, and subject bibliography. Each of these divisions requires a technique to be mastered and used as a tool by those who are asked to compile buying lists, to search for accurate information about published material in book form, and to answer questions about books in print.[30]

Booksellers must on occasion trace and record details of authorship, editions, scope, contents, and grade of selected literature of a subject. They may also be expected to evaluate books on subjects within their particular areas of expertise.[31]

Antiquarian booksellers will need to pursue this fascinating topic even further, for the demands of book collectors are usually more specialized and erudite than those of the average customer. Dealers in first editions and secondhand, out-of-print, and scarce books and manuscripts will be required to extend their studies to descriptive or other aspects of analytical bibliography.[32]

Scholars as Bibliographers

Analytical bibliography is mostly the domain of the scholar and is designed primarily to provide positive and incontrovertible identification of books. Scholar-bibliographers must be acquainted with the physical characteristics of books: format, number of pages, typography, and the number and description of plates. They must know the important distinctions between editions and the nature of omissions and additions and the reasons for them. When books have been published anonymously or pseudonymously, bibliographers must attempt to indicate the real name of the concealed author and must expose the false attribution when a book has been spuriously or erroneously ascribed to another author. They must provide date and place of publication when it is omitted from the title page or colophon and correct these important items when they have been purposely or inadvertently altered. Bibliographers must know something about rare books and the circumstances that have contributed to their scarcity. Finally they must have more than a nodding acquaintance with the many kinds of literary fraud, with printed editions and, even more reprehensible, editions secretly issued by an unauthorized publisher.[33]

Much of the scholarly activity within analytical bibliography seems to be carried on by literary critics, many of whom teach English or literature on the college level.

Characteristics of the Bibliographer

No matter what their vocation, bibliographers seem to have a penchant for detail and a liking for penury. Quoted below is a doggerel written by a noted bibliographer that gives us some insight into the bibliographer's plight.

TO A BIBLIOGRAPHER, WITH A
PRESENT OF DRIED BAY LEAVES

When Homer smote his bloomin' lyre
The people flocked from croft and town:
Most came to hear and to admire,
But one man came to write it down,
Another matched him, note for note,
Observing with a clerky air
Not what but how it was he wrote.

Thus bard and scribe and bibliog-
Rapher began their endless race;
Sing, publish, and then catalogue
Whatever issues we can trace.

The poet won his wreath of bays;
The publisher gained cold hard cash;
The third man earned nor coin nor praise;
But old leaves out of Homer's trash.

These leaves are withered, sere, and dry,
And if you flaunt them, men will stare;
So cook them in a pizza pie,
Don't try to wear them in your hair.[34]

A bibliographer's work is often quite technical. The search for information, especially in the absence of definite clues, not only consumes time, energy, and eyesight but causes great consternation, often all out of proportion to the importance of the items sought. But bibliography can hardly be recommended as an occupation for completely sane persons. What really intelligent individual would spend hours leafing through the files of a daily newspaper or issues of a periodical for a single minor contribution just to be able to list it? Or pay a high price for some piece of trivia because there seemed to be no other way of locating a copy? Or pester a publisher, printer, or binder in order to establish the number of copies actually issued of a particular book?[35]

And all for what purpose? Not for financial gain, surely. As the doggerel points out, there are very few bibliographers who have earned substantial sums for either their compilers or their publishers. And not for lasting fame either: most bibliographies are out of date before they are published. Furthermore, if a bibliography is published on a subject of continuing importance, it will soon be superseded, and, otherwise, be quickly forgotten.[36]

In spite of all this, bibliographers seem determined to continue their work, even though at times beset by ridiculous difficulties. Elliott Coues, writing in 1897 about his monumental but never-completed *Universal Bibliography of Ornithology*, stated:

> I never did anything else in my life which brought me such . . . praise . . . and immediate . . . recognition, at home and abroad, from ornithologists who knew that bibliography was a necessary nuisance and a horrible drudgery that no mere drudge could perform. It takes a sort of inspired idiot to be a good bibliographer, and his inspiration is as dangerous a gift as the appetite of the gambler or dipsomaniac—it grows with what it feeds upon, and finally possesses its victim like any other invincible vice.[37]

The noted bibliographer Robert L. Collison has said that

> there is something very satisfying in handling a well-constructed bibliography; the care and enthusiasm with which the bibliographer has applied himself to the task is reflected in the thoughtful annotations, the ample cross-references, and the careful selection of material, so that users are continually being directed to new and unsuspected resources, their minds stimulated by new ideas, and their conception of their subjects enriched by the indication of new fields as yet unexplored. The finished product, if good, reads so easily that few give thought to the arduous and exacting nature of the task that confronts every bibliographer anew.[38]

Every bibliographer, whether a student, a bookseller, a collector, a librarian, or a scholar, faces the same series of questions. When we pick up a book, for instance, we want to identify it as precisely as possible, locate where it stands in the hierarchy of editions, determine what its importance is, and generally settle its hash. Needless to say, we give the questions different weights depending on whether we happen to want to buy a book, sell a book, or study some aspects of a book. Bibliography provides the motive power to move a book into a shop, out of a shop, into a private collection or a library, and off the shelf into a critical or historical study of an edition.[39]

Alfred William Pollard, in a presidential address to the Bibliographical Society (London) said: "What then is the business of the bibliographer? Primarily and essentially, I should say, the enumeration of books. His is the lowly task of finding out what books exist, and thereby helping to secure their preservation, and furnishing the specialist with information as to the extent of the subject matter with which he has to deal."[40] Daily, throughout the world, a spate of books and other graphic materials is published or produced. Within many subjects, in many languages, huge numbers of ideas spill out in random order, much as do stock quotations on the high-speed ticker of the New York Stock Exchange. So that most people can understand them, the stock quotations must be arranged in a regular alphabetical table, with the day's high, low, and closing prices indicated. Bibliographers do much the same with the mass of material they find. They collect, classify, describe, and arrange.[41] The process of description of books in many cases involves analytical bibliography, so that a true enumeration of the editions, states, and issues of the same title may be made, for how can lists be made unless the objects are really identified? Of books this is true, but of ideas and words, not so. They are not physical objects and therefore cannot be studied as such. Bibliography is now extended to cover ideas. Here the idea is supreme, and the physical object is all but forgotten.[42]

Enumerative bibliography has become a tremendously broad field and threatens to become even more extensive as books and ideas multiply. The bibliographer in today's world is faced with an almost infinite number of tasks that might be undertaken. The labor is often arduous and difficult and has minimal monetary remuneration, but for those who like this kind of work, the satisfaction is great. Esdaile has written that the bibliographer, in the seclusion of libraries, is not the dusty and bloodless creature often pictured but a bona fide detective engaged in a thrilling kind of hunt.[43]

Summary

Arising out of a basic need to bring order to and provide access to the mass of written and printed documents produced by human beings since the beginning of recorded time, bibliography has emerged as a primary element in this ordering and access process. Many definitions have been given to describe what bibliography is and does but there is still disagreement among practitioners as to bibliography's precise meaning and functions.

In practice, bibliography can be structured into two broad areas of activity, one dealing with graphic materials as physical entities or material objects (Analytical or Critical), or as intellectual entities (Enumerative or Systematic), with various subdivisions.

Both analytical and enumerative bibliography have a variety of functions all of which assist in the ordering and retrieval of information and the advancement of knowledge in almost every subject field. With the activities of bibliographers working in a number of related professions down through the centuries, we have seen the development of vast information networks and sophisticated bibliographic tools that aid in the ordering and dissemination of recorded information.

For those whose work is concerned with these records a knowledge of the forms and conventions of bibliography becomes a necessity, because a bibliography is the line that links scholar to scholar across geographical boundaries and offers unlimited possibilities.[44]

Selected Related Writings

BIBLIOGRAPHY

Clapp, Verner W. "Bibliography." *Encyclopedia Americana,* 3 (1983), pp. 721–724.

Francis, Sir Frank C. "Bibliography." *The New Encyclopaedia Britannica,* 1 (1983), pp. 978–981.

Shoemaker, Richard H. "Bibliography (General)." *Library Trends,* 15 (January 1967), pp. 340–346.

Stokes, Roy *The Function of Bibliography*. 2nd ed. Aldershot, Eng.: Gower, 1982.

BIBLIOGRAPHERS

Bond, William H. "Bibliography and Bibliographers." *AB Bookman's Weekly,* 47 (April 26, 1971), pp. 1395–1397.

D'Aniello, Charles. "Bibliography and the Beginning Bibliographer." *Collection Building,* 6 (Summer 1984), pp. 11–19.

Kumar, Girja and Krishan. *Bibliography*. New Delhi: Vikas Publishing House, 1976. See Chapter XVII (pp. 215–225).

Smith, F. Seymour. *Bibliography in the Bookshop*. 2nd ed. London: Deutsch, 1972.

Notes

1. David C. Weber, "Bibliographical Blessings," *Papers of the Bibliographical Society of America,* 61 (October/December 1967), p. 307.

2. Neal R. Harlow, "The Well-Tempered Bibliographer," *Papers of the Bibliographical Society of America,* 50 (1956), p. 28.

3. Ibid.

4. Michael Keresztesi, "The Science of Bibliography: Theoretical Implications for Bibliographic Instruction," In: *Theories of Bibliographic Education, Designs for Teaching*. Edited by Cerise Oberman and Katarina Strauch. (New York: Bowker, 1982), p. 5.

5. Roy Stokes, *The Function of Bibliography*. 2nd ed. (Aldershot, Eng.: Gower, 1982), p. ix. Stokes deals somewhat with the problem of specialization within the field which is possibly more prevalent than we realize.

6. Charles Barrett Brown, *The Contribution of Greek to English*. (Nashville, TN: Vanderbilt University Press, 1942), pp. 29, 78.

7. The origin and changes that have occurred in the use of the term "Bibliography" are treated at some length in the following works: Rudolph Blum, *Bibliographia: An Inquiry into its Definition and Designations*. (Chicago: American Library Association; London: Dawson, 1980), pp. 12–77; Louise-Noëlle Malclès, *Bibliography*. (Metuchen, NJ: Scarecrow Reprint, 1973), © 1961, pp. 1–9; and Roy Stokes, *The Function of Bibliography*. 2nd ed. (Aldershot, Eng.: Gower, 1982), pp. 1–15.

8. G. Thomas Tanselle, "The State of Bibliography Today," *Papers of the Bibliographical Society of America,* 73 (July/September 1979), p. 289.

9. Walter Wilson Greg, "What is Bibliography?" *Transactions of the Bibliographical Society* (London), 12 (1914), p. 40.

10. Ross Atkinson, "An Application of Semiotics to the Definition of Bibliography," *Studies in Bibliography,* 33 (1980), p. 56.

11. G. Thomas Tanselle, "Bibliography as a Science," *Studies in Bibliography,* 27 (1974), p. 88.

12. Percy Freer, *Bibliography and Modern Book Production*. (Johannesburg: Witwatersrand University Press, 1954), pp. 1–13.

13. Paul S. Dunkin, *Bibliography: Tiger or Fat Cat?* (Hamden, CT: Anchor Books, 1975), p. 7. Dunkin further states that "any definition of bibliography is a statement of personal experience and belief."

14. Terry Belanger, "Descriptive Bibliography," In: *Book Collecting: A Modern Guide*. Edited by Jean Peters. (New York: Bowker, 1977), p. 99.

15. Lawrence J. McCrank, "Analytical and Historical Bibliography: A State of the Art Review," In: *Annual Report of the American Rare, and Out-of-Print Book Trade, 1978/79*. Edited by Denis Carbonneau. (New York: BCAR Publications, 1979), p. 175.

16. See Belanger, pp. 99–100.

17. Verner W. Clapp, "Bibliography," *Encyclopedia Americana*. (1983), Vol. 3, p. 721.

18. Richard H. Shoemaker, "Bibliography (General)," *Library Trends,* 15 (January 1967), p. 340.

19. *The ALA Glossary of Library and Information Science*. Edited by Heartsill Young, et al. (Chicago: American Library Association, 1983), p. 72.

20. See Clapp, p. 721.

21. Back in the early 1950s it was estimated that there were possibly 9,600 to 147,456 different kinds of bibliographies. Unesco/Library of Congress Bibliographic Survey. *Bibliographical Services, Their Present State and Possibilities of Improvement. . .* .(Washington, D.C.: 1950), paragraph 2.1. Also cited in Neal R. Harlow, "Bibliographers in an Age of Science," *Revue de l'Université d'Ottawa*, 23 (January/March 1953), p. 41.

22. See Clapp, p. 722.

23. Ibid., p. 724.

24. For a treatment of the Hofmann forgeries see "A Scandal In America: Part I." (authorship unclear) appearing in *The Book Collector*, 36 (Winter 1987), pp. 449–470.

25. William A. Katz, *Introduction to Reference Work: Volume I. Basic Information Sources*. 5th ed. (New York: McGraw-Hill, 1987), pp. 58–59.

26. Ibid., p. 59.

27. Ibid.

28. Neal R. Harlow, "The Well-Tempered Bibliographer," *Papers of the Bibliographical Society of America*, 50 (1956), p. 28.

29. Manuel D. Lopez, "A Guide for Beginning Bibliographers," *Library Resources and Technical Services*, 13 (Fall 1969), pp. 463–464.

30. F. Seymour Smith, *Bibliography in the Bookshop*. 2nd ed. (London: Deutsch, 1972), pp. 18–19.

31. Ibid.

32. Ibid.

33. Gustave O. Arlt, "Bibliography—An Essential Piece of Equipment," *Library Journal*, 86 (April 15, 1961), p. 1540.

34. William H. Bond, "Bibliography and Bibliographers," *AB Bookman's Weekly*, 47 (April 26, 1971), p. 1395. Dr. Bond was the head librarian at Harvard's Houghton Library for many years. He is a true scholar-librarian-bibliographer.

35. Donald Clifford Gallup, *On Contemporary Bibliography, with Particular Reference to Ezra Pound*. (Austin, TX: Humanities Research Center, University of Texas, 1970), p. 7.

36. Ibid., p. 8.

37. Elliott Coues, "Dr. Coues' Column," *The Osprey*, 2 (November 1897), p. 39.

38. Robert Collison, *Bibliography, Subject and National*. 3rd ed. (New York: Hafner, 1968), p. xiii.

39. See Bond, p. 1395.

40. Alfred William Pollard, "Practical Bibliography," *The Library* (London), New Series, 4 (April 1903), p. 158.

41. See Shoemaker, p. 341.

42. Ibid.

43. Arundell J. K. Esdaile, *A Student's Manual of Bibliography*. 3rd ed., revised by Roy Stokes. (New York: Barnes and Noble, 1954), p. 32.

44. Girja and Krishan Kumar, *Bibliography*. (New Delhi: Vikas Publishing House, Ltd., 1976), pp. 215–216.

Chapter Two

HISTORICAL SURVEY

Although bibliography had its beginnings in antiquity, it is a lusty infant in swaddling clothes. Sired scarcely four centuries ago by Conrad Gesner, christened during the eighteenth century by DeBure when he produced his *Bibliographie instructive*, the entry of bibliography into the field of learning has been comparatively recent.[1] Throughout its historical development, bibliography has been a flexible yet persistent discipline which has endured by constant adaptation to changing needs.

Beginnings

The listing of books is of ancient origin. There had been such lists of clay tablets even in the library of Sennacherib at Nineveh in the 7th century B.C.[2] Thus, in tracing the beginnings of bibliographical study one can detect, in the compilation of catalogs of books contained in the great collections of classical times, the embryo of an aspiring discipline. Another example is the famous library at Alexandria in the third century B.C., which contained the most extensive collection of Greek literature in the ancient world. At least two catalogs were prepared by order of Ptolemy Philadelphus, one listing tragedies, and the other comedies. Librarians of the Alexandrian library were primarily bibliographers and this was a major part of their responsibilities. It is certainly true that collection building and the preparation of a catalog, both essentially bibliographic functions, were very highly developed arts in Alexandria.[3]

For a period of time the Greek poet Callimachus was a librarian at Alexandria. He compiled a critical catalog, entitled *Pinakes* (Lists), that included the more important books in the library, which he arranged under 120 subjects. Another well known Greek, Galen, a physician of the second century A.D., on a somewhat smaller scale compiled a list of his own books. Since Galen was such a prolific writer, it is not at all surprising that he would need such a catalog. This work, entitled *De Libris Propriis Liber*, is a classified arrangement of his writings into seventeen groups under such headings as commentaries, moral philosophies, grammar, and so on.[4]

A close relationship to biography is quite evident in early bibliographies because most of them were lists of an author's works included in a biography. It has not been possible to determine at what point bibliographies became separated from these biographies and became the main object of a compiler. We do know, however, that during the fifth century A.D. St. Jerome, 347–420, the translator of the Vulgate Bible into Latin, and Gennadius of Marseilles (fl. late 5th century, Marseilles), a theologian and priest, both compiled separate bibliographies that bore the same title, *De viris illustribus* ("On Famous Men"). St. Jerome did say that his work should have been more correctly entitled *De Scriptoribus Ecclesiasticis* ("On Ecclesiastical Writers"). Throughout succeeding centuries many bio-bibliographies made their appearance.[5] The first example of a bibliography appended to a book other than a biography was *The Ecclesiastical History of Britain* (A.D. 731) by English historian and scholar the Venerable Bede.

Middle Period

The need to record the books contained in large collections was felt even in early medieval times. This trend was well documented by the catalogs that are known to have existed of various medieval libraries. During this period there was also some isolated examples of catalogs which recorded the existence of books on a much wider scale. As an example, a catalog compiled by Franciscan monks in the 14th century entitled *Registrum librorum Angliciae*, contains a list of manuscripts in over 180 English monasteries. In about the same period of time a similar but single-handed attempt at the same thing was made by John Boston, a Benedictine monk of Bury around 1410. In this work entitled *Catalogus scriptorum ecclesias*, Boston cataloged the collections of some 195 religious houses in England and Scotland. He listed, under their names, the writings of about 700 authors and also included their names under the books of the Bible about which they had written. The locations of the books are shown by numbers used to identify the holding libraries, a method used by bibliographers today. Although it is far from complete, many consider this work to be the first example of a union catalog, i.e., a catalog showing locations of titles in several libraries.[6]

So far the examples discussed above have been catalogs rather than bibliographies. The point here is that materials contained in a bibliography are not necessarily restricted to a single collection, library, or group of libraries. Bibliographies may confine themselves to one topic, a particular period of time, the works by or about a particular author, or both, and so on, but the works listed and described may well be located throughout libraries in many countries. The first true bibliographies, as separate entities, were those produced by Johann Tritheim (1462–1516), abbot of Sponheim, toward the end of the fifteenth century. He compiled an extensive bibliography of ecclesiastical writers, entitled *Liber de scriptoribus ecclesiasticis* (1494), published in Basle by Johann Amerbach.[7] In this work he lists about 7,000 books under their authors, arranged in chronological order from Alexander, bishop of Cappodocia, down to himself. He also added an alphabetical index of authors, arranged by their Christian names.[8] In the following year (1495), Tritheim's second bibliography, *Catalogus illustrium virorum Germaniae,* was published in Mainz at the press of Peter von Frieberg, recording the writings of the most prominent German authors. Over 2,000 works are listed by more than 300 authors, also arranged chronologically.[9]

The Modern Period

Following the invention of printing toward the middle of the fifteenth century, and the resulting increase in book production, the need to record and control bibliographically this literary outpouring also increased. However, it was a number of years before any significant attempt was made. Eventually, in 1545 Conrad Gesner (1516–1566), the Swiss-German doctor, writer, and naturalist, published his monumental *Bibliotheca universalis* (Universal bibliography), in which he recorded about 12,000 books written as printed in Latin, Greek, and Hebrew. The entries are arranged alphabetically by author (complete with biographical details) and include title, date, place of publication, and the name of the publisher. Gesner frequently gives an indication of a book's contents or extracts from the book itself. For sources of information Gesner visited many libraries and secured booksellers' catalogs and their published works, including Tritheim's bio-bibliography.[10]

LIBER

Quæstiones uarias:	li.	j	
In libros Ethicorū:	li.	x	
In Philosophia morali:	li.	j	

Hic etiam composuit officium stigmatum sancti Francisci ordinis minorum institutoris. In multos denique Bibliæ libros cōmētarios edidisse dicitur: qui ad manus nostras adhuc minime uenerūt. Claruit sub Ludouico bauaro imperatore quarto & Iohanne papa. xxij. Anno domini Millesimo. CCC. XXX.

n Icolaus de Lyra: natione Anglicus: ordinis fratrum minorū: uir in scripturis sanctis studiosissimus: & longa exercitatione peritus: hebraica lingua ad perfectum instructus: ingenio promptus: sermone scholasticus: nec minus conuersatione q̄ scientia uenerandus: Scripsit in sacris uoluminibus multa præclara opuscula: quibus nomē suum ad noticiā posteritatis deuenit. Quæ q̄ utilia quāq; necessaria sint oīibus sacrā scripturā discere cupientibus: nemo melius nouit: q̄ qui se in eorum lectione exercitauit. Sunt eñ qui eum ob eloquij simplicitatē estimēt cōtemnēdū: qui mihi uidētur & uani & imperiti ac sacræ scientiæ salutaris philosophiæ indigni: quoniā & simplicitatē ecclesiasticā uituperant: & uerba non res amplectuntur. De opusculis autem huius deuoti & eruditi uiri subiecta feruntur:

Super sententias:	li.	iiij	
In Genesim ad litterā:	li.	j	In principio &c̄. Omissis.
In Exodum:	li.	j	Scd'm qd' dicit Isidorus.
In Leuiticum:	li.	j	Vocauit aūt Mo. &c̄. Sicut
In Numeros:	li.	j	Locutus est dn̄s &c̄. Ex.
In Deuteronomiū:	li.	j	Declaratio sermonū tuoꝝ.
In Iosue:	li.	j	Introduces eos & plan.
In Iudicum:	li.	j	Suscitauit dn̄s iudices.
In Ruth:	li.	j	In dieb⁹ &c̄. Hic cōsequē.
In Regum:	li.	iiij	Per me reges regnant.
In Paralipomenon:	li.	ij	Colligite fragmenta.
In Esdram & Neemiā:	li.	iij	Erit sacerdos super sol'.
In Tobiam:	li.	j	Hæc oportuit facere &c̄.
In Iudith:	li.	j	Arfaxat &c̄. Post historias.
In Hester:	li.	j	In diebus &c̄. Postquam.
In Iob:	li.	j	Patientiā habe in me &c̄.
In Psalterium:	li.	j	Propheta magn⁹ surrexit.
In Prouerbia Salomonis.	li.	j	Ecce descripsi eam tibi tri.
In Ecclesiasten:	li.	j	Verba ecclia stes. sicut dic.
In Canticacanticorū:	li.	j	Osculetur me &c̄. Expedi.
In librū Sapientiæ:	li.	j	Post libros historiales.
In Ecclesiasticum:	li.	j	Oīis sapiētia &c̄. Hic inci.
In Esaiam ꝓphetam:	li.	j	Hierusalē euangelistā da.
In Hieremiā:	li.	j	Prophetā in gentib⁹ dedi.
In Threnos hieremiæ:	li.	j	Quō sedet. In præcedēti.
In librū Baruch:	li.	j	Hæc uerba &c̄. Post librū.
In Ezechielem:	li.	j	Aperti sunt cæli &c̄
In Danielem:	li.	j	Danieli aūt dedit deus.
In. xij. ꝓphetas minores:	li.	j	Duodecim ꝓphetarū ossa.
In Machabæorū:	li.	ij	Et factū est &c̄. Post histo.
In euangeliū Matthæi:	li.	j	Quattuor facies uni et.
In Marcum:	li.	j	Facies leonis a dextris.
In Lucam:	li.	j	Facies bouis a sinistris.

Figure No. 2. Page from Tritheim's *Liber De Scriptoribus Ecclesiasticis* (1494)
Courtesy the Grolier Club

BIBLIOTHECA

Vniuerſalis, ſiue Catalogus omni-
um ſcriptorum locupletiſſimus, in tribus linguis, Latina, Græca, & Hebraica: extantium & non extantiũ, ueterum & recentiorum in hunc uſq;
diem, doctorum & indoctorum, publicatorum & in Bibliothecis laten-
tium. Opus nouum, & nõ Bibliothecis tantum publicis priuatisue in-
ſtituendis neceſſarium, ſed ſtudioſis omnibus cuiuſcunq; artis aut
ſcientiæ ad ſtudia melius formanda utiliſſimum: authore
CONRADO GESNERO Tigurino doctore medico.

TIGVRI APVD CHRISTOPHORVM
Froſchouerum Menſe Septembri, Anno
M. D. XLV.

Figure No. 3.
Title Page from Gesner's
Bibliotheca Universalis (1545)
Courtesy the Grolier Club

In 1548 the first national bibliography, or one devoted to the writers of one nation, entitled *Illustrium majoris Brittaniae Scriptorum hoc est Angliae, Cambriae ac Scotiae summarium,* was compiled by John Bale, chronicler and perhaps the earliest playwright in the English language.[11] This bio-bibliographical work, in which English writers were arranged in chronological order, was prepared in order to save from oblivion the rich resources of monastic libraries that had been suppressed or partially destroyed. Bale, like Gesner, visited libraries and corresponded with scholars when he did not have access to specific books.

Of course, the most far-reaching impact upon the development of bibliography was the invention of the printing press in the fifteenth century and the resulting increase in the number of published books. Trade bibliographies, and book lists prepared by booksellers made their appearance in Germany, where Frankfurt and Leipzig became the centers of the German and foreign book trade. Along with the establishment of seasonal book fairs in these cities, first the dealers and later city governments published what can be considered genuine trade bibliographies.[12]

We find that by the eighteenth century, bibliography had become recognized as a distinct area of knowledge. The number of bibliographical classification schemes increased, and the theoretical foundations of the field were explored by various writers. Libraries began printing catalogs of their collections. Among the most notable of these were Leyden (1710), Oxford (1738), and the Bibliothèque Royale (1743).[13]

Close on the heels of Germany in the development of bibliography was France, particularly after the book fairs had ceased in the eighteenth century. One of the more important French bibliographies was J. C. Brunet's *Manual du libraire et de l'amateur de livres,* first published in 1810, but frequently enlarged. Brunet arranged his entries by authors and added an index of subjects. For each work he provided a reasonably detailed description, which included technical information on the pagination, the number of lines to the page, the signing of gatherings, and so forth, as well as notes on editions and sale prices.[14] The first bibliographies of bibliographies were lists of library catalogs. Philippe Labbé's *Bibliotheca bibliothecarum* (1671) is a good example.[15] Julius Petzholdt published in 1866 his *Bibliotheca bibliographica,* which in arrangement, fullness of bibliographical detail, accuracy, and reliability is still the authority for the books included.

With the advent of the nineteenth century, bibliography had become firmly established as a major tool in academic research, which it continues to be today. Basic works on the theoretical aspects of bibliography began to consider the problems of enumerative, critical, historical, and selective bibliographies. Also bibliographical journals were created to keep abreast of current trends.[16]

An important aspect in the development of bibliography as a discipline was the emergence of the bibliographical society toward the end of the nineteenth century. Generally these societies are associations of professional scholars or amateurs interested in collecting information about books. Some promote the study of literature, the art of bookmaking, book preservation, or book collecting. Others sponsor historical research on books and issue papers or transactions containing such research. The membership of these groups includes college and university professors, librarians, teachers, rare-book dealers, and collectors.[17]

Of these societies the oldest is the Bibliographical Society, London, founded in 1892. The Bibliographical Society of America was founded in 1904 as a continuation on a national scale of the Bibliographical Society of Chicago, which was founded in 1899.[18] Perhaps the most scholarly society in the United States is the Bibliographical Society of the University of Virginia, founded in 1947, a leader in analytical bibliography, with worldwide membership. As a whole these organizations provide a vehicle for growth and development of their members within the discipline.

Contemporary Period

At the turn of the present century, came the next great change in bibliographical study. The groundwork for the physical examination and description of books had been laid by such earlier bibliographers as Ludwig Hain in his monumental work *Repertorium bibliographicum*, 4 vols. (1826–38); Henry Bradshaw (1831–1886), for many years librarian of the Cambridge University Library; Robert Proctor, who in the nineties was engaged in cataloging incunabula in the Bodleian Library and later in the British Museum; and numerous others of lesser note.[19] Now instead of simply compiling lists, the bibliographer was gradually being influenced to undertake a study of all the processes involved in the making of books. This in turn led to the belief that the bibliographer could, by such investigation, shed some light on certain literary problems concerned with the transmission of text, from the author's manuscript to the completed printed book.[20]

This "new bibliography" is now the field of analytical or critical bibliography. It flourished mostly in Great Britain during the first years of this century with the works and writings of such well know bibliographers as Sir Walter Wilson Greg, Sir Stephen Gaselee, Alfred William Pollard, and Ronald Brunlees McKerrow. McKerrow's *An Introduction to Bibliography for Literary Students*, first published in 1927 was the first general attempt to examine the use of printing materials and methods of Elizabethan times and to relate them both to the transmission of text from the author's manuscript to the printed copy and to the changes appearing in later editions.[21] About mid-century the main activity in this area of bibliographic study seemed to swing to the other side of the Atlantic with the publication of *Principles of Bibliographical Description* (1949) by Fredson Bowers and many of subsequent studies. In recent years there have been a number of new works published, the most notable of which is *A New Introduction to Bibliography* by Philip Gaskell, published in 1974.

Related to enumerative or systematic bibliography there have been several important works published over the past few decades. There is Anthony M. L. Robinson's *Systematic Bibliography* now in its 4th edition (1979), and more recently Donald W. Krummel's extensive study *Bibliographies: Their Aims and Methods* (1984).

Current Status of Bibliography

The outlines of bibliography have thus expanded greatly since the beginnings of recorded history. Even with this extensive history of growth and development it has only been in the last fifty years that bibliographic study has achieved recognition as a separate and distinct branch of scholarship. This trend indeed reflects the current state of civilized society with its tremendous expansion of scientific and technical knowledge. The result of this information explosion is that the demands now made on bibliography are as vast as the scientific and technical advances themselves that it must document and control.[22]

Perhaps the leading exponent of analytical bibliography today is G. Thomas Tanselle, who believes that analytical bibliography is not simply an ancillary discipline but is of interest in its own right, by providing statistical evidence about printing and publishing practices. He admonishes analytical bibliographers to integrate their study into, and expand in conjunction with, the body of work on printing, publishing, and book-trade history. Analytical bibliography, Transelle asserts, must mature in developing a more rigorous self discipline.[23]

In discussing the relationship of analytical and enumerative bibliography, Marcia J. Bates indicates that there has been a longstanding dispute among bibliographers as to the primacy of each branch. She suggests that enumerative bibliography has possibly earned disdain only because it has been woefully underdeveloped, not because it is intrinsically a trivial activity. Her analysis attempts to establish a rationale for the disciplinary equality of enumerative bibliography.[24]

A contrasting view is offered by Jackson R. Bryer, who contends that the value of enumerative bibliography surpasses that of analytical bibliography in that the finished products are of more practical use if they are done well. He points out that an enumerative bibliography is probably used by a wider readership than a descriptive bibliography or textual study.[25]

There seems to be little doubt as to the status of bibliographic study today regardless of the branch. Over the years there have evolved many classic works in the field, a solid theoretical foundation, and a disciplinary self-awareness, all hallmarks of a vibrant and valid field of application and study. Now with the addition of electronic databases and information networks, bibliography is taking on new dimensions which have far reaching implications.

Selected Related Writings

Besterman, Theodore. *The Beginnings of Systematic Bibliography*. 2nd ed. New York: Burt Franklin, 1968, © 1936. (Reprint)

Blum, Rudolph. *Bibliographia: An Inquiry into Its Definition and Designations*. Translated from the German by Mathilde V. Rovelstad. London: Dawson; Chicago: American Library Association, 1980.

Breslauer, Bernard H. and Roland Folter. *Bibliography: Its History and Development*. New York: Grolier Club, 1984.

Condit, Lester. "Bibliography in Its Prenatal Existence," *Library Quarterly*, 7 (October 1937), pp. 564–576.

Fulton, John Farquhar. *The Great Medical Bibliographers: A Study in Humanism*. Philadelphia: University of Pennsylvania Press, 1951.

Harlow, Neal R. "The Well-Tempered Bibliographer," *The Papers of the Bibliographical Society of America*, 50 (1956), pp. 28–39.

Malclès, Louise Noëlle. *Bibliography*. Translated by Theodore Christian Hines. Metuchen, NJ: Scarecrow Reprint, 1973, © 1961.

Nash, N. Frederick. "Enumerative Bibliography from Gesner to James," *Library History*, 7, No. 1 (1985), pp. 10–20.

Padwick, Eric William. *Bibliographical Method: An Introductory Survey*. Cambridge, Eng.: James Clarke, 1969. See Chapter I (pp. 1–12).

Pollard, Alfred William. *Alfred William Pollard: A Selection of His Essays*. Compiled by Fred W. Roper. Metuchen, NJ: Scarecrow Press, 1976.

Schneider, Georg. *Theory and History of Bibliography*. Translated by Ralph Robert Shaw. New York: Columbia University Press, 1934. See Part 5 (pp. 271–293).

Notes

1. Lester Condit, "Bibliography in its Prenatal Existence," *Library Quarterly*, 7 (October 1937), p. 564. Condit is referring here to Guillaume François DeBure (1731–1782).

2. Mukunda Lal Chakraborti, *Bibliography in Theory and Practice*. 2nd ed., rev. (Calcutta: World Press, 1975), p. 4.

3. Sir Stephen Gaselee, "The Aims of Bibliography," *The Library*, 13, no. 3 (December 1932), p. 229.

4. Eric William Padwick, *Bibliographical Method: An Introductory Survey*. (Cambridge: James Clarke, 1969), p. 1. A more detailed survey of Galen's bibliographical work is given by Theodore Besterman in his *The Beginnings of Systematic Bibliography*. 2nd ed., rev. (New York: Burt Franklin, 1968, © 1936), pp. 2–3. The library of Alexandria is covered in Chapter III of Elmer D. Johnson's book *Communication. . . .* 4th ed. (Metuchen, NJ: Scarecrow Press, 1973), pp. 28–43. Other ancient libraries are discussed as well in this book.

5. Bohdan S. Wynar, *Introduction to Bibliography and Reference Work*. 4th ed. (Littleton, CO: Libraries Unlimited, 1967), p. 44. See also Louise Noëlle Malclès, *Bibliography*. (Metuchen, NJ: Scarecrow Reprint, 1973, © 1961, p. 3.

6. See Besterman, p. 6.

7. See Padwick, p. 2.

8. See Besterman, p. 8.

9. See Padwick, p. 2. Since both of these works came equipped with alphabetical indexes, they were practical works of reference. For further discussion see Besterman, pp. 8–10 and N. Frederick Nash, "Enumerative Bibliography from Gesner to James," *Library History*, 7, No. 1 (1985), pp. 12–13.

10. Malclès, pp. 19–22. There is some disagreement among historical bibliographers as to which man, Tritheim or Gesner, should be considered the "Father of Bibliography." Besterman argues (p. 10) that since Tritheim was the first genuinely bibliographically minded scholar to compile bibliographies, that the title rightfully belongs to him. On the other hand, for perhaps nationalistic reasons, Georg Schneider, in his *Theory and History of Bibliography* (New York: Columbia University Press, 1934), p. 273, emphatically states that Gesner is the "Father of Bibliography."

11. See Besterman, pp. 22–23. An illustration of Bale's *Scriptorum illustrium majoris Brytannie catalogus* (1557) is included.

12. See Schneider, pp. 272–273.

13. See Wynar, p. 45.

14. See Padwick, pp. 5–6.

15. See Malclès, pp. 31–32, 36, 133.

16. See Wynar, p. 46.

17. John Cook Wyllie, "Bibliographical Societies," *Encyclopedia Americana*, 3 (1978), p. 721.

18. Isadore Gilbert Mudge, *Bibliography*. (Chicago: American Library Association, 1915), pp. 18–21.

19. See Padwick, pp. 6–8.

20. Ibid., p. 8.

21. Ibid. p. 12.

22. See Wynar, p. 46.

23. G. Thomas Tanselle, "The State of Bibliography Today," *Papers of the Bibliographical Society of America*, 73 (July/September 1979), pp. 296–297. Keep in mind that Tanselle here is talking only about analytical or critical bibliography.

24. Marcia J. Bates, "Rigorous Systematic Bibliography," RQ, 16 (Fall 1976), p. 7.

25. Jackson R. Bryer, "From Second-Class Citizenship to Respectability: The Odyssey of an Enumerative Bibliographer," *Literary Research Newsletter*, 3 (Spring 1978), pp. 60–61.

Chapter Three

THE OBJECTS AND ARTIFACTS OF BIBLIOGRAPHY

Since the existence of bibliography is dependent upon graphic objects or artifacts, it will be helpful to introduce those that have had the greatest impact upon the discipline. The survey below will not only provide a brief overview of each area, but also assess their relationship to the study of bibliography.

A Brief Historical Survey of the Book and Printing

Part of bibliography is the study of books as physical objects as distinguished from their literary content. A book is basically a written or printed record of some length and sustained purpose, inscribed on materials light and compact enough to be carried around by someone interested in its contents. Consequently, as this kind of common transmitter of information and ideas, the book has survived many radical changes in format over the centuries. No one knows for sure how old they really are, but it is thought that books probably appeared in several places at the same time.

One of the earliest forms of the book was the cuneiform clay tablet used in Mesopotamia by the Sumerians, Babylonians, Assyrians, and Persians somewhere between 3000 B.C. and 500 B.C., when it was superseded by alphabetic writing on papyrus.[1] We know that the Assyrian king Ashurbanipal (669–626 B.C.) had a library of some 30,000 clay tablets housed in his palace at Nineveh.[2] Almost equally ancient was the Egyptian papyrus scroll used until about A.D. 300. These scrolls were made by gluing sheets of papyrus together on alternate edges. Spreading the scroll out horizontally, the scribe wrote in vertical columns, rolling up the finished manuscript to make a book. In another area of the globe Chinese books of the fifth century B.C. and earlier were constructed of bamboo strips that were bound together by cords. Some of the world's great literature was first recorded on these obsolete materials. For example, Hammurabi's code of laws and the Gilgamesh epic were written on clay. Works of the great Greek and Roman poets, dramatists, and philosophers, as well as the books of the Bible, were inscribed on papyrus scrolls. The sayings of Confucius were recorded on bamboo. Other early writing materials included leather rolls, bark, and palm leaves.

The next major step in the history of the book was a product of the early Christian era. The codex was developed by the Christian writers to accommodate their more lengthy texts. Much like the modern book, it consisted of vellum leaves piled on top of each other and fastened on one end. This form of the book was much handier than the scroll in that it did not need to be rolled out to gain access to a complete text, and the vellum leaves could be folded and could accommodate writing on both sides, which papyrus could not.[3]

In most of the ancient civilizations reading and writing was done mainly by scholars and priests of court and temple. The invention of the alphabet, and its improvement by the Greeks, simplified writing. By 400 B.C. reading was a general, though surely not universal, accomplishment in Athens. At its height the Roman Empire supported a thriving book trade, with commercial writing rooms and many book shops. Cultured and wealthy Romans commonly had private libraries in their homes. Following the famous Greek examples at Alexandria and Pergamum the Roman emperors also established libraries. The break-up of the Western Roman Empire after 476 brought an end to that literary culture. In the centuries that followed, writing again became the activity of the clergy, and it was a matter of considerable note when a ruler like Charlemagne or Alfred the Great of England was literate or patronized scholarship.[4]

During the Medieval period, from the sixth to the twelfth centuries, almost all of the centers of book production and use in Western Europe were in the monasteries. In fact, these monastic scriptoria thrived from Italy to Ireland. Some of the books produced by these monkish scribes, such as the Book of Kells (Ireland, eighth century), are famous for their exquisite beauty in lettering and illumination.[5] The flowering of monastic learning during the time of Charlemagne produced the Caroline minuscule letter, the model for the modern printed Roman lower-case alphabet. However, monastic books were restricted largely to Latin religious texts. The development of vernacular tongues sharply divided the written literary language from the spoken tongue of the people.[6]

In the thirteenth century the flourishing of universities created a book trade in university towns. Stationers supplied books for students. At the same time the rising middle class in the expanding cities provided the stimulus for the development of a broader commercial book trade.[7] When Richard de Bury compiled his famous treatise on book collecting, *Philobiblon* in 1345, this trade was well developed. During the thirteenth and fourteenth centuries the vernacular languages were also firmly established as written literary languages through the work of such writers as Dante, Boccaccio, Petrarch, and Chaucer.

The social and cultural climate of the fifteenth century in Europe provided the impetus for a revolution in the book trade. With the rise of humanism came the development of vernacular literature, which broadened the interest in books. Craft guilds of manuscript-book dealers were organized to supply the demand for books from different classes of people. At the same time technological advances matched cultural needs. Paper, invented in China during the first century A.D., had reached Europe by way of the Arab lands and by 1400 had replaced vellum for manuscript books. It is possible that the block-printing process, developed in China and exemplified in the *Diamond Sutra* (A.D. 868), also came to the West via the Orient, but it is generally considered to have been independently discovered in Europe around 1400. The screw press was used for wine crushing and other jobs, and metallurgical skills and techniques were developing. Sometime around 1450 Johann Gutenberg of Mainz and his collaborators were printing with movable type. The use of this printing process spread rapidly, so that by 1500 it was found in every major country in Europe except Russia.[8]

With the growth of the book trade the scribes of the earlier era were replaced by entrepreneurs of sufficient means to operate printing establishments that could produce an edition and take the risk of selling enough copies to make a profit. Although the Gutenberg Bible and other early printed books were imitations of expensive manuscripts, printers soon learned that the advantage of the printing press was in producing large, cheap editions of books in popular demand. For example, the small Latin grammar of Donatus was printed more frequently during the fifteenth century than any other book.[9]

Printing and publishing during the sixteenth century were marked by a flood of Reformation tracts. It is quite evident that the printing press contributed to the endurance of that religious revolt.[10] Another innovation

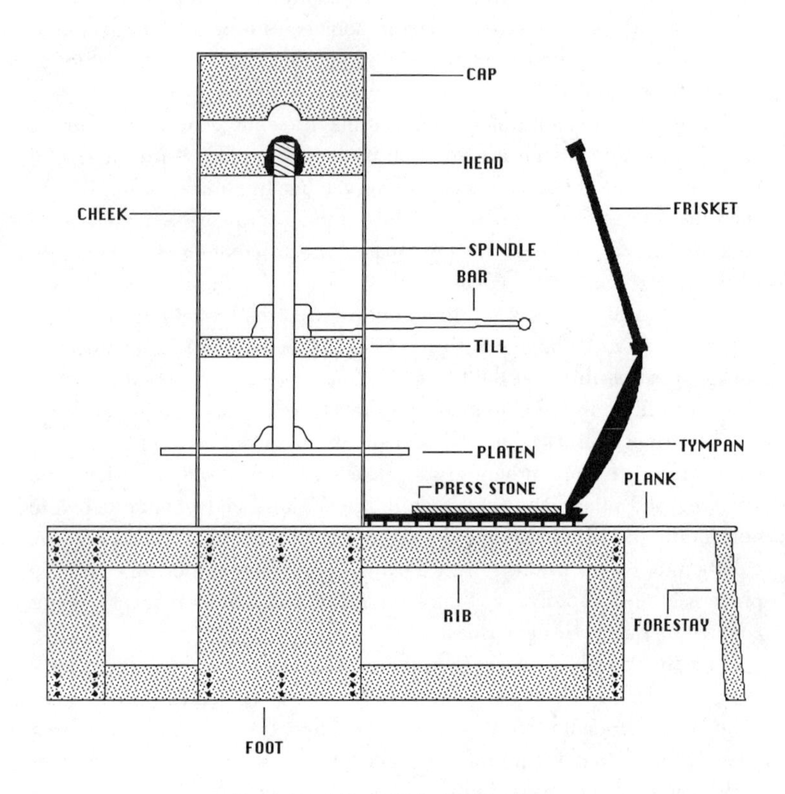

Figure No. 4 Early Style Printing Press

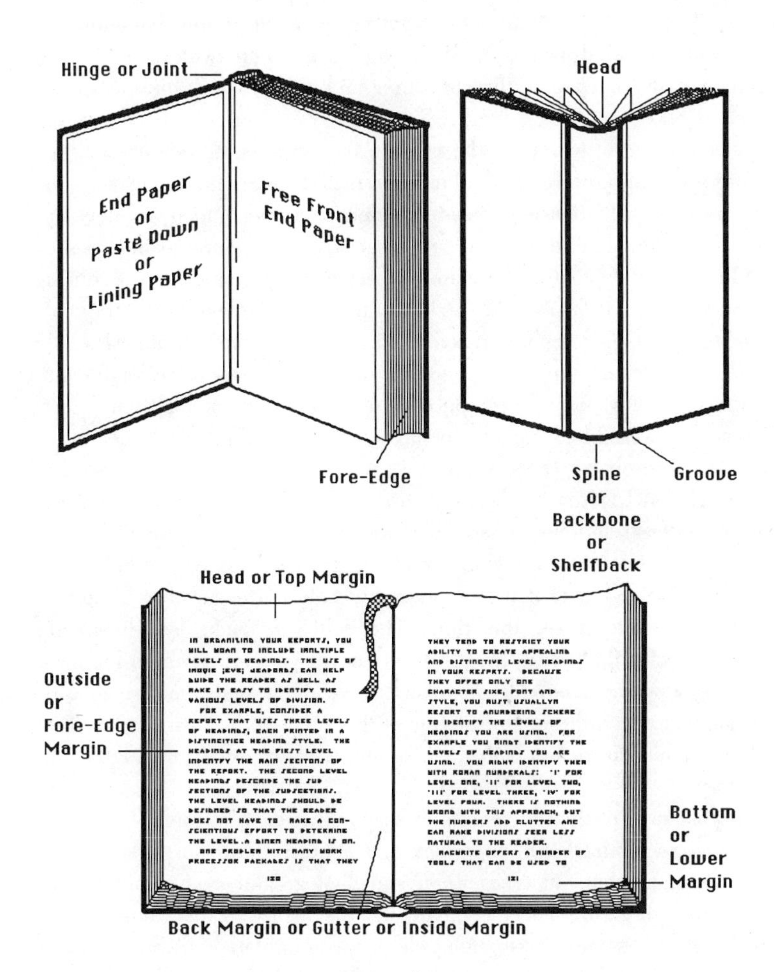

Figure No. 5. Parts of the Book

of the printing press was its ability to reproduce drawings. In effect it was now possible to publish technical books that depended on the accuracy of their illustrations for their value. Consequently during the sixteenth century anatomical drawings, herbals, and maps were widely published. Great artists, such as Albrecht Dürer and Sebastian Brant, illustrated printed books.[11]

Notable in the history of the book in the seventeenth century was the flowering of literature in England, France, and Spain, along with the issuance of early classics of modern science. An accompanying development was the rise of the periodical press. With its beginnings in Germany and the Netherlands the newspaper experienced its greatest growth during the English Civil War (1642–1649). Magazines developed from the periodically published reports of scientific societies organized after 1660.[12]

With the ever-increasing popularity of books by the early eighteenth century, it was possible for publishers to pay authors for their efforts although it would be some time before successful authors would be able to live comfortably on the royalties received from their publications. The copyright law passed by the English Parliament in 1709 established the basic modern relationship between author and publisher.[13] Another influence on the book in the eighteenth century was the increasing literacy of women. Appealing to that new group of readers, the novel as a literary form flourished during this time. The belief in books as educational devices was reflected in the growth of encyclopedias, of which the most famous was the *Encyclopedie* of Denis Diderot and the French encyclopedists. Another manifestation of this same belief was the growth of subscription libraries in both England and America during the eighteenth century.

In the wake of the nineteenth-century industrial revolution, bookmaking was mechanized with papermaking machines, power presses, sewing machines, mechanical typesetters, and photographic techniques for reproducing illustrations. Accompanying this mechanization was a great acceleration of book production, which was stimulated by the spread of democracy and free public education, the rapid advances in historical and scientific scholarship, the growth of cities with easy internal communication, and the related increase in leisure time.[14]

This industrialization of publishing gave rise to a number of developments related to the history of the book. One of the most notable of these was the private-press movement, introduced by William Morris and his Kelmscott Press, which he founded in 1891. The attempt here was to preserve the craft traditions of printing lost in the mechanization process.

Later developments include the production of large editions at low cost, aided by new inventions and processes like the offset press and perfect binding in producing the inexpensive paperback, and microprint and microform publications, which mark the most radical change in the format of the book since the invention of the codex.

From 1900 to the present the book has been challenged by such new media as the motion picture, radio, and television. On the whole it is difficult to deny that there has been a decline in the relative importance of the book. On the other hand, book production and the rate of literacy throughout the world are increasing. The book continues to be a convenient means of communication because it can be readily adapted to individual needs, is portable, and can provide a medium of communication over which the individual has the greatest control.

Bookmaking Materials

Books have been made out of a variety of materials in the past. Other than printing, the basic component of the book is the paper on which the type impression is made. The following is an overview of the history of paper, type, printing ink, and bindings as they apply to the making of books.

Bibliographers are vitally interested in the history of printing, papermaking, binding, and so on because they assist in the task of identifying specific states, issues, and editions and of dating undated books. Bibliographers use the histories of these materials to detect and expose literary forgeries.

Paper

As noted earlier, humankind's intellectual achievements progressed with the development of writing. The early writing materials were both bulky and often tended to be heavy which became an increasing problem as a measure of portability became desirable. Clay, metal, wax, and skins were in use around 4000 B.C., and papyrus around 2400 B.C. in Egypt. Papyrus is a tall reed that grows along such rivers as the Nile, the Tigris, and the Euphrates. The layers of fiber around the plant's pith were stripped off, laid crosswise, and laminated by means of a flour paste glue and pressure. Since papyrus was a crosswise-layered product, it was not truly the paper that was later used in books.[15] An interesting parallel to the use of papyrus occurred in Central America, where a very similar material was made by the Maya and later by the Aztecs. The Maya's *huun* paper, made from wild fig tree bark, was superior to papyrus because of its flexibility.[16] It helped to advance the early Central American civilizations as papyrus did those of Egypt and Mesopotamia.

It was about A.D. 75 that Tsi-Lun, a young Chinese scholar, started experimenting on the development of a better writing surface. With the help of Emperor Hoti, himself a scientist, Tsi-Lun succeeded by the year 105 in producing a fair grade of paper. He didn't leave us his recipe, but it is fairly certain that he used a mixture of bamboo fiber and old rags, plus the inner fibers of the mulberry tree. He beat the ingredients into a mass, mixed it with water, and poured it on grass molds. The excess water seeped through and left a flat film of matted fiber. This was pulp in sheet form. When it was dried in the sun, then rubbed smooth with a stone, the result was paper.[17]

History records that the Chinese later used hand molds made from horsehair cloth lashed to bamboo frames. The magic formula for paper remained secret for 600 years. But in 704, when Arab armies captured the city of Samarkand in western China, several papermakers were abducted to Baghdad and put to work making their product. Other raw materials were developed. In 794 the Chinese workers of Baghdad made paper from linen rags.[18]

Surprisingly, it was not until the eleventh century that paper made its way to Europe, due mainly, according to historians, to the socioreligious gulf existing between East and West. Both Spain and Italy lay claim to being the first European nations to establish paper mills, perhaps as early as the eleventh century. Historians generally concede the edge to Spain, with 1150 given as the date for the appearance of a mill at Jativa. From there papermaking slowly spread through Europe. England did not produce paper until around 1494, but the British recognized paper's importance and took the lead in its manufacture. Paper was soon used for designing English ships.[19]

English settlements in America developed rapidly and soon needed paper in ever-increasing amounts. In 1690 William Rittenhouse established the first American papermill in Philadelphia. Using linen rags as raw material, this plant averaged 100 pounds of paper per day even though the process was still very crude. Paper pulp was prepared by letting wet rags ferment for six to seven weeks. The rotting process loosened the fibers although it also gave the pulp a coffee-brown color.

This stock was then bleached in lime-water, broken up by stamping, placed in bags, and washed in a stream. One-third of the original stock had rotted and was washed away. The washed residue was again bleached in the sun, suspended in water, and dipped from the water with a wooden frame that had a screen on the bottom. The frame was shaken as the water drained, leaving a wet mat. These mats were removed from the screens with felt blankets, stacked between the blankets, pressed to remove the water, and finally hung in a loft to dry. Most paper was made in this manner until the middle of the nineteenth century. Since this process was painstakingly slow and rags were hard to get, paper was always in short supply.[20]

In 1801 the Fourdrinier paper machine was invented. This involved a process in which a pulp suspension was spread on a moving wire screen; after the water drained off, a continuous wet sheet was removed. The paper machines on which most of our paper is made today are simply improved versions of the Fourdrinier mechanism.[21]

Another development occurred in the 1820s with the invention of the cylinder machine. On this machine sheets were formed on rolls. Several sheets were pressed together when wet, and boardlike laminate was formed. The resulting layers can be seen in cardboard and book matches. Drying the wet sheets of paper and board continued to be a serious problem until 1826, when steam-heated cylinders were employed to dry them. Unfortunately, this equipment had to be cranked by hand or water power.[22]

As the process was improved papermakers were limited mainly by the scarcity of rags. During the Civil War some desperate papermill executives even imported mummies from Egypt to make pulp from the wrappings. There was a constant search for other sources of fiber, including straw, rope, and wood. Wood provided a good source if the individual fibers could be separated. Mechanical and chemical pulping processes, slowly developed during the last century, overcame the rag shortage and made the modern paper and book industries possible.

Type

Although the processes of type production have been revolutionized many times over the years, the essential stages have actually changed very little. After a typeface is designed it is then cut as a die, from which a matrix is made. Finished type is then cast from this matrix. Each of these processes is subject to many smaller operations and calculations before the font can be produced either by machine or hand casting. A font of type is a complete range of one sort of a size and a uniform face, including upper-case (capital) letters, lower-case (small) letters, punctuation marks, small capital letters, italic letters (originally a font in itself and not regarded as a integral part of any other), and anything else that has been required at different times to produce a printed page.[23]

Books printed before 1500 are termed *incunabula*, or "cradle" books. Many of these are printed in *black letter* (Gothic) type. Because printing started in Germany, where the Gothic letter was standard for the scribes, Gothic was the first typeface used in printing—including the printing of the Gutenberg Bible, which had great impact on the new craft. This type was used for many years, but with less and less frequency after 1500, usually for books of a religious nature.[24]

In modern times photographic processes have for the most part taken the place of type cast for the letterpress process. Most type today is composed by highly specialized and intricate machines that look much like large typewriters. Despite this, the bibliographer should know something about both printing and type and the history of their development.[25]

Printing Ink

Like paper, ink was first developed in China between 3000 and 2500 B.C. It is believed that these inks were made by mixing lampblack with oil and gum. The prototypes of our modern printing inks were first developed in Europe during the fifteenth century. The ingredients, much the same as those thought to be used by the ancient Chinese, consisted of carbon black that had been ground into a varnish and was made by cooking linseed oil together with a natural resin.[26]

Printing inks today must satisfy many more requirements than those manufactured for writing purposes, and they vary widely in composition depending on the printing method used. The kind and speed of the press are important in the selection of ink. Also printing inks must be suitable for application to a great variety of surfaces, such as paper, rubber, textiles, metal, wood, or plastic. Printing inks must also serve widely diverse purposes—say, the creation of a brightly colored poster—as well as a production of a regular printed page. The inks in both cases are quite different from each other in composition. Each must last for a different period of time and must withstand different conditions during use.[27]

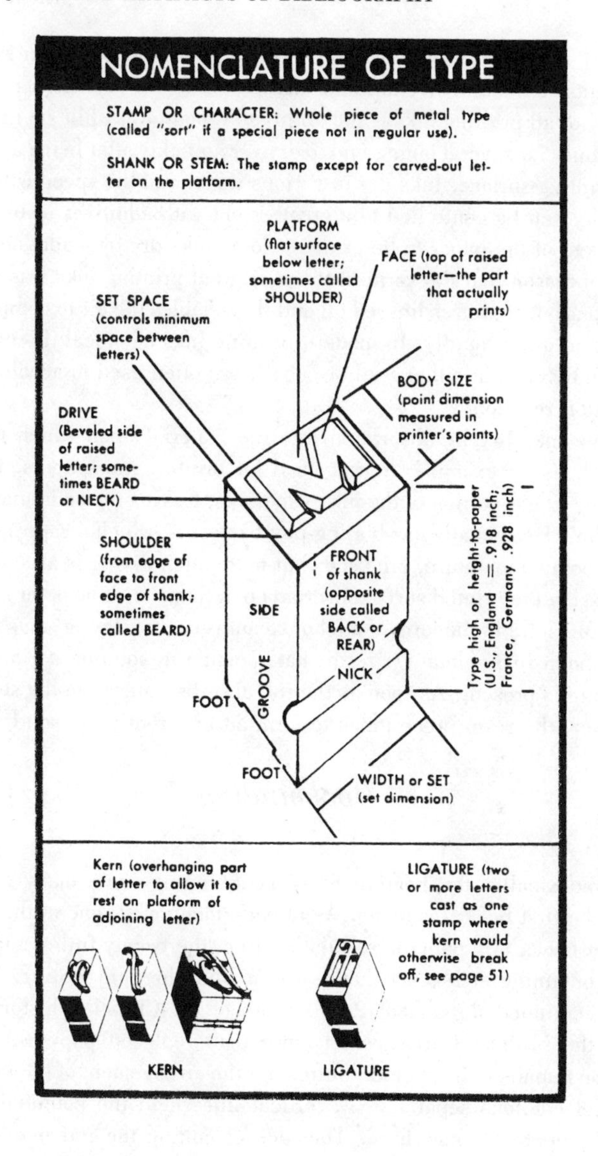
NOMENCLATURE OF TYPE
STAMP OR CHARACTER: Whole piece of metal type (called "sort" if a special piece not in regular use).
SHANK OR STEM: The stamp except for carved-out letter on the platform.
PLATFORM (flat surface below letter; sometimes called SHOULDER)
FACE (top of raised letter—the part that actually prints)
SET SPACE (controls minimum space between letters)
BODY SIZE (point dimension measured in printer's points)
DRIVE (Beveled side of raised letter; sometimes BEARD or NECK)
Type high or height-to-paper (U.S., England = .918 inch; France, Germany .928 inch)
SHOULDER (from edge of face to front edge of shank; sometimes called BEARD)
FRONT of shank (opposite side called BACK or REAR)
SIDE
GROOVE
NICK
FOOT
FOOT
WIDTH or SET (set dimension)
Kern (overhanging part of letter to allow it to rest on platform of adjoining letter)
LIGATURE (two or more letters cast as one stamp where kern would otherwise break off, see page 51)
KERN
LIGATURE

Figure No. 6. Illustration of Type
Courtesy the Myriade Press

Most modern printing inks are viscous liquids that contain synthetic pigments, binders, solvents, and ingredients to aid drying. A necessary quality of all printing inks is the ability to remain wet while on the press, sometimes for several hours, and to dry very quickly after being applied to the printing surface. Inks dry in various ways, and the speed with which they dry can be controlled to a great extent with additives or by special treatment of the paper to be printed. Some inks dry by oxidation. It was for this reason that the varnish of the original printing inks was cooked. Heat partially oxidizes linseed oil and this enables the air to complete the oxidation quite rapidly. In modern printing inks chemical driers, which frequently contain either lead or cobalt, are often used to accelerate the oxidation reaction.[28]

Some inks dry by absorption into the material upon which they are printed, as for example the ink used for printing newspapers. In other inks the liquid portion of the ink evaporates, leaving the solid matter as a dry film. Occasionally low-boiling-point solvents, which disappear quickly at room temperature, are used, but more often drying is accomplished by passing the printed surface over an open flame or some other source of heat. Moisture in the form of a jet of steam is use for drying some printing inks. Such inks contain a resin that remains in solution as long as no moisture is present. As soon as the ink absorbs water from the steam jet, however, the resin precipitates to form an apparently dry solid.[29]

Bookbinding

Paradoxically, the beginnings of bookbinding came many centuries after the first book was made. As already mentioned, one of the earliest known books is a papyrus roll dating from the twenty-fifth century B.C. and containing eighteen columns of Egyptian hieratic writing. The roll form continued throughout 2,000 years of pre-Christian history. Even after the birth of Christ, when parchment replaced papyrus, the roll volume remained the standard form. But the arrangement of the writing in parallel columns separated by vertical lines held the potential for the development of a new form. The idea of cutting the roll into separate panels, each containing three or four columns, eventually gave birth to the book as we know it. Consequently the first bound book was constructed of single sheets, hinged along one edge by means of sewing or lacing. In the Latin codex, or manuscript book, the columnar arrangement of writing continued, with typical examples from the Roman period

Figure No. 7. Binding Styles

having three or four columns to the page. Down to the present day, two and three-column pages have proven practical and easy to read.[30]

It might come as a surprise to some to know that early bindings had all of the basic construction elements that modern bindings have. The early bindings were constructed of folded sheets, collected into gatherings, and sewn into cords running across their backs. The leaves of the books were large, the size probably determined by the size of the animal skins from which the parchment was made. After a time wooden boards were placed on either side of the book proper, in positions corresponding to the front and back covers. Later it was discovered that the cords onto which the gatherings were sewn could as easily be laced directly into the edges of the boards to form a more compact, sturdy, and durable unit. The evolution of bookbinding was completed when the whole volume was covered with a sheet of leather to conceal the sewing and provide additional reinforcement to the hinges.[31]

The history of bookbinding is thus part and parcel with that of the book itself. But, in the past 1,800 years there has not been one single change in the primary construction of the book. It is still made up of a series of folded gatherings, or signatures, sewn together at the folds and contained between two boards whose outer surfaces are covered. Just as the development of any technique cannot be isolated from concurrent factors, so bookbinding has been influenced by many events having nothing to do with books, or even literature.[32]

Most of the early bindings were the products of monastic orders during the Middle Ages and therefore are closely allied with the Church. There are many examples extant of the fine craftsmanship of this era, with manuscript books bound in leather, richly tooled, and frequently decorated with settings of gems and rare stones or heavy gold-leaf designs.[33]

With the introduction of papermaking from China the binder's art was extended to handle this new material. Good strong thread was used in the sewing, and silk was employed in making headbands. Leather was attached to the wooden cover boards in its full thickness; shaving it thin, or paring, was unknown.

The invention of printing from movable type in the middle of the fifteenth century brought a revolution in bookbinding. The greatest factor affecting this revolution, along with the printing press, was the greatly increased popular demand for books. Consequently, bookbinding was transferred from the monasteries to printers' shops, and later to separate binding establishments. As a covering, leather continued to be the most suitable and durable. Improvements in materials and tooling gave bookbinding a fresh impetus. From this period there are also many examples of fine bindings, especially from among royalty and the aristocratic classes who sponsored the development of distinct binding styles.[34]

Naturally the bookbinding trade was greatly affected by the Industrial Revolution. To many connoisseurs of the binding art the machines of mass production invented and developed during this period undermined the quality of the finished product. Of course, these machines did make it possible for every reader to own a book with the appearance of quality at a low price. The drive to reduce costs also resulted in cheaper materials and shortcuts in the binding process. For example, when flat tapes were introduced to replace cords, commercial bindings continued to be influenced by the traditional look of elegance, even to the extent of attaching false bands to the backbone. In true flexible-leather binding the leather is glued directly to the backs of the gatherings or signatures. But a hollow back was invented for use with tape sewing that places almost all the strain upon the two hinges, instead of distributing it over the backs of the signatures.[35]

Case bindings were developed to speed up the binding process. Covers and backbone were made up independently of the sewn signatures, in one flat unit consisting of the two cover boards, the backbone stiffener, and the cloth or paper cover material. All titling, decoration, and finishing were done while the case was flat. Then the sewn signatures and case were brought together and fastened one of the other on a special machine. Most books today are bound by this method.[36]

Until the seventeenth century bookbinding was a handicraft practiced by skilled workers who used the finest materials available. Following the changes brought about by the introduction of machine technology, books lacked artistic taste and utilitarian construction according to critics. The art of fine bindings now became a specialized craft practiced by only a few workers catering to libraries and private collectors.

Manuscripts

Possibly greater than the mass of printed books accumulated throughout history are the manuscript records of humankind. It is almost impossible to estimate the physical bulk of the records of businesses, institutions, official agencies, and individuals. Everything, from the records of the U. S. Department of State to acting copies of Broadway plays, has its documentary value. Throughout time the variety and complexity of manuscripts have been vastly greater than that of the printed book and have remained a relatively homogeneous artifact for the last five centuries.[37]

The oldest manuscripts, those found in Egyptian tombs, were written on papyrus. It has been estimated that the earliest of these dates from around 3,500 B.C. Parchment, which succeeded papyrus as a writing material, was much more durable. Most extant ancient manuscripts are of parchment. Both sides were used and many sheets were erased and reused—these are called palimpsests. In contrast, the manuscripts of the Middle Ages were often beautifully illuminated in colors on vellum, a fine variety of parchment. Initial letters of first lines and titles were often highly decorated.[38]

Some scholars study manuscripts as cultural artifacts for historical purposes mainly as physical objects in order to identify the workshops that produced them. This type of study is currently known as *codicology* and is closely related to analytical bibliography.[39]

Nonprint Materials

Bibliography affects to some degree every available type and source of knowledge. Nonprint materials are information-bearing media that are not in the form of the conventional book, that is to say normally written information in a continuous text organized in a linear order. The kinds of nonprint media can be grouped into broad categories depending upon their essential nature such as microforms, sound recordings, audio-visual materials, databases, etc.

Bibliographic techniques and devices have been created and are being developed to provide improved access to nonprint materials which are expanding both in numbers and types. It is not improbable that in the near future, bibliographic control of nonprint media will approach that of the other artifacts of bibliography.

Selected Related Writings

THE BOOK AND PRINTING

Binns, Norman E. *An Introduction to Historical Bibliography*. 2nd ed. London: Association of Assistant Librarians, 1962.

Eisenstein, Elizabeth L. *Printing Revolution in Early Modern Europe*. New York: Cambridge University Press, 1983.

Esdaile, Arundell James Kennedy. *Esdaile's Manual of Bibliography*. 5th ed. Revised by Roy Stokes. Metuchen, NJ: Scarecrow Press, 1981. Consult Chapters 2, 3 and 6.

Johnson, Elmer D. *Communication: An Introduction to the History of Writing, Printing, Books and Libraries*. 4th ed. Metuchen, NJ: Scarecrow Press, 1973.

Levarie, Norma. *The Art and History of Books*. New York: James H. Heineman, 1968.

McMurtrie, Douglas C. *The Book: The Story of Printing and Bookmaking*. 3rd ed. New York: Oxford University Press, 1943.

Moxon, Joseph. *Mechanick Exercises on the Whole Art of Printing (1683-4)*. Edited by Herbert Davis & Harry Carter. 2nd ed. New York: Dover Publications, 1978, ©1962. (Reprint)

Rider, Alice D. *A Story of Books and Libraries*. Metuchen, NJ: Scarecrow Press, 1978.

Small, Christopher *The Printed Word, An Instrument of Popularity*. Aberdeen, Scot.: Aberdeen University Press, 1982.

Winckler, Paul A., ed. *Reader in the History of Books and Printing*. Englewood, CO: Information Handling Service, 1978.

PAPERMAKING

Blum, André. *On the Origin of Paper*. Translated from the French by Harry M. Lydenberg. New York: Bowker, 1954.

Hunter, Dard. *Papermaking: The History and Technique of an Ancient Craft*. 2nd ed. New York: Knopf, 1947.

________. *Papermaking in Pioneer America*. Philadelphia: University of Pennsylvania Press, 1952.

________. *Papermaking Through Eighteen Centuries*. New York: William Edwin Rudge, 1930.

Lewis, Naphtali. *Papyrus in Classical Antiquity*. Oxford: Clarendon Press, 1974.

Paper Structure and Properties. Edited by Anthony J. Bristow and Petter Koleth. New York: Marcel Dekker, 1986.

Schlosser, Leonard B. "A History of Paper." In: *Paper - Art & Technology*. San Francisco, CA: World Print Council, 1979. See pp. 2–19.

The Structure and Physical Properties of Paper. Edited by H. F. Rance. New York: Elsevier Scientific, 1982.

U. S. Library of Congress. *Papermaking: Art and Craft*. Washington, DC: Library of Congress, 1968.

TYPOGRAPHY

Biggs, John R. *Basic Typography*. London: Faber and Faber, 1973.

Johnson, Alfred F. *Type Designs: Their History and Development*. 3rd ed. London: Deutsch, 1966.

Lawson, Alexander. *Printing Types, An Introduction* Boston: Beacon, 1972.

Lieberman, J. Ben. *Type and Typefaces: A Treasury of Typography Book*. 2nd ed. New Rochelle, NY: The Myrinde Press, 1978.

Simon, Oliver. *Introduction to Typography*. 2nd ed. Edited by David Bland. London: Faber and Faber, 1963.

Tracy, Walter. *Letters of Credit: A View of Type Design*. Boston: Godine, 1986.

Updike, Daniel B. *Printing Types: Their History, Forms and Use: A Study of Survival*. 3rd ed. Cambridge, MA: Belknap Press of Harvard University, 1967.

PRINTING INK

Beard, J. "How Medieval Printers Put Bibles Together." *New Scientist,* 114 (April 16, 1987), p. 15.

Bloy, Colin H. *A History of Printing Ink, Balls and Rollers, 1440–1850*. London: Wynkyn de Worde Society; New York: Sanstone Press, 1980, © 1967.

Hutchinson, Geoffrey H. "Developments in the Technology and Application of Offset Lithographic Printing Inks." *Chemistry and Industry,* No. 22 (November 17, 1986), pp. 764–769.

Voet, Andries. *Ink and Paper in the Printing Process*. New York: Interscience, 1952.

Wilborg, Frank B. *Printing Ink: A History with a Treatise on Modern Methods of Manufacture and Use*. New York: Harper, 1926.

BOOKBINDING

Burdett, Eric. *The Craft of Bookbinding: A Practical Handbook*. Newton Abbot, Eng.: David and Charles, 1975.

Comparato, Frank E. *Books for the Millions: A History of the Men Whose Methods and Machines Packaged the Printed Word*. Harrisburg, PA: Stackpole, 1971.

Darley, Lionel S. *Introduction to Bookbinding*. London: Faber and Faber, 1978, © 1965.

Diehl, Edith. *Bookbinding: Its Background and Technique*. New York: Reinhart, 1946.

Johnson, Pauline. *Creative Bookbinding*. Seattle, WA: University of Washington Press, 1963.

Lewis, Roy H. *Fine Bookbindings in the Twentieth Century*. New York: Arco, 1985, © 1984.

Needham, Paul. *Twelve Centuries of Bookbindings, 400–1600*. New York: Pierpont Morgan Library; Oxford University Press, 1979.

Watson, Aldren A. *Hand Bookbinding: A Manual of Instruction*. New York: Bell, 1963.

MANUSCRIPTS

Braswell, Laurel N. *Western Manuscripts from Classical Antiquity to the Renaissance: A Handbook*. New York: Garland, 1981.

Deuel, Leo. *Testaments of Time: The Search for Lost Manuscripts and Records*. New York: Knopf, 1965.

Madan, Falconer. *Books in Manuscript, A Short Introduction to Their Study and Use*. 2nd ed. New York: Empire State Book Co., 1927.

Sinks, Perry W. *The Reign of the Manuscript*. Boston: R. G. Badger, 1917.

Thorpe, James Ernest. *The Use of Manuscripts in Literary Research: Problems of Access and Literary Property Rights*. New York: Modern Language Association of America, 1974.

NONPRINT MATERIALS

Croghan, Antony. *A Bibliographic System for Non-Book Media: A Description and List of Works*. 2nd ed. London: Coburgh Publishers, 1979.

Fothergill, Richard and Ian Butchart. *Non-Book Materials in Libraries: A Practical Guide*. London: Clive Bingley; Hamden, CT: Linnet Books, 1978.

Grove, Pearce S. *Nonprint Media in Academic Libraries*. Chicago: American Library Association, 1975.

Thompson, Anthony H. "Knowledge or Format—Which Comes First?" *Audiovisual Librarian,* 12 (November 1986), pp. 184–188.

Wall, Thomas. "Nonprint Materials: A Definition and Some Practical Considerations on their Maintenance," *Library Trends,* 34 (Summer 1985), pp. 129–140.

Notes

1. Gertrude Buford Rawlings, *The Story of Books*. (New York: Appleton, 1904), pp.11–13.

2. Lester Condit, "Bibliography in Its Prenatal Existence," *Library Quarterly,* 7 (October 1937), p. 564–565. For a somewhat more extensive account see Elmer D. Johnson and Michael H. Harris, *History of Libraries in the Western World,* 3rd ed., rev. (Metuchen, NJ: Scarecrow Press, 1976), pp. 19–21.

3. Arundell J. K. Esdaile, *Esdaile's Manual of Bibliography,* 4th ed., revised by Roy Stokes (New York: Barnes and Noble, 1967), pp. 184–185. Papyrus codices also exist as well as those made from vellum.

4. Alice Damon Rider, *A Story of Books and Libraries*. (Metuchen, NJ: Scarecrow Press, 1976), pp. 51–55.

5. Ibid., pp. 77–79.

6. Daniel Gore, *Bibliography for Beginners,* 2nd ed. (New York: Appleton-Century-Crofts, 1973), pp. 20–23.

7. Derek Williamson, *Historical Bibliography*. (Hamden, CT: Archon, 1967), pp. 93–94.

8. Douglas Crawford McMurtrie, *The Book: The Story of Printing & Bookmaking,* 3rd ed., rev. (London: Oxford University Press, 1943), pp. 132–135.

9. Lucien Febvre and Henri-Jean Martin, *The Coming of the Book: The Impact of Printing, 1450–1800*. (London: NLB; Atlantic Highlands, NJ: Humanities Press, 1976) p. 253.

10. Ibid., pp. 287–290.

11. See McMurtrie, p. 246.

12. Henry Bartlett Van Hoesen, *Bibliography, Practical, Enumerative, Historical: An Introductory Manual*. (New York: Scribner's, 1928), p. 346.

13. See Esdaile, p. 304.

14. See Williamson, pp. 41–48.

15. For a detailed examination of the papyrus manufacturing process see Naphtali Lewis, *Papyrus in Classical Antiquity*. (Oxford, Eng.: Clarendon Press, 1974), pp. 34–69.

16. Dard Hunter, *Papermaking: The History and Technique of an Ancient Craft*. (New York: Dover Publications, 1978), p. 25. This is a reprint of the 1947 second edition.

17. Crown Zellerbach Corporation, *Paper . . . Its Story,* rev. ed. (San Francisco: The Corporation, 1952), p. [2].

18. *The Paper Handbook,* 3rd ed. (Portland, OR: Boise Cascade Paper Group, 1976), p. 8.

19. Leonard B. Schlosser, "A History of Paper," In: *Paper—Art & Technology*. (San Francisco: World Print Council, 1979), pp. 4–7. See also Hunter, pp. 63–66. In many countries, especially in Europe and North America, the use of paper preceded its manufacture for some time, which accounts for paper's commercial future and importation long before the manufacturing process was developed.

20. The early development of papermaking in America is expertly covered by Dard

Hunter, *Papermaking in Pioneer America*. (Philadelphia: University of Pennsylvania Press, 1952), pp. 9–19. The Rittenhouse Mill is discussed in some detail in Chapter 3, pp. 20–27.

21. See Schlosser, pp. 15–16.

22. See Hunter, *Papermaking: The History and Technique of an Ancient Craft*, p. 361.

23. David B. Boswell, *A Text-Book on Bibliography*. (London: Grafton, 1952), p. 41.

24. J. Ben Lieberman. *Type and Typefaces: A Treasury of Typography Book*. (New Rochelle, NY: The Myriade Press, 1978), pp. 31–36.

25. For one of the better short treatments of typography see Esdaile, pp. 74–99.

26. The history of printing ink from its invention in China to modern times is well documented in Frank B. Wilborg, *Printing Ink, A History with a Treatise on Modern Method of Manufacture and Use*. (New York: Harper, 1926); see especially Chapters I–VII, pp. 1–96.

27. Thomas Landau, *Encyclopedia of Librarianship*, 3rd ed., rev. (London: Bowes and Bowes, 1966), p. 358.

28. Andries Voet, *Ink and Paper in the Printing Process*. (New York: Interscience, 1952), pp. 3–7.

29. Ibid.

30. Aldren A. Watson, *Hand Bookbinding, A Manual of Instruction*. (New York: Bell, 1963), p. 9. Watson further indicates that since modern trade books predominantly single column, their pages are smaller, in contrast to the much larger books of earlier times.

31. Ibid.

32. Ibid., pp. 9–10.

33. Douglas Cockrell, *Some Notes on Bookbinding*. (London: Oxford University Press, 1929), p. 1.

34. Ibid., p. 4.

35. See Watson, p. 12.

36. Philip Gaskell, *A New Introduction to Bibliography*. (New York: Oxford University Press, 1972), pp. 231–234.

37. Lawrence S. Thompson, "Manuscripts," *Encyclopedia of Library and Information Science*, 17 (1976), p. 130.

38. *The New Columbia Encyclopedia*, edited by William H. Harris and Judith S. Levey (New York: Columbia University Press, 1975), p. 1689.

39. For an excellent, concise discussion of codicology and bibliography see, Lawrence J. McCrank, "Analytical and Historical Bibliography: A State of the Art Review," In: *Annual Report of the American Rare, Antiquarian and Out-of-Print Book Trade, 1978/1979*, edited by Denis Carbonneau (New York: BCAR Publications, 1979), pp. 176–177.

Chapter Four

ENUMERATIVE OR SYSTEMATIC BIBLIOGRAPHY

Introduction

The term "enumerative" and "systematic" refer both to the techniques used by bibliographers and to the instruments they create. Consequently Tritheim's *Liber de scriptoribus ecclessiasticis,* the result of a painstaking recording and enumeration of titles, is an enumerative bibliography. This, as we have seen, was the earliest form of bibliographic activity and it remains the starting point of all bibliographical study for, unless a book or other item is known to exist, it cannot be found so as to be analyzed or described. Basically the word implies a listing in alphabetical or chronological order but in many cases entries are arranged systematically for a particular purpose such as a selection of books by their subject matter to form a subject bibliography. Normally the enumerative or systematic bibliography requires only brief entries with enough information to identify the work and to enable the user to evaluate the significance in their field of the materials listed.[1]

Enumerative bibliography has become a tremendously broad field and threatens to become even larger as books, other graphic materials, and ideas multiply. The bibliographer today is faced with an almost infinite number of tasks which might be undertaken.[2] Generally the enumerative bibliographer sets out to identify all the materials on a given topic, to range them in order of precedence to suggest their relationship to another, and in so doing to guide the user to those that are most likely to be important and valuable for his or her purposes whatever those purposes may be.[3]

Historical Background

In order to understand the current dimensions of enumerative bibliography more fully it might be helpful to recapitulate a little bit of history.

Both books and readers were needed before bibliography could get well under way, and by the time cradle books had evolved titles and dates (in the mid-1460s), enumerative bibliography came into existence.[4] Beginning with the first commercial book lists of the German publishers it was a short step to compilations for dealers and the entire German book trade. Before the end of the sixteenth century, national bibliographies also appeared in Italy, France, and England. The earliest attempt at universal or world bibliography was made in 1545, with the publication of Conrad Gesner's *Bibliotheca universalis*.[5] A number of these lists were elementary subject bibliographies, being divided after the manner of contemporary university faculties, into theology, philosophy, and medicine. About the middle of the seventeenth century a French bookseller by the name of Louis de Saint-Charles improved upon the German models by the addition of critical notes, followed by Nicolas Antonio's *Bibliotheca Hispana*.[6] England's *Term Catalogues* (1668)[7] was the first successful book list issued periodically. True subject bibliographies developed slowly, both as lists of material on specific subjects and by internal arrangement under leading entry words.[8]

In the early part of the eighteenth century, printed catalogs of both public and private libraries were fairly numerous, and critical bibliographies in the form of notes and book reviews appeared, first in the *Journal des Savants* (1665–). The earliest professional scholar-bibliographers were found among the Jesuits and Benedictines in the same century, and the first work on applied bibliography, the *Bibliographie instructive*[9] by the librarian François DeBure was published during the years 1763–1793; this title, which was probably the first to use the term "bibliography" in its modern sense, marked the birth of the profession of bibliography.[10]

From these simple beginnings, enumerative bibliography has evolved to its present state. Once used only to link printer and buyer, it is now employed in many ways to advance our intellectual horizons. It is concerned with the communication of all knowledge; with the discovery, identification, description, and classification of documents; with printing, publishing, and the book arts; with book hunting and collecting; with library administration and use; and, in its most specialized sense, with the formal application of bibliographic principles of arrangement without respect to content.[11]

Nature and Uses

Enumerative bibliography has long been considered the poor stepsister of analytical bibliography. Enumerative bibliographers have too often conceded that the other branch involves more technical complexity,[12] but there are those who argue, with much substance, that enumerative bibliography in its finest sense has always been the basic discipline and will be more and more widely recognized as such.[13]

Here we are dealing with the most practical product of the bibliographic art—a bibliography. Broadly speaking, a bibliography is an intermediary instrument or device that assists in the transfer of information from the producer to the ultimate consumer. More specifically, it is the list or sequence of descriptions of graphic materials on a given subject or area.[14] The arrangement or sequence of descriptions varies widely, usually depending on the use for which the bibliography is intended. For example, descriptions may simply be arranged alphabetically, chronologically, or by major subdivisions of a subject. The descriptions also may vary in completeness and style. At the lower end of the scale of complexity—not necessarily of usefulness—the enumerative bibliography can be simply a checklist, containing only the essential information to identify the item and nothing more.[15]

Enumerative bibliographies usually have one or more common characteristics. They may attempt to be comprehensive in the coverage of a subject area or very selective. Comprehensiveness or selectivity is often the result of the bibliographer's aim in compiling the bibliography. The bibliography may be retrospective or current in nature. Currency is at times difficult to achieve, since most enumerative bibliographies are out of date even before they are published. Bibliographies serve as bridges to a larger body of information and ultimately also lead to more specialized types of information.

The main objective of an enumerative bibliography is to collate and list information about individual books and related material in a logical and useful order. This means that some sort of selection has taken place to determine what to include. Enumerative or systematic bibliography is basic to other areas of the field because the prerequisite for studying the book or any other piece of graphic material is that it is known to exist. This process of discovery and verification is only accomplished with the assistance of an enumerative or systematic bibliography.[16]

In terms of basic functions, enumerative bibliography is purely a recording one. Therefore, the recording activity must be distinguished from the selection activity. Selecting requires critical evaluation of the subject content that only a subject specialist is capable of doing well. At the same time, the bibliography should be as complete as possible and non-critical in its approach. Naturally, selection in this case involves accepting those items for inclusion which fall within the scope of the topic concerned or meet the purpose for which the bibliography is being compiled.[17]

Bibliographical Organization and Control

Enumerative bibliographies have three basic functions: 1) to identify and verify, 2) to locate, and 3) to select.[18] The descriptions collected for the bibliography identify such things as author, title, edition, coauthors, publisher, and place and date of publication. Location refers to where the item can be found in a library or some other place. Because they indicate what materials are available in a certain area, bibliographies serve as selection aids for the user.

If bibliographies are indeed supposed to accomplish these three things, then we must consider several related problems, of which bibliographical organization and control are paramount. The amount of literature available today is vast and expanding rapidly. In spite of efforts to solve the problem created by the current information explosion, the situation continues to worsen. Given this condition, librarians, information specialists, and bibliographers are playing an important role in attempting to bring order out of chaos. They are exerting every effort to provide satisfactory service to scholars and other patrons through existing bibliographic tools or are taking the initiative in improving bibliographic service in all areas.[19]

Because recorded knowledge has grown so rapidly in size and complexity, the need to have it organized in some systematic fashion has become imperative. As a consequence we are led to the concept of bibliographic organization which is the pattern of effective arrangement that results from the systematic listing of the records of human communication.[20] These listings are, of course, bibliographies of various kinds, mostly of an enumerative nature both in the form of printed graphic materials or available as online databases.

Related to the problem of bibliographic organization is that of bibliographic control. Perfect bibliographic control would imply a complete record of the existence and location of every book, every document, every article, even every written thought. The probability of ever reaching such a utopia is remote. The problem of bibliographical control is as ancient as the beginning of writing.[21] Bibliographic control emphasizes the need for mastery over materials in all branches of knowledge through enumerative bibliographies. However, in a broader sense, it implies the need for control in the bibliographic organization of the publishing trade and library profession.[22]

In summary, bibliographic organization is concerned with the pattern of effective arrangement achieved by means of a systematic listing of recorded knowledge. Satisfactory bibliographic organization of recorded knowledge will automatically lead to proper bibliographic control; both attempt to achieve the same objective.[23] Both of these problems are complex and immense and cannot be adequately discussed in this short space.

The work of modern enumerative bibliographers is very exacting, because the bibliographies they compile exhibit a wide range of types designed to fulfill various needs. Generally speaking, the types may cover universal, national, and trade bibliographies; author and subject bibliographies; publisher's catalogs; indexes to periodicals; abstracting journals; bibliographies of bibliographies; periodical-literature surveys; and machine-readable databases. Such bibliographers have to make extensive searches through the vast mass of graphic materials to compile dependable repertoires.[24]

Enumerative bibliographies expand the records of human civilization. They come to our aid whenever we try to verify a title, or gather information regarding the literature available on a subject, or appraise materials by annotations or references to critical and evaluative reviews, or find out the basic and best books on a subject, or ascertain bibliographic data about an author. The need of such activity for everyone in pursuit of knowledge, direct or indirect, is quite obvious.

Types and Functions of Enumerative Bibliographies

Primarily as the practical aspect of the discipline, enumerative and systematic bibliography is concerned with the production and study of lists of recorded knowledge. Variety of interest and purpose is reflected in the production and use of bibliographies. One person just wants to know some books to read on a particular subject or by an author; another wants to know about everything written on a subject; yet another is searching for the best or standard books.[25] Some are engaged in book selection; some want to investigate the record of the printing output of a nation; some are interested in book rarities and their location; and others need a general repertory, say, a combination of catalogs of several big libraries, so as to avoid consulting scattered sources; and there may be yet another group who want to know about the existing bibliographies in a particular subject discipline or on specific authors.

Bibliographies of various types are available to meet all such needs. Arundell Esdaile has broadly classed then as *primary* bibliographies—the original record of material—and *secondary* bibliographies—those in which materials recorded in scattered works have been rearranged to aid in research. Thus, the general, national, and trade bibliographies, as well as the bibliographies of bibliographies, are all primary, and the subject, author, and personal bibliographies are secondary.[26] In considering the types of enumerative bibliographies, the analogy of the sieve is useful. Bibliographies can be likened to a series of sieves that sift and resift the books and other graphic materials of the world, first coarsely and then more finely, until the desired materials are separated out. There are sieves for different purposes: author, language, subject, nationality, period, or what you will. Enumerative bibliography is the art of combining sieves to separate out the desired materials.[27]

The more prominent classes include: 1) General, or Universal Bibliographies; 2) National and Trade Bibliographies; 3) Subject Bibliographies; 4) Author Bibliographies; 5) Selective, or Elective Bibliographies; 6) Bibliophilic Bibliographies; 7) Specialized catalogs; 8) Bibliographies of Bibliographies; and 9) Guides to the Literature. Several categories are not discussed here either because of their esoteric nature or because of their size. For example, there are inventories of rare books, such as Ludwig Hain's *Repertorium Bibliographicum . . . ad Annum MD*[28] or the many periodical indexes like the *Humanities Index*[29] or abstracting services, such as *Biological Abstracts*.[30]

General or Universal Bibliographies

The achievement of a general or universal bibliography which would identify, list and describe all publications issued from the presses of the world in all languages, in all periods, and in all subjects has been a dream of scholars and bibliographers throughout history.[31] Unfortunately the ultimate or ideal universal bibliography is still a dream, because such a work that meets this criterion is yet to be compiled. As the name implies, a general or universal bibliography must be a wide, comprehensive and complete as possible survey of the records of civilization in every field of knowledge and is not, therefore, restricted to any time, place, language, subject or country. Even though there is not a true universal bibliography currently available, attempts have been made at this even though they are incomplete (and probably always will be). Nonetheless, they are frequently of immense value. Universal bibliographies are particularly valuable to scholars who require the identification of materials for which they have incomplete bibliographical information. They also assist those who need to know what books have been written by a certain author. A close familiarity with major universal bibliographies also helps the researcher track down required items more quickly than would otherwise be possible.[32]

THE LIBRARY OF CONGRESS CATALOG (UNITED STATES)

Since 1942, when the first volumes of the Library of Congress Catalog were published,[33] this series of sets has been an invaluable asset to libraries where research is done mainly because of the immensity of the collections, the excellence of the cataloging, and the full bibliographical descriptions. It serves a variety of audiences, most of all librarians involved in cataloging, acquisitions, and reference work. Also it provides an excellent source for author bibliography, verification of bibliographic information, historical notes, location of copies and so on.

Several cumulative sets of volumes reproducing the Library of Congress cards are important. There is the massive Mansell set covering up to 1956, and two others, one covering 1942 to 1962 and the other 1956 to 1967.[34] From 1950 to 1982 the Library of Congress published various cumulative and annual sets covering entries arranged under LC Subject Headings.[35] These sets are continued by the microfiche version from 1983 to the present. Additional cumulative sets are now in preparation.[36]

Beginning in 1983 the Library of Congress ceased publishing the *National Union Catalog* in hard copy and adopted instead a microfiche format which it currently publishes. This format, of course, requires a microfiche reader in order to be used. The microfiche version utilizes a "register/index" arrangement in which all of the information traditionally found on Library of Congress cards now appear in a separate register in a numbered sequence according to the order in which the items are entered. Access to the register is provided by separate indexes for 1) names used as main or added entries; 2) titles; 3) LC series; and 4) LC subjects. Indexes display a shortened form of the record, with reference to the register number for full information. There are cumulative indexes for each year only.[37] In some ways this set is much more difficult and time consuming to use than the previously hardbound cumulative sets.

THE BRITISH LIBRARY (UNITED KINGDOM)

The British Library was created in 1973 from the holdings of the British Museum Library to serve as the national library. Comprising approximately 8.5 million titles in all European languages, the British Library administers one of the largest collections of books in the world.

The printed catalog of this vast library is a new cumulation of the old British Museum *Third General Catalogue* with its three supplements and all subsequently cataloged titles, plus many changes and additions. It includes all entries for pre-1975 imprints acquired and cataloged since 1976. Entries are listed in a single alphabetical sequence by author and the main entries are supported by cross references. Large or complex subject areas such as Aesop and the Bible include specially prepared indexes of sub-sections for quick reference.[38]

No subject catalog has been available from the British Library since the *British Museum Subject Index of Modern Books* concluded with the volumes covering 1971 to 1975. Now there is *The British Library General Subject Catalogue 1975–1985*.[39] Entries are cataloged according to AACR2 and arranged in an alphabetical sequence based on the subject headings of PRECIS (PREserved Context Index System), developed by the British Library Bibliographic Services Division and used in the *British National Bibliography*. Complete entries for a term may be found under several different subject headings. Each work cataloged is given a string of subject terms which are rotated by computer. The significant terms in the string are found as access points (or "lead terms") in the catalog. Each lead term may have other term to its right, which establish the context of the term, or indented on the line below it, which narrow its meaning as illustrated in the example below:

> SWEDEN
>   New towns. Environment planning
> NEW TOWNS, Sweden
> ENVIRONMENT PLANNING. New towns. Sweden

BIBLIOTHÈQUE NATIONALE (FRANCE)

The Bibliothèque Nationale is the national library of France. It has the largest collection of books published in the French language due to

French copyright law, which requires one copy of each book published to be deposited in its collection. It also has extensive collections in other languages, of course.

The catalog of this collection[40] includes entries that are arranged alphabetically by personal author. There are no entries for anonymous classics, periodicals, or corporate authors. Each volume includes the titles acquired up to the date of publication of that volume; thus there is a difference in coverage between the first volumes, which include the entries for the early part of the alphabet and which were published around 1900, and later volumes, which cover the middle and latter part of the alphabet and which were published fifty years later. Beginning with volume 189 (Tissonière) no entries after 1959 are included. Quinquennial supplements, beginning with 1960–1969 are published to keep this catalog up-to-date. These supplements include corporate entries and anonymous authors.

National and Trade Bibliographies

For bibliographic detail about most books the national and trade bibliographies are frequently consulted. They include primarily material published in one country and are directed to its book trade by supplying information needed in buying or selling books. There is a chain of comprehensive national and trade bibliographies for many countries that tend to record every book published from the beginning of printing. The record, of course, is not complete, but the concerted effort of bibliographers over the centuries is steadily decreasing the number of missing items.

UNITED STATES NATIONAL AND TRADE BIBLIOGRAPHIES

Covering publication in the United States there is a nearly comprehensive chain of national and trade bibliographies. The sources of information on current publications are reviewed first, followed by a chronological account of the retrospective sources.

For many years *Publishers Weekly*,[41] the official organ of the book trade, included a section called the "Weekly Record"[42] which listed alphabetically by author or title a selection of books released for publication during the week. For each entry, author, title, imprint, collation, price, and subject headings are given. Since 1974 this section has been issued as a separate publication. It serves as the basis for the *American*

Book Publishing Record which has the entries rearranged by subject according to the Dewey Decimal Classification and indexed by author and title. The monthly issues are then cumulated annually.[43]

A good source for current bibliographical information on recently published books is the *Cumulative Book Index* (CBI).[44] It is faster to use than the *Weekly Record* because entries are listed under author, title and subject interfiled in a dictionary arrangement. The CBI includes books published not only in the United States but also in the English language in other countries.

To locate books by publisher the *Publishers' Trade List Annual* (PTLA)[45] is a good source to consult. This annual publication consists of publishers' catalogs arranged alphabetically by publishers' names and bound together in sets of volumes. A separate section in the front of the first volume contains a table of contents and a listing of books from smaller publishers. These are arranged in several alphabets according to the length of the publication and can best be located by consulting the table of contents, which covers both the supplements and the main section. Because PTLA lacks a uniform system of arrangement, and because a decreasing number of important publishers are contributing their catalogs (due to fiscal constraints), the comprehensiveness and usefulness of this source has diminished.

Beginning in 1948, and originally conceived as an index to PTLA, *Books in Print*[46] was created. Issued annually, this work presently consists of seven volumes: two author volumes, one covering A-K and the other L-Z; two title volumes, and two subject volumes. The seventh volume contains a listing of publishers and addresses. Information is arranged alphabetically in each volume with author, title, publisher, editor, and date of publication along with price and some additional ordering information. This work is now available on CD-ROM.

For projected books there is *Forthcoming Books*.[47] Each issue provides a cumulated list of most books published in the United States since the compilation of the current issue of *Books in Print* and continues to offer information on titles announced for publication in the next five months. Each issue overlaps and updates the preceding one. There are separate author and title sections, in which publisher, price, and publication data are given. A subject guide is also part of this work.

Books published in soft covers are listed in *Paperbound Books in Print*.[48] The frequency of this publication has varied from its inception, but since 1972 it has been issued in two cumulated hardbound volumes per year, in March and November, and is arranged in three sections: title index, author index, and subject index.

A nearly unbroken chain of American retrospective national and trade bibliography starts with four major sets, each covering a particular period, that record with varying degrees of thoroughness the American books published from the introduction of the printing press into the colonies in 1639 to the beginning of comprehensive trade bibliography in 1876. A fifth set, spanning all of American history, but with many limitations, is usually considered as part of American retrospective bibliography.[49]

Covering the earliest period is a work compiled by Charles Evans, a noted American librarian who spent more than thirty years on his *American Bibliography*. This work includes books, pamphlets, and periodicals arranged chronologically by date of publication. There is an index of authors, and index for classified subjects, and an index for printers and publishers in each volume. Evans was only able to complete his work up to the letter M in the entries for 1799 when he died in 1935. Clifford Kenyon Shipton started with the letter N for 1799 and continued through the alphabet for 1800, with an author and subject index. Roger P. Bristol edited volume 14, which is a cumulative author-title index to the entire set, including pseudonyms, attributed authors, governmental agencies, and group entries for newspapers and almanacs. Related to Evans is the *National Index of Imprints Through 1800: The Short-Title Evans,* compiled by Shipton and James E. Mooney.[50] Here the 39,000 Evans items and 10,000 items not in Evans but numbered by Shipton and Mooney are arranged in one alphabetical list. Each entry gives the author when known, author's dates, short title, place of publication, printer and publisher, date of publication, pagination, Evans number, and location of the copy reproduced in the microprint edition of *Early American Imprints*.[51] It also lists the libraries that have the microprint cards. A checklist of 1,289 books in the Rare Books Division of the New York Public Library but not contained in Evans was published in 1960.[52]

The years from 1800 to 1820, which Evans had planned to cover, remained for many years in bibliographic limbo. Finally, in 1958, there began to appear a series of volumes compiled by Ralph R. Shaw and Richard H. Shoemaker which cover the bibliography of this period.[53] Generally this work follows the methods used by Evans and, like the older bibliography, gave the location of copies of the books listed. Unfortunately, this set was not as carefully compiled as was Evans due to a lack of time and funds; the inability of the compilers to examine first-hand all the works listed forced them to rely heavily on descriptions in secondary sources. Consequently, in some entries author's first names are omitted, in some cases only brief titles are given, and in others the name of the publisher is omitted as well as the number of pages and the size of the volume. Errors were inevitable, so this set should be used with some caution.[54] There are index volumes for authors, titles, and another that lists sources and library symbols. In 1983 appeared an index of printers, publishers, and booksellers, plus a geographical index.

A third major bibliography covering the period from 1820 to 1861 was compiled by Orville Augustus Roorbach,[55] a bookseller who intended this compilation mainly for the use of booksellers. Volume one (1820–1852) includes periodicals, sections on law books, state reports, and digests. The second (October 1852–May 1855), the third (May 1855–March 1958), and the forth (March 1858–January 1861), are less comprehensive. All four volumes are arranged alphabetically by author and title, and the entries include the publisher and occasionally the date of publication, but the bibliographical information supplied is generally scanty. Authors' names are often incomplete, and dates of publication and number of pages are omitted. Incomplete and often inaccurate as it is, however, Roorbach's work is currently the only general bibliography for the period.[56]

Another bibliographic set has been created to provide better coverage for these years. The *Checklist of American Imprints* was started by Richard H. Shoemaker before his death in 1970. The volumes in this series are planned to cover books published from 1820 to 1875 and are being compiled by various bibliographers.[57]

Continuing the Roorbach set is the *American Catalogue* (1861–1871),[58] which James Kelly, a young Irishman, managed to compile in spite of the devastating effects of the Civil War. Given the upheaval of the times it is not surprising that Kelly's work has many inaccuracies. He intended this publication to be a continuation of Roorbach's, but because of its large number of inaccuracies he was denied permission to designate it as such. Nevertheless, it forms the best available record for books published during this period.[59]

With the publication of *The American Catalogue of Books in Print*[60] (not to be confused with Kelly's *American Catalogue*), the United States had its first comprehensive national and trade bibliography. Books are listed in the first volume under both authors and titles. A subject list is provided in the second volume. Supplementary volumes followed at more or less regular intervals until 1910, when it was succeeded by its rival, the *United States Catalog*,[61] which the H. W. Wilson Company had been publishing since 1898. This catalog of books in print and for sale was supplemented by the *Cumulative Book Index*, issued periodically with cumulations. When the *United States Catalog* ceased publication in 1928, it was replaced by the permanent cumulations of CBI. The periodical supplements continue to list new books as they appear.[62]

Possibly the most ambitious national and trade bibliography spanning the field of American history, but with continually diminishing completeness is Joseph Sabin's *Bibliotheca Americana*, begun in 1868 and requiring the assistance of many others to complete.[63] Sabin was born and educated in England and learned bookbinding from a bookseller in Oxford. In 1848, he emigrated to the United States and spent the rest of his life working as a bookbinder, auctioneer, and bookseller in New York and Philadelphia. His original plan was to include in his bibliography all works related to the political, military, social, and religious history of the entire Western Hemisphere, from its discovery until his day. It is perhaps ironic that he, like Charles Evans, attempted more than he was able to accomplish in his lifetime. Only thirteen volumes had been completed when he died in 1881. The work was continued by Wilberforce Eames, librarian of the Lenox Library, who carried it through volume twenty by 1892. Nothing further was done until 1927, when a Carnegie grant made it possible for R. W. G. Vali to finally complete the work. It was published by the Bibliographical Society of America in 1936.[64] Sabin's bibliography contains 106,412 numbered entries. Added editions and titles are cited only in the notes and are counted. Arrangement is by author and each entry includes title, imprint, format, and collation. Many entries also have bibliographic notes and library location. Originally it was intended to include titles about America wherever published, however, with the passage of time it became clear that if the work were to be completed its scope would have to be drastically reduced. After volume twenty, therefore, all titles published since 1876 were dropped. (These were being listed in the new trade bibliographies anyway.) Broadsides published after 1800 were also excluded. Further restrictions followed: government publications were omitted, as were unimportant sermons, collections of world travel, general poetry, drama, and fiction after 1800 (unless of historical value, in which case it was included until 1830), and so on. Sabin's patchwork type of national bibliography, which is the result of overambitious planning and lack of time and funds, is a graphic example of what is all too common.[65] An additional related work is Lawrence S. Thompson's, *The New Sabin*.[66] This set covers works from the period,

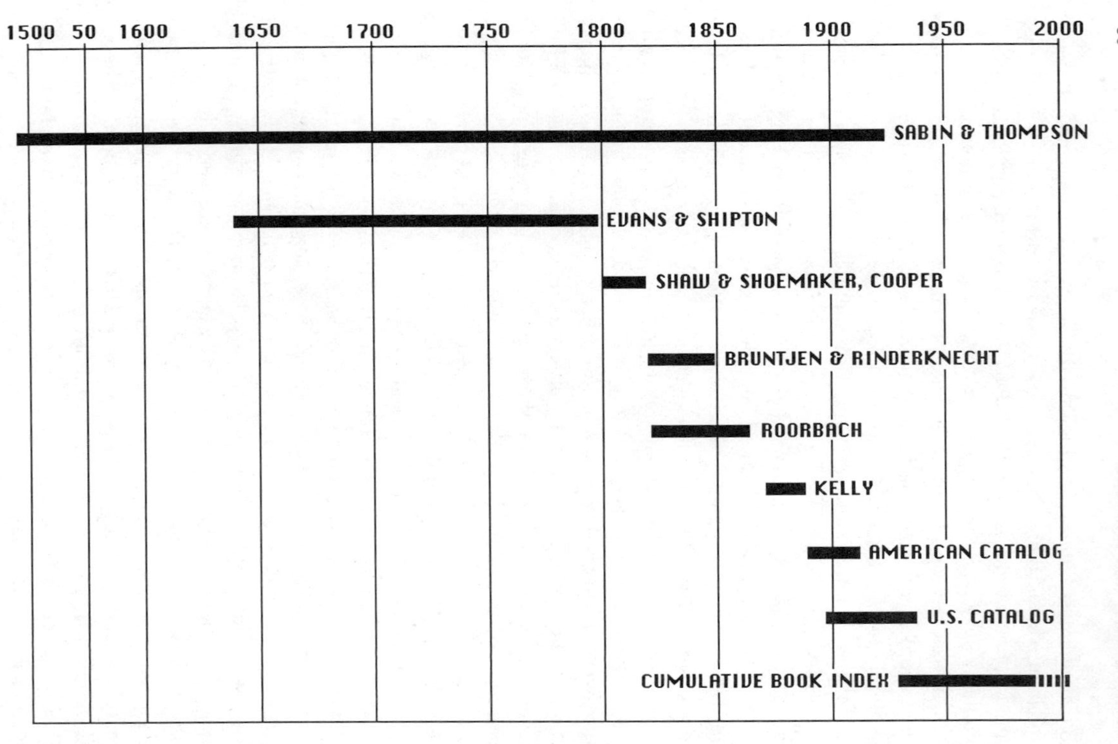

Figure No. 8. Chronology of American Retrospective National and Trade Bibliography

not all of which are in Sabin, that were examined by Thompson before his death. Entries are numbered serially, with each volume containing a separate author alphabet. The superb index for this set is found in volumes 5 and 10.

UNITED KINGDOM NATIONAL AND TRADE BIBLIOGRAPHIES

The chain of United Kingdom national and trade bibliography is much larger than that of the United States. For current books it must be recalled that the *Cumulative Book Index* is "a world list of books in the English language" and therefore will be useful for locating many British publications.

The major national bibliography in the United Kingdom is the *British National Bibliography*.[67] Often referred to as the BNB, this work is a subject list arranged by the Dewey Decimal Classification System, with alphabetical author, title, and subject indexes. Issued monthly, with annual and five-year cumulations, each cumulation has three sections: 1) a classified subject section; 2) an author and title section; and 3) a subject index. The lists are compiled from books and pamphlets received under the provision of the Copyright Act of the British Museum. Full bibliographic information is provided for each entry.

One of the more prominent United Kingdom trade bibliographies is *British Books in Print*.[68] In the late nineteenth century, Joseph Whitaker began to issue the *Reference Catalogue of Current Literature*, listing all the books in print at that time. Since 1965 it has been published under the title *British Books in Print*, and is now issued annually in four volumes. Publishers' names and addresses are listed in the front of the first volume. It includes authors, titles, and catchwords in a single alphabetical sequence.

Another important trade publication is *Whitaker's Cumulative Book List*.[69] In the 1920s this series, based on the records in a periodical publication called *The Bookseller*, was started. It is a classified list—that is arranged by subject, with author and title indexes. It provides comprehensive, but not complete coverage. Full bibliographical information is given for each entry including prices.

OTHER FOREIGN NATIONAL AND TRADE BIBLIOGRAPHIES

Like the United States and the United Kingdom, there are comparable national and trade bibliographic chains in many countries of the world.

No attempt is made here to list those of all countries. Instead, as an example the chain for France is indicated and two major sources for locating others are cited.

In France the main national and trade bibliography is *Bibliographie de la France-Biblio*.[70] Issued weekly and arranged in three parts: 1) classified; 2) titles; and 3) authors, this work is cumulated annually into the publication *Les Livres de l'Année-Biblio*.[71] For retrospective coverage one of the most extensive sources is *Bibliographie de la France* for the years 1811–1971.[72]

Two principal guides to national and trade bibliographies are Barbara L. Bell's *An Annotated Guide to Current National Bibliographies* and G. E. Gorman and J. J. Mills' *Guide to Current National Bibliographies in the Third World*.[73]

Subject Bibliographies

Subject bibliographies are lists in which both the purpose of compilation and the common characteristics of the listed materials are related to the subject matter of their contents. Such lists, like other bibliographies, may be current or retrospective, comprehensive or selective, and may or may not include annotations. They may be issued as periodicals or monographs, in book form or on separate cards, and even in the form of film, tape, or bibliographic information stored in a computer in machine-readable form so that the information can be retrieved on demand. Subject bibliographies range in importance and comprehensiveness from tools for the work of major disciplines and great industries, like *Chemical Abstracts*,[74] to brief lists of scattered references on some minute point of interest. In total, subject bibliographies form the majority of bibliographic output today and are so numerous that bibliographies of bibliographies are necessary to keep track of them. Surveyed below are six subject bibliographies, each representing a different subject, to illustrate the wide diversity of approaches and formats used in compilations of this kind.

Published bibliographies utilizing a strictly alphabetical arrangement are rarely used currently. Richard D. Woods in his bibliography, *Reference Materials on Mexican Americans*,[76] arranges 387 entries alphabetically by author covering bibliographies, checklists, indexes, guides, directories and other materials. The annotations are well written and there are complete author, title, and subject indexes.

Another infrequently used format is one where entries are arranged by type of material, such as monographs, dictionaries, indexes and the like. Guides to the literature often employ, at least partially, this type of arrangement. Dederick C. Ward and others have utilized this approach extensive in their work, *Geologic Reference Sources*.[77] It is a ready-reference guide to materials in the geological sciences. Coverage includes articles, books, maps, etc. arranged by type under sections on general, subject and regional sources. Access is provided by subject and geographic indexes.

Subject bibliographers using mostly a chronological arrangement of entries are also not very common currently. Obviously this approach is most applicable to historically related subjects. A good example is *Footnotes to History*, by Harold S. Sharp.[78] Three hundred and thirteen events or episodes from American history are arranged in chronological sequence. Each episode is discussed followed by a list of related readings. The citations provide complete bibliographic information.

The most common arrangement employed by subject bibliographers is a classified one by broad or narrow topics or a combination of both. To illustrate a well-organized classified arrangement is a compilation by Graham C. Kinloch entitled, *Race and Ethnic Relations*.[79] Kinloch annotates and indexes 1,068 sociological studies, including books, journal articles, and some doctoral dissertations issued on race from 1960 to 1979.

An excellent example of a current subject bibliography utilizing a classified arrangement is, *Recent Publications on Governmental Problems*.[80] Issued twice monthly, this publication is a checklist that indexes articles, books, pamphlets, and other materials relating to state and local government. Most useful as a source for identifying documents, research reports, and other nontrade materials. Internal arrangement is under such broad topics as "Reference" and "Energy," and by sub-headings under these. Full bibliographic information is given, including price (when available) and the publisher's address. Since 1978 the annual cumulation apparently has had a subject and author index.

Author Bibliographies

Certain basic aims constitute the purposes of modern author bibliographies: the location, identification, and recording of the significant forms of all a writer's utterances that have been disseminated through the printed word. There are problems associated with achieving these aims. The most obvious is attempting to establish the canon when it becomes difficult to identify anonymous or pseudonymous contributions. There is also a problem in discovering the existence of unrecoverable attributions of undeterminable size and depth.[81] There are, of course, other difficulties, but most author bibliographies do achieve a reasonable amount of definitiveness despite the existence of unknown or unrecorded items.

Over the past two decades, production of author bibliographies has accelerated many fold. They appear in numerous publications and formats—full-length books, journal articles, bibliographies attached to critical works, and the like. Of course, these compilations vary in coverage from extensive to highly selective. They may include an author's full canon, works by and about an author, criticism only, a special aspect of an author's life and works, or may be a listing of the holdings of a particular library or bookseller's collection. Using John Steinbeck as an example, the bibliographic works discussed below represent some of the major forms that comprise this branch of enumerative bibliography.

Very few authors have the need for a separate bibliography of bibliographies, but John Steinbeck is one of them. *Steinbeck Bibliographies: An Annotated Guide*, by Robert B. Harmon,[82] provides an example. Entries are arranged in alphabetical sequence by author or title along with extensive annotations. For each of the 202 citations, full bibliographic information is given along with applicable subject headings. Access is provided by author, title, subject, series, and journal indexes.

One of the most useful types of author bibliographies is one that is both descriptive and enumerative in nature. The most definitive bibliography of this type covering the writings of John Steinbeck is Adrian Homer Goldstone and John R. Payne's, *John Steinbeck: A Bibliographical Catalogue*.[83] This work is by far the most extensive record by and about John Steinbeck. First editions are described according to the rules for descriptive bibliography, and other works less fully. It provides bibliographical information on each Steinbeck title in chronological order, including major editions of each title. Other sections cover his contributions to books, periodicals, translations, and those works produced for stage, screen, television, and radio. There is a rather short section on books and articles about Steinbeck.

Catalogs of special collections located in libraries containing materials by and about a specific author are becoming more prevalent. One of the more extensive relating to John Steinbeck has been published by the

Salinas Public Library, *John Steinbeck, A Guide to the Collection of the Salinas Public Library*.[84] Materials in this catalog are listed under broad headings such as Books, Contributions to Books, Contributions to Periodicals, Manuscripts, Correspondence, and so on. Included are many photographs and illustrations. Unfortunately there is no index.

There are many bookseller's catalogs that can be considered as legitimate author bibliographies. Among those published relating to John Steinbeck, perhaps the most extensive and esthetically pleasing is Morrow (Bradford) Bookseller Ltd., *John Steinbeck: A Collection of Books and Manuscripts*.[85] This compilation is an exceptionally attractive, useful sales catalog of the collection gathered by Harry Valentine of Pacific Grove, California. The seven hundred numbered entries cover a range of Steinbeck materials from manuscripts and printed works to photographs, film posters, and ephemera. The annotations provide excellent descriptions and frequently refer to related entries. Included are illustrations comprising about fifty black-and-white photographs, most quite clear, of selected items. There is no index, which is indeed unfortunate.

Specialized bibliographies covering a particular aspect of an author's life and works are appearing in ever greater numbers. A relevant example concerning the development of John Steinbeck as a writer is Robert J. DeMott's, *Steinbeck's Reading*.[86] This compilation is the first full-length list of books that passed through Steinbeck's hands during his lifetime, some of which influenced his writing. The 934 items are arranged in alphabetical sequence by author and annotated with Steinbeck's own comments in many cases, thus making it of double interest to the Steinbeck collector or scholar. DeMott also furnishes a lengthy, closely analytic introduction, some engaging illustrations, more than 50 pages of notes, and an authoritative bibliography. Author and title indexes facilitate the use of this bibliography.

Lists of critical works about authors are common and often quite extensive. Related to critical writings about Steinbeck is Maurice Beebe and Jackson R. Bryer's article, "Criticism of John Steinbeck: A Selected Checklist."[87] This extensive list covers both critical books and articles about Steinbeck and his writings. The body of the bibliography is divided into two main sections: Part I consists of general studies dealing with Steinbeck's life and writing; and Part II lists discussions of individual novels and stories, with an index to the general studies listed in Part I as well as special studies not previously listed. Titles of the major works on Steinbeck are capitalized. Books and essays by the same writer are listed chronologically, but no attempt was made to list all appearances of the same work, generally giving priority to books over periodicals. Omissions include foreign criticism, unpublished theses or dissertations, transient reviews, and routine discussions in encyclopedias, handbooks, and histories of literature.

Selective or Elective Bibliographies

Bibliographies of this kind list selected items, which are arranged systematically, usually according to subject. They are most useful in selecting retrospective material, especially for small and medium-sized libraries. Some of these are guides to best or standard works. Selective or elective, bibliographies may be either retrospective or current, and most vary in terms of format and coverage.

For current materials, an excellent source is *The Booklist*.[88] Issued semimonthly except for August, this periodical is a general review source for all types of books, emphasis being on materials thought suitable for small to medium-sized public libraries. It is arranged by broad classes. Complete bibliographical information is given for each entry, including price.

For those who are looking for guidance on what to read in a number of different areas there is *Good Books: A Book Lover's Companion*, by Steven Gilbar.[89] Gilbar's list is arranged under 500 general subject headings and the almost 9,000 books cover both fiction and nonfiction. Under the subject headings the books are listed alphabetically by author. Each title included has a brief description attached, and for some there are references to related titles. Unfortunately not all pertinent bibliographic information is included, only author, title and date of publication. There are author and subject indexes.

Selecting good books to read from a writer's perspective can be gained from *Writer's Choice: A Library of Rediscoveries*, by Linda S. and William A. Katz.[90] Entries are arranged in two main sections, fiction and nonfiction. Under fiction the entries are arranged alphabetically by author. For nonfiction, entries are organized alphabetically by author under sixteen broad subject headings such as biography, sports, etc. There is full bibliographical information provided for each entry and a note on the author, and something about the book. Included is an index of recommended readings and one covering authors and titles.

Somewhat similar to Clifton Fadiman's *Lifetime Reading Plan*,[91] is

British writer Philip Ward's, *A Lifetime's Reading: The World's 500 Great Books*.[92] Arranged in chapters designated Year 1, Year 2, etc., are the suggested readings. Starting with Year 5, he devotes each segment to a geographic location. Items are described to assist users in their selections. Access is provided via an author/title index.

Since the early 1920s a standard reference guide to the best in reading has been the *Reader's Adviser*.[93] This work is a guide to the best in print in different literary forms and subject fields, such as literature, biographies, classics, drama, poetry, fiction, dictionaries and encyclopedias, history, travel, science, and philosophy. The thirteenth edition 1986–1988, is in 6 volumes with volumes 4 through 6 being published in 1988.

A series of catalogs published by H. W. Wilson called the *Standard Catalog Series*[94] has assisted in the selection of materials for various types of libraries and groups. These catalogs are carefully selected lists with well-written annotations, quoting source. They are generally arranged in three parts: 1) classified catalog, arranged by the Dewey Decimal Classification; 2) author, title, subject, and analytical index; 3) directory of publishers. This series includes the following publications: 1) *Children's Catalog;* 2) *Junior High School Library Catalog;* 3) *Senior High School Library Catalog;* 4) *Public Library Catalog;* and 5) *Fiction Catalog*.

Bibliophilic Bibliographies

A bibliophile is someone who loves or collects books. Quite often this person collects books because of their physical characteristics. Consequently a bibliophile may be interested in artistically distinguished bindings, kinds of typefaces, illustrations, and so on. Acquiring first editions is a specialty of many book collectors.[95]

Bibliophiles seem to have a personal attachment to each book they obtain. Very often they are well-read persons or scholars. A book collector is able to acquire a passion for bibliographic learning, at times as great as the passion for the physical features of books. Bibliophiles have assisted in the development of the care, preservation, and decoration of books, which has led to a greater appreciation of them. In many ways they have contributed a great deal to scholarship.[96]

There are numerous lists of books of interest to bibliophiles, such as those dealing with first editions. Often the chief motive in compiling such lists is self-satisfaction, though they may incidentally possess certain distributive value. These lists place great emphasis on the description of books, which are outstanding from the point of view of peculiarities in their physical makeup. Because bibliophiles are mainly interested in early books, bibliophilic bibliography forms an important part of early bibliography.[97]

Serious book collectors, libraries, scholars, booksellers as well as the general reader will find Van Allen Bradley's compilation, *The Book Collector's Handbook of Values,*[98] very useful. Entries are arranged alphabetically by author, or title if an author is unknown. Inclusions are mostly limited to nineteenth- and twentieth-century British and American publications. For each item listed, a price range is indicated for copies in good condition.

A contemporary work covering American authors from colonial times to the present is, *First Printings of American Authors*.[99] Each volume of this five-volume set presents a group of authors arranged alphabetically. A photograph of each author accompanies a chronological listing of his or her works, including major distinguishing features of first and other editions. Some entries feature facsimile title pages. Volume 4 has an author index to the first four volumes. Volume 5 has been recently published and has a separate index. Some secondary works relating to each author are also included including bibliographies.

Still considered by many booksellers to be the standard in the field is *Merle Johnson's American First Editions*.[100] Given is information concerning the identification of first editions desired by collectors and booksellers.

Specialized Catalogs

Catalogs could well fit within the universal, or general classification; they are, however, a distinct type of enumerative bibliography. They are ordinarily lists, inventorial in character, of books of which the common characteristics are not that they have the same author or subject matter (although either or both of these may be true) but that they are issued by a particular publisher or group of publishers, are offered for sale by a particular bookseller, or are owned by a particular library or group of libraries.[101]

An example of a catalog representing the collection of a specialized agency of an academic institution is the *Subject Catalog of the Institute of Governmental Studies Library, University of California, Berkeley*.[102] All material is classified by a specially developed adaptation of the Library of

Congress system with more than 2,000 subject headings. Also covered are major periodicals, which are analyzed for pertinent articles. Each subject heading includes a geographical subdivision.

A representative catalog of a scholarly organization is the *Catalog of the Foreign Relations Library*.[103] This is the catalog of the library of the Council on Foreign Relations. The collection totals approximately 55,000 volumes. The catalog is arranged in dictionary form—author, subject, and title interfiled.

Many booksellers issue specialized catalogs of important collections that are extensive. One by John H. Jenkins entitled, *Works of Genius*,[104] is a very beautifully printed and illustrated bookseller's catalog of 100 antiquarian books. Extensive bibliographical and additional information is provided for each item. Most booksellers' catalogs are not this well done.

Specialized collections within large libraries have catalogs that are useful. One of these is located in the Newberry Library, Chicago, entitled, *A Catalogue of the Everett D. Graff Collection of Western Americana*.[105] The Graff collection consists of approximately 10,000 books, pamphlets, maps, broadsides, and manuscripts of high quality relating to exploration, settlement, and development of the country west of the Mississippi River. This catalog (4,801 items) is limited mainly to source materials and includes only those secondary works of exceptional interest or value.

Bibliographies of Bibliographies

Multiplication of bibliographies of different types in many subject fields has resulted in the compilation of bibliographies of bibliographies. These bibliographies illustrate the existence of materials on particular subjects or on specific authors, sometimes from the very beginning of printing to the present time. No one knows for sure just how many separately published bibliographies have been compiled—but the number must be immense. The bibliography of bibliographies is particularly useful as a means of gaining access to the literature of an obscure or limited topic or one not adequately covered in the standard bibliographies. The person who has never consulted one of these works can have no conception of the wealth and diversity of information provided by bibliographical writing or the varied and complex forms in which such writings occur.[106]

An example of this genre of bibliography is *A World Bibliography of Bibliographies*, by Theodore Besterman.[107] Besterman's work is considered a classic general bibliography of bibliographies and is the most extensive work of its kind, listing some 117,000 items. It is a classified bibliography of separately published bibliographies of books, manuscripts, and patent abridgments. Besterman is especially useful for old bibliographies of all countries and periods.

For current coverage as well as retrospective bibliographies there is the *Bibliographic Index*.[108] This work records new bibliographies as they are issued, whether they appear as separate books or pamphlets or as lists accompanying other works. It is issued twice a year in paperback form and cumulated annually in a bound volume. Items are arranged alphabetically under subject. Because of its extensive coverage, this work is very valuable in itself and as a complement to Besterman.

Out-of-date but still useful is *Bibliographies, Subject and National*, by Robert Lewis Collison.[109] It is a handbook containing 400 to 500 carefully selected and annotated citations to bibliographies. Part 1 covers subject bibliographies arranged in Dewey Classification order, and Part 2 covers universal and national bibliographies. Includes an index of subjects and personal names.

Many bibliographies of bibliographies related to specific subject areas are being compiled currently. For example, *Peace and War:* A Guide to Bibliographies,[110] compiled by Berenice A. Carroll, Clinton F. Fink, and Jane E. Mohraz is an annotated bibliography of 1,398 bibliographies related to war and peace. Entries are arranged under broad subject headings and are accessed via author and subject indexes.

Guides to the Literature

These compilations are not strictly subject bibliographies in the ordinary sense, because they usually go beyond the normal limits of enumerative bibliography in including not simply lists of references but also discussions of the functions and uses of the types of literature. Some go further, in providing information on careers, instructions on how to use the library, or work assignments for student development. Denis Grogan (cited below) has identified two principal types of guides to the literature: 1) textbook, and 2) reference book. The chief difference between these two is the format: in the textbook, sources are considered in the context of an essay on the subject matter of a particular field or area, whereas the reference-book guide is a subject bibliography often accompanied by very brief introductions to each type of material listed.

An excellent example of the textbook approach is Denis Joseph Grogan's, *Science and Technology: An Introduction to the Literature*.[111] Written in essay form, the chapters deal with encyclopedias, dictionaries, handbooks, etc., describing their principal uses and citing individual sources or guides.

Exemplifying the reference book approach is Frederick L. Holler's, *Information Sources of Political Science*.[112] This extensive work lists and annotates 2,423 printed or computerized reference works in political science including public administration and international relations. Holler provides lengthy, critical annotations and tables illustrating interrelationships of titles. Access is made possible through author, title and subject indexes.

An example of a mixture between the textbook and reference book approaches is contained in, *Sources of Information in the Social Sciences*, edited by William H. Webb, et al.[113] Formerly edited by Carl Milton White, this work provides bibliographic essays as well as annotated lists of reference works. It covers the social sciences in general and nine subdivisions. Each one consists of two sections: 1) a bibliographic essay written by a specialist to explain the history and methodology of the discipline and to cite a substantial number of pertinent, significant monographs; and 2) annotated lists of reference sources, grouped by form, type, or specialized aspect—e.g., guides to the literature, abstracts, bibliographies, encyclopedias, and handbooks. Periodicals are listed in each category. A detailed table of contents and index of authors, titles, and subjects are included.

The standard guide to reference works such as this one is, *Guide to Reference Books*, edited by Eugene Paul Sheehy, et al.[114] The successor to Winchell and Mudge, Sheehy has carried on the excellent reputation of this outstanding reference guide. While Sheehy uses the reference-book approach, the coverage is extensive and the annotations well designed.

Selected Related Writings

GENERAL

Bates, Marcia J. "Rigorous Systematic Bibliography," *RQ*, 16 (Fall 1976), pp. 7–16.

Bryer, Jackson, R. "From Second-Class Citizenship to Respectability: The Odyssey of an Enumerative Bibliographer," *Literary Research Newsletter*, 3 (Spring 1978), 55–61.

Clapp, Verner W. "Bibliography," *Encyclopedia Americana*, 3 (1983), pp. 721–724.

Downs, Robert B., and Frances B. Jenkins, eds. *Bibliography: Current State and Future Trends*. Urbana: University of Illinois Press, 1967.

Hackman, Martha L. *The Practical Bibliographer*. Englewood Cliffs, NJ: Prentice-Hall, 1970.

Krummel, Donald W. *Bibliographies: Their Aims and Methods*. London: Mansell, 1984.

Robinson, Anthony M. L. *Systematic Bibliography: A Practical Guide to the Work of Compilation*. 4th ed., rev. New York: Saur, 1979.

Van Hoesen, Henry Bartlett, and Frank Keller Walter. *Bibliography: Practical, Enumerative, Historical: An Introductory Manual*. New York: Scribners, 1929.

BIBLIOGRAPHIC CONTROL

Davinson, Donald E. *Bibliographic Control*. 2nd ed. London: Bingley, 1981.

Downs, Robert B. "Problems of Bibliographical Control," *Library Trends*, 2 (April 1954), pp. 498–508.

Shera, Jesse Hauk. Bibliographic Management," *American Documentation*, 2 (January 1951), pp. 47–54.

________, and Margaret E. Egan, eds. *Bibliographic Organization*. Chicago: University of Chicago Press, 1951.

Stokes, Roy. *Bibliographical Control and Service*. New York: London House and Maxwell, 1965.

Wilson, Patrick. *Two Kinds of Power: An Essay on Bibliographical Control*. Berkeley: University of California Press, 1978, c1968.

NATIONAL AND TRADE BIBLIOGRAPHY

Bell, Barbara L. *An Annotated Guide to Current National Bibliographies*. Alexandria, VA: Chadwyck-Healey, 1986.

Cameron, Shelia H. M. "Compiling a National Bibliography," *SLA News* (Scottish Library Association), No. 156 (March/April 1980), pp. 53–56.

Conover, Helen F. *Current National Bibliography*. Washington, D.C.: Library of Congress, General Reference and Bibliography Division, 1955; Reprinted by Greenwood Press, 1968.

Gorman, G. E., and J. J. Mills. *Guide to Current National Bibliographies in the Third World*. 2nd rev. ed. London: Zell, 1987.

SUBJECT BIBLIOGRAPHY

Bibliography and the Historian. Edited by Dagmar Horna Perman. Santa Barbara, CA: Clio, 1968.

Hale, Barbara M. *The Study of Subject Bibliography of the Social Sciences and Humanities*. Oxford: Pergamon Press, 1970.

Needham, Christopher D., ed. *The Study of Subject Bibliography with Special Reference to the Social Sciences*. College Park, MD: School of Library Services, University of Maryland, 1970.

Staveley, Ronald. *Notes on Subject Study*. London: Deutsch, 1962.

________, Ia C. McIlwaine and John H. St. J. McIlwaine. *Introduction to Subject Study*. London: Deutsch, 1967.

AUTHOR BIBLIOGRAPHY

Edwards, Anthony S. G. "Some Problems in Modern Enumerative Bibliography," *Text: Transactions of the Society for Textual Scholarship*, 1 (1981), pp. 327–336.

Laurence, Dan H. "A Portrait of the Author as a Bibliography," *The Book Collector*, 35 (Summer 1986), pp. 165–177.

McKitterick, David. "Author Bibliographies," *The Book Collector*, 32 (Winter 1983), pp. 391–406.

Notes

1. Eric William Padwick, *Bibliographical Method: An Introductory Survey*. (Cambridge, Eng.: James Clarke, 1969), p. 13.
2. Richard H. Shoemaker, "Bibliography (General)," *Library Trends*, 15 (January 1967), p. 5.
3. William H. Bond, Bibliography and Bibliographers," *AB Bookman's Weekly*, 47 (April 26, 1971), p. 1395.
4. Neal R. Harlow, "Bibliographers in an Age of Science," *Revue de l'Université d'Ottawa*, 23 (January/March 1953), p. 40.
5. Conrad Gesner, *Bibliotheca Universalis sive Catalogus Omnium Scriptorum Locupletissmus in Tribus Linguis Latina, Graeca, et Hebraica*. . . . (Zurich: Christoph Froschauer, 1545).
6. Nicolas Antonio, *Bibliotheca Hispana* . . . (Rome: Nicolaus Angelus Tinassius and Antonius de Rubeis, 1672–1696), 4 vols.
7. Edward Arber, *Term Catalogues, 1668–1709*. . . . (London: Arber; New York: Dodd, 1903–1906), 3 vols.
8. See Harlow, p. 40.
9. Guillaume François DeBure, *Bibliographie Instructive: ou traite de la connoissance de livres rares et singuliers*. . . . (Paris: G. F. DeBure, 1763–1782), 10 vols.
10. Georg Schneider, *Theory and History of Bibliography*. Translated by Ralph Robert Shaw. (New York: Columbia University Press, 1934), pp. 5, 277.
11. Roy Stokes, *The Function of Bibliography*. 2nd ed. (Aldershot, Eng.: Gower, 1982), p. 44.
12. Marcia J. Bates, "Rigorous Systematic Bibliography," *RQ*, 16 (Fall 1976), p. 7.
13. Ibid.
14. Ibid., p. 9.
15. See Bond, p. 1395.
16. Girja Kumar and Krishan Kumar, *Bibliography*. (New Delhi: Vikas, 1976), p. 9.
17. Ibid.
18. William A. Katz, *Introduction to Reference Work, Volume I, Basic Information Sources*. 4th ed. (New York: McGraw-Hill, 1982), p. 41.
19. See Kumar, p. 177.
20. Verner W. Clapp, "The Role of Bibliographic Organization in Contemporary Civilization," In: *Bibliographic Organization*, edited by Jesse H. Shera and Margaret E. Egan. (Chicago: University of Chicago Press, 1951), p. 4.
21. Robert B. Downs and Frances B. Jenkins, "Introduction," *Library Trends*, 15 (January 1967), p. 337.
22. See Kumar, p. 178.
23. Ibid., p. 179.

24. Ajit Kumar Mukherjee, *Book Selection and Systematic Bibliography*. (Calcutta: World Press, 1960), p. 72.

25. Ibid., p. 74.

26. Arundell J. K. Esdaile, *A Student's Manual of Bibliography*, 3rd ed., revised by Roy Stokes. (New York: Barnes and Noble, 1954), p. 283.

27. Raynard C. Swank, "Cataloging Cost Factors," *Library Quarterly*, 26 (October 1956), p. 305.

28. Ludwig Hain, *Repertorium Bibliographicum, in quo libri omnes ab arte typographica inventa usque ad annum MD typis expressi ordine alphabetico . . . recensentur* (Stuttgart & Tübingen: J. G. Cotta; Paris: J. Renouard, 1826–1838), 2 vols. in 4 parts.

29. *Humanities Index* (New York: H. W. Wilson, 1974—date), v.1-date.

30. *Biological Abstracts* (Philadelphia: Biological Abstracts, 1926—date), v.1—date.

31. Ray Astbury, *Bibliography and Book Production*. (New York: Pergamon Press, 1967), p. 123.

32. Mukunda Lal Chakraborti, *Bibliography in Theory and Practice*. 2nd rev. and enl. ed. (Calcutta: World Press, 1975), pp. 347–348.

33. U.S. Library of Congress, *A Catalog of Books Represented by Library of Congress Printed Cards Issued to July 31, 1942* (Ann Arbor, Mich.: Edwards Bros., 1942–1946), 167 vols., Reprinted, (New York: Rowman and Littlefield, 1963). This was followed by *Supplement: Cards Issued August 1, 1942–December 31, 1947* (Ann Arbor, Mich.: Edwards Bros., 1942), Reprinted, (New York: Rowman and Littlefield, 1963), 42 vols., and by *Library of Congress Author Catalog: A Cumulative List of Works Represented by Library of Congress Printed Cards, 1948–1952* (Ann Arbor, Mich.: Edwards Bros., 1953), Reprinted, (New York: Rowman and Littlefield, 1964), 24 vols. It is continued by the *National Union Catalog: A Cumulative Author List Representing Library of Congress Printed Cards and Titles Reported by Other American Libraries, 1953–1957* (Ann Arbor, Mich.: Edwards Bros., 1958) 28 vols. Other sets in this series include: *1958–1962* (New York: Rowman and Littlefield, 1962), 54 vols., *1963–1967* (Ann Arbor, Mich.: Edwards Bros., 1973), 119 vols., and *1973–1977* (New York: Rowman and Littlefield, 1978), 135 vols. From 1978 to 1982, the Library of Congress published separate sets for each year: *1978*, 16 vols., *1979*, 16 vols., *1980*, 18 vols., *1981*, 15 vols., and *1982*, 21 vols. From 1983 to the present a microfiche format (see text) has been employed for this catalog.

34. *National Union Catalog, Pre-1956 Imprints. A Cumulative Author List Representing Library of Congress Printed Cards and Titles Reported by Other American Libraries* (London: Mansell, 1968–1981), 754 vols. Volumes 687–754 are a supplement to the basic set of 686 volumes. The other two cumulative sets include, *Library of Congress* and *National Union Catalog Author Lists, 1942–1962: A Master Cumulation* (Detroit: Gale Research, 1969–1971), 152 vols., which overlaps the Mansell set and *National Union Catalog, 1956 Through 1967. A Cumulative Author List Representing Library of Congress Printed Cards and Titles Reported by Other American Libraries* (Totowa, NJ: Rowman and Littlefield, 1970–1972), 125 vols.

35. U.S. Library of Congress, *Library of Congress Catalog—Books: Subjects* (Washington, D.C.: Library of Congress, 1950—date). This series of volumes were issued in the following cumulations: *1950–1954*, (Ann Arbor, Mich.: J. W. Edwards, 1955), 20 vols., *1955–1959*, (Paterson, NJ: Pageant Books, 1960), 22 vols., *1960–1964* (Ann Arbor, Mich.: J. W. Edwards, 1965), 25 vols., *1965–1969* (Ann Arbor, Mich.: J. W. Edwards, 1970), 42 vols., *1970–1974* (Totowa, NJ: Rowman and Littlefield, 1976), 100 vols. The years 1975–1982 were published annually in separate sets. From 1983 to date subjects are

part of the microfiche version of the *National Union Catalog*. Motion pictures, films, etc. have been covered in U.S. Library of Congress, *Library of Congress Catalog—Motion Pictures and Filmstrips, 1953–1957, 1958–1962, 1963–1967, 1968–1972* (Ann Arbor, Mich.: Edwards, 1958–1973). Continued by U.S. Library of Congress, *Films and Other Materials for Projection, Oct. 1972/June 1973–78* (Washington, D.C.: Library of Congress, 1974–1979). Motion pictures, video recordings, filmstrips, transparency sets etc. are now listed in *NUC Audiovisual Materials* [*microform*]. *Jan./Mar. 1983—date* (Washington, D.C. Library of Congress, 1983—date). This is the microfiche version. Covering music is, U.S. Library of Congress, *Library of Congress Catalog—Music and Phonorecords, 1953–1972* (Washington, D.C.: Library of Congress, 1953–1972). Continued by *National Union Catalog. Music, Books on Music, and Sound Recordings. Jan./June 1973—date* (Washington, D.C.: Library of Congress, 1973—date).

36. The K. G. Saur Company is now engaged in a monumental bibliographic service for the scholarly community by making available on microfiche the entire Library of Congress catalog for the years 1898 to 1980 in its *Main Catalog of the Library of Congress* (New York: Saur, 1984—date). The 10,000 fiche includes author, title, subject series, etc. cards in a single dictionary sequence.

37. Eugene P. Sheehy, ed., *Guide to Reference Books*. 10th ed. (Chicago: American Library Association, 1986), p. 13.

38. *The British Library General Catalogue of Printed Books to 1975* (New York: Saur; London: Bingley, 1979–1987), 360 vols. Two single volume indexes accompany this set. There is a *Subheadings Index* (New York: Saur, 1982), 197p., and a *Title Index* (New York: Saur, 1982), 654p.

39. *The British Library General Subject Catalogue 1975–1985* (New York: Saur, 1987), 75 vols.

40. Paris. Bibliothèque Nationale, *Catalogue Général des Livres Imprimés: Auteurs* (Paris: Impr. Nationale, 1900—date), consists of 231 volumes as of 1981. There is an additional important set, *Catalogue Général des Livres Imprimés, Auteurs-Collectivités-Auteurs—Anonymes, 1960–1969* (Paris: Impr. Nationale, 1972–1978), 27 vols.

41. *Publishers Weekly* (New York: Bowker, 1872—date), v.1—date.

42. *Weekly Record* (New York: Bowker, 1974—date).

43. *American Book Publishing Record* (New York: Bowker, 1876—date), v.1-date. Annual cumulations have been published since 1965. Also Bowker has issued two cumulative sets to date (1876–1949), 15 vols., and (1950–1977), 15 vols.

44. *Cumulative Book Index: A World List of Books in the English Language* (New York: H. W. Wilson, 1898—date).

45. *Publishers' Trade List Annual* (New York: Bowker, 1873—date). A microfiche version covering 1903–1963 has been published by Meckler Publications, Westport, CT.: 1980 (containing 4,100 fiche) with an index compiled by Anthony Abbott which indicates the fiche numbers and position on the fiche, of the catalog of a given publisher for a given year.

46. *Books in Print: An Author-Title-Series Index to the Publisher's Trade List Annual* (New York: Bowker, 1948—date).

47. *Forthcoming Books* (New York: Bowker, 1966—date).

48. *Paperbound Books in Print* (New York: Bowker, 1955—date).

49. Martha L. Hackman, *The Practical Bibliographer* (Englewood Cliffs, NJ: Prentice-Hall, 1970), p. 21.

50. Charles Evans, *American Bibliography: A Chronological Dictionary of All Books,*

Pamphlets and Periodical Publications Printed in the United States of America from the Genesis of Printing in 1639 Down to and Including the Year 1800 (Chicago: Printed for the Author, 1903–1959), 14 vols. Volumes 13–14 were published by the American Antiquarian Society, Worcester, Mass. Reprinted (New York: Peter Smith, 1941–1967). Added to this set is Roger P. Bristol's, *Supplement to Charles Evans' American Bibliography* (Charlottesville, VA: Published for the Bibliographical Society of America and the Bibliographical Society of the University of Virginia by the University Press of Virginia, 1970), 636p. Later Bristol compiled his *Index to Supplement. . . .* (Charlottesville, VA: Published for The Bibliographical Society of the University of Virginia by the University Press of Virginia, 1971), 191p., and an *Index to Printers, Publishers, and Booksellers Indicated by Charles Evans in His American Bibliography* (Charlottesville, VA: Bibliographical Society of the University of Virginia, 1961), 172p. See also Clifton Kenyon Shipton, and James E. Mooney, *National Index of American Imprints Through 1800: The Short-Title Evans* (Worcester, MA: American Antiquarian Society and Barre Publishers, 1970), 2 vols. This is a combined index to Evans and Bristol, with corrections.

51. *Early American Imprints* has been published from 1955 to the present by Readex Microprint, New York, in two series. The first series published from 1955 to 1983 covered Evans (1639–1800) and consisted of two different formats. The first was issued on microcards (31,000 cards) published from 1955 to 1983 and the second on microfiche (approximately 22,000 fiche) up to 1983 when the series was considered as complete as possible. The second series covers the same period as the Shaw-Shoemaker bibliography, i.e. 1801–1819, published in microprint consisting of over 52,000 cards up to December of 1980. This set is apparently still in progress.

52. New York. Public Library. Rare Book Division, *Checklist of Additions to Evans' American Bibliography in the Rare Book Division of the New York Public Library*. Compiled by Lewis M. Stark and Maud D. Cole (New York: The Library, 1960), 110p.

53. Ralph Robert Shaw, and Richard H. Shoemaker, *American Bibliography: A Preliminary Checklist* (Metuchen, NJ: Scarecrow Press, 1958–1966), 22 vols.

54. See Hackman, p. 23.

55. Orville Augustus Roorbach, *Bibliotheca Americana, 1820–61* (New York: Roorbach, 1852–1861), 4 vols. Reprinted, (New York: Peter Smith, 1939).

56. See Hackman, p. 23.

57. Richard H. Shoemaker, *A Checklist of American Imprints for 1820–1829* (Metuchen, NJ: Scarecrow Press, 1964–1971), 10 vols. The volume for 1830 was compiled by Gale Cooper (Scarecrow, 1972); those for 1831–1833 (Scarecrow, 1973–1979), by Scott and Carol R. Bruntjen. A title index was compiled by M. Frances Cooper (Scarecrow, 1972), and an author index with corrections and sources to the 1820–1829 set (Scarecrow, 1973). Later years are covered by the series, *Checklist of American Imprints for [date]* (Metuchen, NJ: Scarecrow Press, 1964–date). The volume for 1834 was compiled by Carol R. and Scott Bruntjen (Scarecrow, 1982) and the years 1835 to 1839 (Scarecrow, 1985–1988), by Carol Rinderknecht.

58. James Kelly, *American Catalogue of Books Published in the United States from Jan. 1861 to Jan. 1871* (New York: Wiley, 1866–1871), 2 vols. Reprinted, (New York: Peter Smith, 1938).

59. See Hackman, p. 26.

60. *American Catalogue of Books, 1876–1910* (New York: Publishers' Weekly, 1880–1911), 8 vols. in 13. Reprinted, (New York: Peter Smith, 1941).

61. *United States Catalog: Books in Print, 1899–1928* (New York: H. W. Wilson,

1900–1928), 4 vols. Published in conjunction with the *Cumulative Book Index* until approximately 1945. See Sheehy, p. 54, AA576–AA577.

62. See Hackman, p. 26.

63. Joseph Sabin, *Bibliotheca Americana. A Dictionary of Books Relating to America from Its Discovery to the Present Time* (New York: Sabin, 1869–1892; Bibliographical Society of America, 1928–1936), 29 vols. Reprinted, (New York: Mini-Print, 1966, i.e., Metuchen, NJ: Scarecrow Press). An index was compiled by John Edgar Molnar, *Author-Title Index to Joseph Sabin's Dictionary of Books Relating to America* (Metuchen, NJ: Scarecrow Press, 1974), 3 vols., which lists author and titles in a single sequence with some identification of pseudonyms.

64. See Hackman, pp. 29–30.

65. Ibid.

66. Lawrence Sidney Thompson, *The New Sabin: Books Described by Joseph Sabin and His Successors, now Described Again on the Basis of Examination of Originals, and Fully Indexed by Title, Subject, Joint Authors, and Institutions and Agencies* (Troy, NY: Whitson, 1974–1983), 10 vols.

67. *British National Bibliography* (London: Council of the British National Bibliography, British Library, 1950—date), v.1—date.

68. *British Books in Print: The Reference Catalogue of Current Literature* (London: Whitaker, 1874—date).

69. *Whitaker's Cumulative Book List* (London: Whitaker, 1924—date), v.1—date.

70. *Bibliographie de la France-Biblio* (Paris: Cercle de la Librairie, 1972—date). *Biblio* (1934—1971) merged with this publication in 1972.

71. See Sheehy, p. 70, AA753–AA754.

72. Ibid.

73. See Katz, p. 74. Extensive coverage of national, trade and regional bibliographies with annotations is provided by Sheehy on pages 51 to 106, giving both current and retrospective citations. For a checklist of current national bibliographies of 98 countries see the *ALA World Encyclopedia of Library and Information Services*. 2nd ed. (Chicago: American Library Association, 1986), pp. 575–580. An even more extensive work is *An Annotated Guide to Current National Bibliographies*. By Barbara L. Bell. (Alexandria, VA: Chadwyck-Healey, 1986). See also Gary E. Gorman and J. J. Mills, *Guide to Current National Bibliographies in the Third World*. 2nd rev. ed. (London: Zell, 1987).

74. *Chemical Abstracts* (Easton, PA: Chemical Abstracts, 1907—date), v.1—date.

75. Verner W. Clapp, Bibliography," *Encyclopedia Americana*, 3 (1983), p. 723.

76. Richard D. Woods, *Reference Materials on Mexican Americans: An Annotated Bibliography* (Metuchen, NJ: Scarecrow Press, 1976), 190p.

77. Dederick C. Ward, *Geologic Reference Sources: A Subject and Regional Bibliography of Publishers and Maps in the Geological Sciences*. 2nd ed. (Metuchen, NJ: Scarecrow Press, 1981), 560p.

78. Harold S. Sharp, *Footnotes to History: A Bibliographic Source Book* (Metuchen, NJ: Scarecrow Press, 1977), 639p.

79. Graham C. Kinloch, *Race and Ethnic Relations: An Annotated Bibliography* (New York: Garland, 1984), 250p.

80. *Recent Publications on Governmental Problems* (Chicago: Merriam Center Library, University of Chicago, 1933—date), v.1—date.

81. Anthony S. G. Edwards, "Some Problems in Modern Enumerative Bibliography," *Text: Transactions of the Society for Textual Scholarship*, 1 (1981), pp. 327–328.

82. Robert B. Harmon, *Steinbeck Bibliographies: An Annotated Guide* (Metuchen, NJ: Scarecrow Press, 1987), 137p.

83. Adrian Homer Goldstone, and John R. Payne, *John Steinbeck: A Bibliographical Catalogue of the Adrian H. Goldstone Collection* (Austin, TX: Humanities Research Center, University of Texas at Austin, 1974), 240p.

84. Salinas Public Library, *John Steinbeck, A Guide to the Collection of the Salinas Public Library*. Edited by John Gross and Lee Richard Hayman (Salinas, CA: The Library, 1979), 196p.

85. Bradford Morrow, Bookseller Ltd., *John Steinbeck: A Collection of Books and Manuscripts Formed by Harry Valentine of Pacific Grove, California*. [Catalog Eight] With a foreword by John R. Payne. (Santa Barbara, CA: Bradford Morrow, Bookseller, Ltd., 1980)

86. Robert J. DeMott, *Steinbeck's Reading: A Catalogue of Books Owned and Borrowed* (New York: Garland, 1984), 239p.

87. Maurice Beebe, and Jackson R. Bryer, "Criticism of John Steinbeck: A Selected Checklist," *Modern Fiction Studies,* 11 (Spring 1965), pp. 90–103.

88. *The Booklist* (Chicago: American Library Association, 1905—date), v.1—date.

89. Steven Gilbar, *Good Books: A Book Lover's Companion* (New York: Ticknor & Fields, 1982), 444p.

90. Linda S. Katz, and William A. Katz, *Writer's Choice: A Library of Rediscoveries* (Reston, VA: Reston Pub. Co., 1983), 255p.

91. Clifton Fadiman, *Lifetime Reading Plan*. Rev. ed. (New York: Crowell, 1978).

92. Philip Ward, *A Lifetime's Reading: The World's 500 Great Books* (New York: Stein and Day, 1982), 368p.

93. *Reader's Adviser* (New York: Bowker, 1921—date)

94. *Children's Catalog* (New York: H. W. Wilson, 1909—date), irregular with the latest edition being the 15th (1986); *Junior High School Libray Catalog* (New York: H. W. Wilson, 1965—date), irregular with the latest edition being the 5th (1985); *Senior High School Library Catalog* (New York: H. W. Wilson, 1926–1928—date), irregular with the latest edition being the 12th (1982); *Public Library Catalog* (New York: H. W. Wilson, 1934—date), irregular with the latest edition being the 8th (1983); and the *Fiction Catalog* (New York: H. W. Wilson, 1942—date), irregular with the latest edition being the 10th (1980).

95. See Kumar, p. 79.

96. Ibid.

97. Ibid.

98. Van Allen Bradley, *The Book Collector's Handbook of Values*. 4th ed., rev. and enl. (New York: Putnam, 1978), 640p.

99. *First Printings of American Authors: Contributions Toward Descriptive Checklists*. Matthew J. Bruccoli, series editor, et al. (Detroit, MI: Gale Research, 1977–1979), 5v.

100. Merle DeVore Johnson, *Merle Johnson's American First Editions*. 4th ed. Revised and Enlarged by Jacob Blanck. (Waltham, MA: Mark Press, 1965, ©1942), 553p. Reprint.

101. See Clapp, p. 722.

102. California. University. Institute of Governmental Studies. Library, *Subject Catalog of the Institute of Governmental Studies Library, University of California, Berkeley*. (Boston: G. K. Hall, 1970), 26 vols.

103. Foreign Relations Library, *Catalog of the Foreign Relations Library* (Boston: G. K. Hall, 1969), 9 vols.

104. John H. Jenkins, *Works of Genius: A Catalogue and a Commentary* (Austin, TX: Jenkins Company, 1974), unpaged.

105. Newberry Library, Chicago, *A Catalogue of the Everett D. Graff Collection of Western Americana*. Compiled by Colton Storm. (Chicago: University of Chicago Press, 1968), 854p.

106. See Clapp, p. 723.

107. Theodore Besterman, *A World Bibliography of Bibliographies*. 4th ed. revised and greatly enlarged throughout. (Totowa, NJ: Rowman and Littlefield, 1965–1966, 1971), 5 vols.

108. *Bibliographic Index: A Cumulative Bibliography of Bibliographies* (New York: H. W. Wilson, 1937—date), v.1—date.

109. Robert Lewis Collison, *Bibliographies, Subject and National: A Guide to Their Contents, Arrangement and Use*. 3rd ed., rev. and enl. (New York: Hafner, 1968), 203p.

110. Berenice A. Carroll, Clinton F. Fink, and Jane E. Mohraz, *Peace and War: A Guide to Bibliographies* (Santa Barbara, CA: ABC-Clio, 1983), 580p.

111. Denis Joseph Grogan, *Science and Technology: An Introduction to the Literature*. 3rd ed. (London: Bingley; Hamden, CT: Linnet, 1976), 343p.

112. Frederick L. Holler, *Information Sources of Political Science*. 4th ed. (Santa Barbara, CA: ABC-Clio, 1986), 417p.

113. *Sources of Information in the Social Sciences: A Guide to the Literature*. Edited by William H. Webb, et al. 3rd ed. (Chicago: American Library Association, 1986), 777p.

114. Eugene Paul Sheehy, et al., *Guide to Reference Books*. 10th ed. (Chicago: American Library Association, 1986), 1560p.

Chapter Five

ANALYTICAL OR CRITICAL BIBLIOGRAPHY

Introduction

The primary distinctions between enumerative or systematic bibliography and analytical or critical bibliography have been made previously and the importance of the former has been indicated with regard to the recording of books so that they can be identified and located. After a book has been discovered and obtained, a variety of different investigations can be performed depending upon the nature and purpose for which the investigation is being conducted. It is these investigations to which the name of analytical or critical bibliography is applied.[1] Consequently when we speak of analytical or critical bibliography, we normally refer to the study of books as physical objects, the details of their production and the effects of the method of manufacture on the text. Therefore, when Sir Walter W. Greg called bibliography the science of the transmission of literary documents, he was referring to analytical bibliography.[2]

There was a time, however, in the development of bibliographical studies when it was considered useful to separate the analytical from the critical work in the definition. The process of analysis of the material under review was considered to be essentially the first operation to discover the facts, following which a critical process of explanation of these facts could be applied. This latter process then would be the realm of critical as distinct from analytical bibliography. In practice the process of analysis and critical comment on the facts are so intertwined that no useful purpose is served by attempting to separate them.[3]

As an independent study, analytical bibliography is comparatively new, and much of its activity has been directed toward finding out about itself, discovering its own procedures, testing its own hypotheses, and increasing the scope of its own applications. It is still growing and developing, but expert knowledge of it is not very widespread.[4] Although it has historical antecedents several centuries back, analytical bibliography has had its greatest development during the twentieth century. Most of this activity, which took place early in this century, was centered on Shakespearian texts in general, and with the nature and authority of the so-called quarto texts and their relation to the text printed in the first folio in particular. Associated with this movement came studies in English literature by three eminent scholars, Alfred W. Pollard, Ronald B. McKerrow, and Sir Walter W. Greg, all interested in bibliography.[5]

Following the work of English antiquarian scholar and librarian Henry Bradshaw and librarian and incunabulist Robert Proctor, Greg, McKerrow, and Pollard developed what is now called analytical bibliography. It has had some notable successes, like the discovery of the true nature of the Pavier quartos and the revelation of the Wise forgeries, and it has played a significant role in shaping a few of the best editions of recent years, like Fredson Bowers' collection of Dekker's plays.[6] Also it has produced some landmark studies such as Charlton Hinman's study of the Shakespeare First Folio, and other works by Bowers, Philip Gaskell, and G. Thomas Tanselle to mention but a few.

Resulting from the work of these and other bibliographers, much has been gained in the way of bibliographical scholarship which involves the critical analysis of the text and its presentation. Using this approach the analytical bibliographer examines the physical form of a book and all of its relations, which claim to transmit the same text, in order to ascertain exact identification, confirm attributions, and determine changes that occurred as an author communicated with an audience. Even though we speak here of books, the analytical bibliographer is concerned also with codices, pamphlets, unbound tracts, broadsides, placards, etc.[7]

Analytical bibliography is associated with printed books, not with the study of manuscripts per se, although manuscripts and intermediate printings such as galley proofs are studied whenever found. An important distinction must be made with regard to manuscripts. A manuscript text may not be the finished version of an item, whereas the printed text is a standardized, fixed, and preserved product. In effect when something appears in print it becomes codified. Consequently, publication of a text in printed form is viewed as the dissemination of a finished product, but prior to the modern ability to produce facsimile copies, variants tended to change or, as some prefer, corrupt a text as it is further removed from its author. Often authorial changes can be introduced following printing, and for that reason the bibliographer finds it unproductive to collect only first editions or to ignore other printed editions altogether in favor of a manuscript text even when the latter is autobiographical.[8]

An interesting counterpart of analytical bibliography is codicology, which is an enlargement of the field of paleography and is the study of manuscripts as cultural artifacts in the historical process. It is a post-World War II term coined by the French and is only now becoming recognized as a viable discipline. In general the methodology of codicology is similar to that of analytical bibliography in that both are based on the techniques developed first in Biblical studies and textual criticism. Both codicology and analytical bibliography may be divided into sub-sets of specialized concerns or study described as historical, textual, and descriptive. Codicology lacks the same vocabulary or hierarchy of concepts based on the idea of an edition, but manuscript copies are similarly identified according to their relationships with prototypes and archetypes. Here the approach is genealogical in nature, tracing ancestry through the descent of a text, and constructing families of manuscripts, which are identified by their variants.[9]

Branches of Analytical Bibliography

Descriptive Bibliography

The principal function of descriptive bibliography is the precise physical description of material. It asks the questions: How is a book put together? What type is used and what kind of paper? How are the illustrations incorporated into the book? How is it bound and what materials make up the binding? What are the main physical characteristics of the material being described if it is not a book? Like the textual bibliographer, the descriptive bibliographer must have a good working knowledge of the state of the technology of the period in order to describe a book's physical appearance both accurately and economically. Descriptive bibliographies are listings that provide full physical descriptions of the books or other material they list, enabling us to tell one edition from another and to identify significant variations within a single edition.

Basically, descriptive bibliography is the precise description of books and other graphic materials as physical specimens that include structure and materials in such description. Commonly the whole picture is sacri-

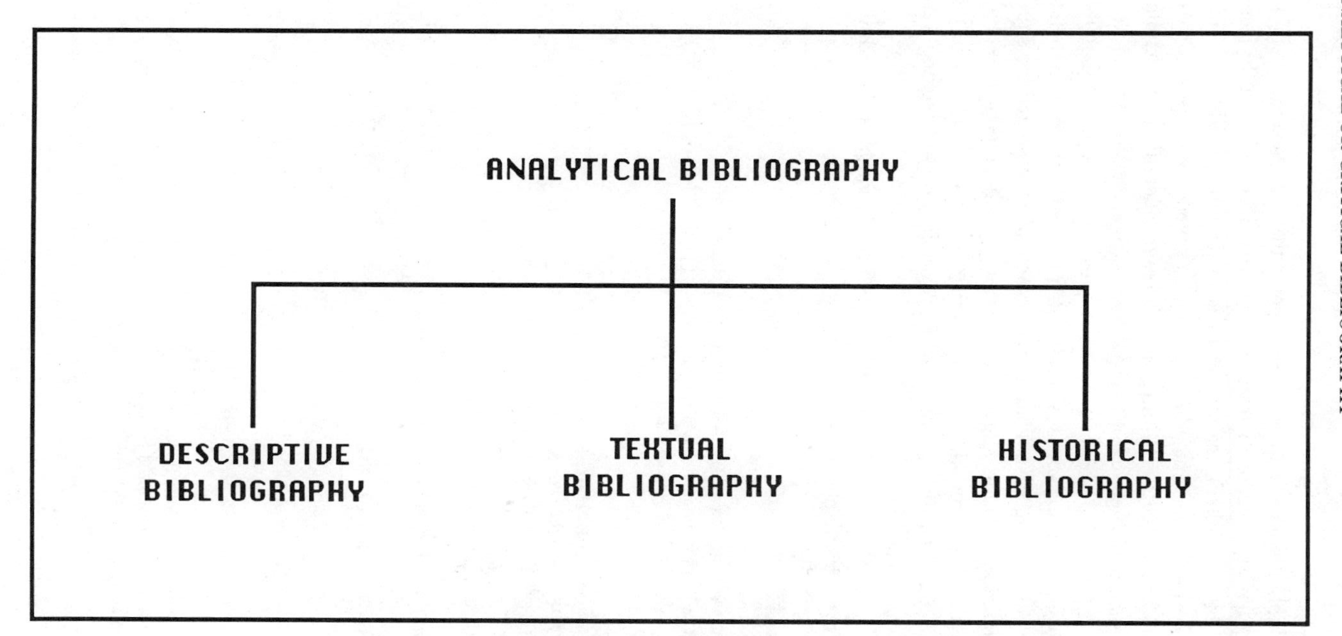

Figure No. 9. Structure of Analytical Bibliography

ficed by bibliographers whose concern is only the text. Descriptive bibliographers tend to confine their focus to imprint data and the title page. Here the bibliographer's main concern is in providing evidence to distinguish between different editions (copies printed from one setting of type), and states (copies within an impression identified by detailed changes such as correction of typographical errors, replacement of worn type, which are called variants), issues (copies of an edition distributed at one time), and variant states and editions produced respectively before and after publication. A standardized approach to collation and the structure of collation formulas allows the descriptive bibliographer to include structure in a description, and quasi-facsimile transcription is widely practiced, although photography and reprography are superseding transcription methods.[10]

Below is an illustration of a full standard bibliographical description showing the various elements:

a) 82. 1755

b) THE | WAY of the WORLD: | A | COMEDY. | Written by Mr.
CONGREVE. | [3-line motto from Horace and ack.] | *EDINBURGH:* |
Printed for G. HAMILTON and J. BALFOUR. | [partial rule] |
M, DCC, LV.

c) *Collation:* 12°. A^4 B-N^4 01, 53 leaves, pp.*1–3* 4–7 *8*
9 *10–11* 12–104 *105* 106, $1 signed
HT] THE | WAY OF THE WORLD.

d) *Contents: A1:* title (verso blank). A2: dedicatory epistle
(cap^2). $A4^v$: prologue (cap^2). Bl^v: dramatis personae
(with cast). B2: HT with text (cap^3). 01: epilogue (cap^2).

RT] THE WAY OF THE WORLD

CW] *$A4^v$ Some* Cl^v *Mira*. [*Mira*] $E4^v$ *Milla*. $G4^v$ the
$I4^v$ confident, $L4^v$ re olv'd $M4^v$ Sir

e) *Type:* text (C2): 39 11., 131 (139) × 70 mm., 66R

f) *Notes:* The edition follows the scene divisions of the 1710
works. The second portion of Scene III, Act II, is
missnumbered. Scene IV, but Scene IV is properly numbered.
No press figures. Bound in blue cloth.

g) PR3364 .W3 1755

In this example, taken from the catalog of the John C. Hodges Collection of the works of William Congreve,[11] element a) is the assigned sequential number in the catalog, b) gives a transcription of the actual title page, c) is the collation or physical description using especially designated symbols signifying size etc., d) gives the contents of the book in sequential order, e) designates the type faces used, f) notes listing important additional information including variations, and g) is the Library of Congress call number by which this volume is arranged on a shelf in the Hodges collection.

Naturally this detailed method sometimes becomes very complex. The collational formula has a misleading scientific look about it—plus signs and minus signs, superscript numbers, and an occasional sprinkling of Greek letters—but it is merely a short hand substitute for one or more simple declarative sentences. No kind of manipulation or mathematical analysis can cause it to divulge hidden truth. Taken for what it is, the collational formula provides an international language converging in compact form much useful information, and in working closely with books published before 1900 one cannot operate without a good grasp of the Greg-Bowers method.[12] Donald Gallup has indicated, however, that this method is unnecessary for most contemporary books except in special cases, and to give such detail for a modern book in a publisher's binding is of little use.[13]

Textual Bibliography

The principal function of textual bibliography is to study the relationship between the printed text and that text as conceived by its author. Handwriting is quite often difficult to decipher. Compositors occasionally make errors, and proofreaders sometimes fail to catch them. But (especially in the period circa 1800) we often have only the printed book itself to tell us what the author intended. It is the basic task of the textual bibliographer to provide us with the most accurate text of a writer's work. The skills that the textual bibliographer should possess are profound knowledge of the works of the writer being edited (and of the writer's time), and an equally profound knowledge of contemporary printing and publishing practices.[14]

In another sense textual bibliography is the application of the principles of analytical bibliography to the correction and interpretation of a text. For all practical purposes, this is the same as textual criticism and it is most often applied in editing. The basic assumption is that the text was unconsciously altered in the process of transmission, mainly through the introduction of variants in printing, and that the removal of non-authorized change allows one to edit a text closer to the author's original text than any single variant. The resulting critical edition is often a codification of what existed previously only as a hypothetical model.[15]

Historical Bibliography

Broadly speaking, historical bibliography involves the history of books and of the people, institutions, and machines producing them. As a study, historical bibliography ranges from technological history to the history of art in its concern with the evidence books provide about culture and society.[16] In this sense historical bibliography becomes archaeological in nature, with a never-ending amount of dated physical evidence. How were these books made? What forces and what options governed their manufacture? There is still so much that we do not know about quite modern books let alone those of an earlier period, and there are so many books to study.[17]

There has been much research conducted among extant records to discover the past about books, but this kind of investigation sometimes is hampered by destroyed records of limited application. On the other hand, some of the discoveries of historical bibliography have immediate and practical application to larger problems, such as the dating of variant editions or the use of certain printing applications. As technology develops, what once was conjecture about the manufacture of books can now be verified fact. Historical bibliography thus provides new weapons for the arsenal of the analytical bibliographer.

Analytical or critical bibliography is, of its very nature, wide ranging. It concerns itself with everything that can have some bearing on the physical nature of the book or other graphic materials. The method by which this information is recorded for the benefit of other researchers is the subject of descriptive bibliography, and the application of this evidence toward the understanding of the text itself is the realm of textual bibliography.[18] Along with this we have the historical factor in the development of materials related to the printed page which is covered under the aegis of historical bibliography.

Current Status of Analytical Bibliography

In 1979 Dr. Lawrence J. McCrank made some observations concerning the status of analytical bibliographical studies that are, for the most part, valid today.[19] Obviously the technology, methodology, and supportive reference services for analytical bibliography have changed considerably from the pioneering days of Greg, Pollard, McKerrow and others of similar stature. With regard to methodology, there is the application of optics to textual studies by use of the Hinman collator,[20] the Vinton Collating Machine,[21] and Rothman's Houston Editing Desk and Editing Frame, all useful for textual comparison.[22] Today we have mechanical collation of texts and computerized scanners that are capable of multi-edition collation.[23]

Now well-developed in literary and historical editing is computer-assisted production of new editions as well as the design of enumerative bibliographies. Advances in recent years of text processing and inexpensive packaged programs such as *Procite* are rapidly revolutionizing the world of bibliographical scholarship and text editing. By using computers, the ability to control variants of minute detail has allowed analyses that were unknown only a few years ago. For example, structural fingerprinting is a method of comparing peculiarities of vocabulary, syntax, and linguistics that builds an argument for authorship based on a mass of otherwise incalcuable minutiae. The primary assumption behind tagmemic clause-analysis is that a person's language and writing abilities provide patterns that can be identified in a comparison of a text of questionable authorship with a text of known authorship; hence its similarity to voice prints for identification, or its popular name of "fingerprinting." The idea has been applied to other forms of bibliographical analysis than textual criticism, such as in the comparison of typographical variants in various editions of a work and similar techniques used in manuscript studies.[24]

Another exciting area of analytical bibliographical studies concerns the technical nature of a book. Rigorous studies of parchment and vellum are influencing both conservation and bibliography. Through certain identification techniques we can now ascertain specimen skins and hides by type of animal, by approximate age, breed, and by estimates of quality and texture. But, such data gathering has not yet allowed scholars to begin to generalize about regional preferences, treatment, and finishing processes or to relate these factors to definite periods.[25] However, identification techniques such as ultraviolet light to locate underpaintings and to decipher erased text,[26] spectroscopy in the study of pigment inks, etc., in both script and type, blow-up photography for critical examination of materials, and x-ray examination for the study of structural patterns of a book without taking it apart, are being used by bibliographers for paper identification, production methods, and materials used by certain printing houses, etc.

One of the major roadblocks to bibliographical investigation has been the inaccessibility of specimens, the need to examine originals, and the lack of location sources. Descriptive bibliographies are now adding locations to their entries which is instrumental in providing access to ever-increasing amounts of valuable material. Large bibliographical databases such as OCLC and RLIN are making it possible to locate materials quickly. Other area bibliographic networks such as the WLN (Western Library Network) are also providing greater access to regional materials.

A final observation relates to the widespread use of microfilm and technical advances in reprography or facsimile reproduction (as by photocopying) of graphic matter. Since many major research libraries are experiencing conservation problems, they are adding to their collections more microfilm materials than ever before. Microfilming projects presently concentrate on manuscripts for preservation purposes, but a rapid deterioration of books is forcing conservation via microfilming printed matter as well.[27] The Library of Congress and other large research libraries are now engaged in large scale microfilming projects of deteriorating materials.

From this brief review, which is obviously discursive, one can see that the field of analytical bibliography is a complex and rapidly developing one replete with new techniques and technology.

Selected Related Writings

GENERAL

Esdaile, Arundell J. K. *Esdaile's Manual of Bibliography*. 5th ed. Revised by Roy B. Stokes. Metuchen, NJ: Scarecrow Press, 1981. Consult pages 10–15.

Francis, Sir Frank C. "Bibliography," *The New Encyclopaedia Britannica: Micropedia*, 2 (1983), pp. 978–981.

McCrank, Lawrence J. "Analytical and Historical Bibliography, A State of the Art Review," In: *Annual Report of the American Rare, Antiquarian and Out-of-Print Book Trade, 1978/1979*. Edited by Denis Carbonneau. New York: BCAR, 1979. See pp. 175–185.

Padwick, Eric W. *Bibliographical Method*. Cambridge: James Clarke, 1969.

Stokes, Roy. "Critical Bibliography," *Encyclopedia of Library and Information Science*, 6 (1971), pp. 276–286.

________. *The Function of Bibliography*. 2nd ed. Aldershot, Eng.: Gower, 1982. A more extensive treatment than the article cited above. See Chapter 3 (pp. 45–71).

Tanselle, G. Thomas. "The State of Bibliography Today," *The Papers of the Bibliographical Society of America*, 73 (1979), pp. 289–304.

Willoughby, Edwin E. *The Uses of Bibliography*. . . . Hamden, CT: Shoe String Press, 1957.

DESCRIPTIVE BIBLIOGRAPHY

Belanger, Terry. "Descriptive Bibliography," In: *Book Collecting, A Modern Guide*. Edited by Jean Peters. New York: Bowker, 1977. See pp. 97–115.

The Bibliographical Society of America, 1904–79, A Retrospective Collection. Charlottesville, VA: Published for the Bibliographical Society of America by the University Press of Virginia, 1980.

Bowers, Fredson Thayer. *Essays in Bibliography, Text, and Editing*. Charlottesville, VA: Published for the Bibliographical Society of the University of Virginia by the University Press of Virginia, 1975.

————. *Principles of Bibliographical Description*. Princeton, NJ: Princeton University Press, 1949. Reprinted in 1986.

Cowley, John D. *Bibliographical Description and Cataloging*. New York: Burt Franklin, 1970, ©1949. (Reprint)

Dunkin, Paul S. *Bibliography, Tiger or Fat Cat?* Hamden, CT: Archon, 1975.

Gaskell, Philip. *A New Introduction to Bibliography*. Corrected issue. New York: Oxford University Press, 1974.

Jones, John B., ed. *Readings in Descriptive Bibliography*. Kent, OH: Kent State University Press, 1974.

McKerrow, Ronald B. *An Introduction to Bibliography for Literary Students*. Oxford, Eng.: Clarendon Press, 1927.

Stokes, Roy. "Descriptive Bibliography," *Encyclopedia of Library and Information Science*, 7 (1972), pp. 1–17.

Tanselle, G. Thomas. *Selected Studies in Bibliography*. Charlottesville, VA: Published for the Bibliographical Society of the University of Virginia by the University Press of Virginia, 1979.

TEXTUAL BIBLIOGRAPHY

Bowers, Fredson Thayer. *Bibliography and Textual Criticism*. Oxford, Eng.: Clarendon Press, 1964.

Brack, O. O., Jr. and Warner Barnes, eds. *Bibliography and Textual Criticism: English and American Literature, 1700 to the Present*. Chicago: University of Chicago Press, 1969.

Standards of Bibliographical Description. Edited by Curt F. Bühler, James G. McMinaway, and Lawrence C. Wroth. Westport, CT: Greenwood Press, 1973, ©1949. (Reprint)

Stokes, Roy B. *The Function of Bibliography*. 2nd ed. Aldershot, Eng.: Gower, Ltd., 1982. Consult Chapter 6 (pp. 107–136).

Tanselle, G. Thomas. *Textual Criticism Since Greg: A Chronicle, 1950–1985*. Charlottesville, VA: Published for the Bibliographical Society of the University of Virginia by the University Press of Virginia, 1987.

HISTORICAL BIBLIOGRAPHY

Binns, Norman E. *An Introduction to Historical Bibliography*. 2nd ed. rev. and enl. London: Association of Assistant Librarians, 1962.

Boswell, David B. *A Text-Book on Bibliography*. London: Grafton, 1952.

McKenzie, Donald F. "Printers of the Mind: Some Notes on Bibliographical Theories and Printing-House Practices," *Studies in Bibliography*, 22 (1969), pp. 1–75.

Mann, George. *Print, A Manual*. . . . London: Grafton, 1952.

Stokes, Roy B. "Historical Bibliography," *Encyclopedia of Library and Information Science*, 36, Suppl. 1 (1983), pp. 219–229.

Tanselle, G. Thomas. *The History of Books as a Field of Study*. Chapel Hill, NC: Rare Book Collection/Academic Affairs Library, The University of North Carolina at Chapel Hill, 1981.

Williamson, Derek. *Historical Bibliography*. Hamden, CT: Archon, 1967.

Notes

1. Roy Stokes, "Critical Bibliography, *Encyclopedia of Library and Information Science,* 6 (1971), p. 277.

2. Terry Belanger, "Descriptive Bibliography," In: *Book Collecting, A Modern Guide*. Edited by Jean Peters. New York: Bowker, 1977, p. 99.

3. See Stokes, p. 277. For the remainder of this chapter I will, for the sake of convenience, refer simply to analytical bibliography instead of analytical or critical bibliography.

4. Robert K. Turner, Jr., "Analytical Bibliography and Shakespeare's Text," *Modern Philology,* 62 (August 1964), p. 52.

5. Sir Frank C. Francis, "Bibliography," *The New Encyclopaedia Britannica: Micropedia,* 2 (1983), p. 980.

6. See Turner, p. 51.

7. Lawrence J. McCrank, "Analytical and Historical Bibliography: A State of the Art Review," In: *Annual Report of the American Rare, Antiquarian and Out-of-Print Book Trade, 1978/1979*. Edited by Denis Carbonneau. (New York: BCAR, 1979), p. 176.

8. Ibid.

9. Ibid., pp. 176–177.

10. Ibid., p. 177.

11. This example is taken from: Tennessee. University. Libraries. *The John C. Hodges Collection of William Congreve in the University of Tennessee Library: A Bibliographical Catalog*. Compiled by Albert M. Lyles and John Dobson. (Knoxville, TN: The Libraries, 1970), p. 53.

12. A number of sources discuss the collation formula in considerable detail, most prominent of which is Fredson Bowers' *Principles of Bibliographic Description*. (Princeton, NJ: Princeton University Press, 1949), pp. 193–254. Others include Paul S. Dunkin, *Bibliography, Tiger or Fat Cat?* (Hamden, CT: Archon, 1974), pp. 23–34; Arundell J. K. Esdaile, *Esdaile's Manual of Bibliography*. 5th ed., revised by Roy Stokes. (Metuchen, NJ: Scarecrow Press, 1981), pp. 290–341; Philip Gaskell, *A New Introduction to Bibliography*. Corrected issue. (Oxford, Eng.: Clarendon Press, 1974), pp. 321–335; Ronald B. McKerrow, *An Introduction to Bibliography for Literary Students*. (Oxford, Eng.: Clarendon Press, 1927), pp. 55–163; and Eric W. Padwick, *Bibliographical Method*. (Cambridge, Eng.: James Clarke, 1969), pp. 142–187.

13. Donald C. Gallup, *On Contemporary Bibliography* . . . (Austin, TX: Humanities Research Center, University of Texas at Austin, 1970), pp. 8–9.

14. See Belanger, p. 100.

15. See McCrank, p. 177.

16. See Belanger, p. 101.

17. William H. Bond, "Bibliography and Bibliographers," *AB Bookman's Weekly,* 47 (April 26, 1971), p. 1396.

18. See Stokes, p. 285.

19. McCrank emphasizes technological advances and their strong impact upon analytical bibliography.

20. Charlton Hinman invented this machine which is an optical instrument for making detailed comparisons of theoretically identical documents. It is used for finding variants in literary texts and for detecting fakes and forgeries. See "Hinman Collator," *Bulletin of the New York Public Library,* 75 (January 1971), pp. 5–6.

21. See Vinton A. Dearing, "The Poor Man's Mark IV or Ersatz Hinman Collator," *Papers of the Bibliographic Society of America,* 60 (1966), pp. 149–158.

22. See Irving N. Rothman, "The Houston Editing Desk and Editing Frame," *Papers of*

the Bibliographical Society of America, 72 (1978), pp. 130–136. The Houston Edition Desk is a portable apparatus designed to facilitate the organization of flat copy during the process of editing or proofreading.

23. The use of computers in text editing and identifying of text variants is expanding. See the following: "The Identification of Text Variants by Computer," by Geogette Silva and Harold Love, *Information Storage and Retrieval*, 5 (October 1969), pp. 89–108; two studies of Trevor H. Howard-Hill the first of which is, "A Practical Scheme for Editing Critical Texts with the Aid of a Computer," In: *Proof: The Yearbook of American Bibliographical and Textual Studies*, Edited by Joseph Katz. (Columbia, SC: University of South Carolina Press, etc., 1973), Vol. 3, pp. 335–356, and the second, "Computer and Mechanical Aids to Editing," in the same source, Vol. 5, pp. 217–235. A survey is provided by Robert L. Oakman, "The Present State of Computerized Collation: A Review Article," In: *Proof: The Yearbook of American Bibliographical and Textual Studies*, Edited by Joseph Katz. (Columbia, SC: University of South Carolina Press, 1972), Vol. 2, pp. 333–348.

24. See McCrank, p. 180. Wordprints are treated to some degree in Andrew Q. Morton, *Literary Detection*. (New York: Scribners, 1978). An interesting use of computer wordprints is being applied by Mormon scholars in an examination of the authorship of *The Book of Mormon*. See "Who Wrote the *Book of Mormon?* An Analysis of Wordprints," by Wayne A. Larsen, Alvin C. Rencher, and Tim Layton, *Brigham Young University Studies*, 20 (Spring 1980), pp. 225–251. A rebuttal to this study was made by James D. Croft, "*Book of Mormon* Wordprints Re-examined," *Sunstone*, 6 (March/April 1981), pp. 15–21.

25. See McCrank, p. 181.

26. For a current example of the use of this type of technology see, "Cameras, Computers Help Decipher Ancient Texts," by Ellen K. Coughlin, *The Chronicle of Higher Education*, 34 (November 11, 1987), pp. A6–A9.

27. See McCrank, pp. 184–185.

Chapter Six

STANDARDS FOR BIBLIOGRAPHIES

Introduction

Standards as used below refer to the quality and character of the elements included in a bibliography with regard to such things as accuracy and sufficient detail that will identify each record included. There are many problems associated with the simplest of bibliographic citations such as what exactly is to be said, in what sequence the elements are to be arranged, how they are to be punctuated, and so on. Naturally for each of these problems there are many solutions in a bewildering range of models and prescriptive style manuals.[1] When it becomes necessary to compile a bibliography, whether it be enumerative or descriptive, where does one find a set of standards for such a task? Luckily there are not as many systems or manuals for this task as there are for citations, and what follows is an attempt to synthesize these into a coherent set of introductory standards that will at least get one started, with references to others for more complex compilations. Obviously there is no one correct way to compile a bibliography, but consistency and common sense dictated in part by the nature of the subject are of paramount importance.

Standards for Enumerative Bibliographies

Compiling enumerative bibliographies can be either a simple or complex undertaking, depending largely on the nature of the subject and the extent to which one intends to treat it. Obviously, a selective checklist on a topic will, in most cases, require less time and effort than a book-length treatment with annotations.

This section is concerned with standards of compilation, from the planning stage to completion of the manuscript. No matter what the purpose or the type of bibliography being prepared, two things are absolutely essential—accuracy and sufficient bibliographical detail to identify each record included. Many precious hours have been lost or wasted by researchers who have been provided with faulty or insufficient information to identify ,an item. Also, it makes no difference whether the bibliography is current or retrospective; the fundamental methods of compilation are the same.

Planning

It is not overstating the case to say that planning is not only the first step in the bibliographic compilation process, but it is perhaps the most important. It is at this point that some necessary decisions will be made and that will guide progress in a orderly, systematic manner. The success of the task undertaken depends greatly upon the attention that is given to planning. Essentially what is at issue is the development of a provisional plan. This plan will be subject to modification as one proceeds through the compiling process. Such flexibility is essential. For example, if a comprehensive bibliography is contemplated, and it is discovered later that the amount of material available is too extensive, then one probably would opt for a selective bibliography instead.[2]

Following the selection of a topic, ask yourself these questions: What types of bibliographic sources are already available on the subject? Are these sources adequate? What level or levels do they cover? Would another bibliography merely duplicate, supplement, or revise? Are these sources retrospective? Do they cover only out-of-print materials? What periods of time do they cover? Also, be careful to consider the potential audience: Try to determine who they are and at what level of education—elementary, high school, or college. What are their needs? Do these needs justify a bibliography, or can they be satisfied with existing tools or other means? What languages other than English should be considered? Also, determine what resources the audience will have available to them.

If the project is determined to be a viable one, following the above approach, then several basic pre-compilation decisions should be made:

1. What period of time will the bibliography cover?
2. Will the coverage be comprehensive, extensive, or selective?

3. What types of materials will be included (e.g., books, articles, government publications, etc.)?
4. What style or format will be most useful for the entries?
5. Shall the entries be annotated, and if so should they be descriptive or evaluative?
6. What arrangement would be most suited for the entries?
7. What types of indexes will provide the best access to materials included?

The answers to these questions will largely depend on the nature of the subject, its size and the funds available.[3]

PERIOD COVERAGE

Most bibliographies are retrospective and require a reasonable consideration of the time span to be covered by their entries. If a subject is too large and the amount of material enormous, it will be essential to limit the period covered. In other words, the period up to which material should be included needs to be determined.

MATERIAL COVERAGE

The decision to make a bibliography comprehensive or selective will be governed by the size and complexity of the subject as well as the quantity of the materials available on it. The choice of selectivity normally is dependent on the familiarity of the subject by the compiler. Here expert choice is essential so that important works will not be omitted and that bias may be minimized. Selective coverage is most useful when it excludes no important material or leaves no large gap.

TYPES OF MATERIALS

The majority of subjects will have a variety of sources related to it such as books or monographs, journal articles, government publications, nonpublished and nonprint materials. Bibliographers should attempt to search out those types of materials that will be particularly useful for the intended user.

ENTRY FORMAT

Many style manuals exist for the major disciplines. For example there is the *MLA Handbook* for students of literature and *A Uniform System of Citation* for legal materials. The main point here is to select a style manual for entries and then stick with it in order to avoid confusion. Be careful, however, that the format chosen is current and includes all pertinent detail for bibliographic identification.

ANNOTATIONS

It goes without saying that annotations add immeasurably to the value of any bibliography. A major problem, however, will be the immensity of the task particularly if the bibliography is designed to be comprehensive. Also, it is necessary to decide on the nature of the annotations whether they will be simply descriptive, critical or both. Whatever the decision, strive for consistency.

ARRANGEMENTS

In order to systematize the collection of material, a tentative arrangement should be worked out based largely on the nature of the subject. Since this is a critical decision, five of the more common arrangements for enumerative bibliographies are outlined below:[4]

A. *Alphabetical*
  a. Author
  b. Title
  c. Subject
  d. Dictionary (a combination of at least two of the above)
  e. Place of publication or some other geographic factor.

This type of arrangement is most useful for bibliographies of subjects that do not lend themselves to subdivision.

B. *Classified*
  a. May adopt one of the existing schemes (Library of Congress, Dewey Decimal System, or Universal Decimal Classification)
  b. Devise special scheme for the situation.

A systematic division or analysis of the subject that can be subdivided in many ways. It is difficult to set up divisions and to put all items into them when a scheme is created. Most useful for subjects that have many logical subdivisions.

C. *Chronological*
  a. Date of publication (individual author, local imprints)
  b. Date covered-periods (subjects with long history).

Obviously the chronological arrangement is more adaptable for author bibliographies and historical subjects where period of time is the dominant factor.

D. *Regional*
   a. Place of publication (e.g. a list of imprints in New York)
   b. Area covered (books related to states or regions).

E. *Type of Material*
   a. Periodicals
   b. Microfilm
   c. Phono-Recordings, etc.

Useful for author lists or when the subject is limited and the types numerous.

Also consider such additional features as a list of abbreviations, table of contents, preface, credits, sources, and cross-references. Of course, any thorough bibliography will have most or all of these.

During the final phase of the planning process, develop a clear, orderly and convenient system for collecting, filing, and keeping track of the entries to be located and recorded. Most experienced bibliographers recommend 3 × 5 inch cards for recording information. They are handy to use because of their size, and can be arranged and rearranged quickly as research progresses. Set up files so that they can be expanded or weeded, or modify organizational patterns as needed. There are also microcomputer programs available today such as *Procite* or some file management programs as *dBase III* that are useful for this purpose.

Collecting and Recording Entries

There are four major steps involved in collecting and recording entries for enumerative bibliographies: a) consulting bibliographic sources and identifying appropriate items, b) recording the bibliographic information according to a predesigned and orderly format, c) obtaining the material and verifying the bibliographic information and recording needed changes, and d) writing annotations and/or other useful descriptive notes.[5] At least the first three steps will undoubtedly be undertaken utilizing a nearby library of some kind. Even if one is familiar with how libraries are organized and function, become acquainted with members of the reference staff who will be more than willing to assist in identifying and obtaining needed materials.

CONSULTING SOURCES AND IDENTIFICATION OF MATERIALS

To achieve comprehensiveness within the limits you have established, you must be thorough in consulting all of the possible sources related to the subject. The following discussion of major sources offers a typology from which one can begin a search for entries and perhaps branch out to consult lesser-used types if necessary.

A good starting point is the card catalog of available libraries. Given the nature of manual and online card catalogs available in libraries presently, a bibliographer can usually find much useful information. Coupled with this is a large number of printed catalogs of special collections in major libraries such as those published by G. K. Hall and Co.

One of the most common types of sources are published bibliographies on a subject as well as those on related topics. These can usually be discovered by using the card catalog of a library or a bibliography of bibliographies such as Besterman or the *Bibliographic Index*. If there is a guide to the literature on a topic or on a related subject area, one is in luck because they are especially useful for identifying relevant bibliographies and possibly collateral materials.

To expand a search for entries, universal, national, and trade bibliographies are essential. Most of these do have subject as well as author/title access. For example the *Cumulative Book Index* lists author, titles, and subjects in a handy dictionary arrangement. Since 1950 the *National Union Catalog*, has provided subject access. However, since 1983 it has been issued only on microfiche and requires a machine in order to be useful. Major trade bibliographies such as *Books In Print* are especially useful for identifying entries by and about authors.

For the majority of subjects, periodical literature is extremely important, especially if the topic is one that is continually developing. The number of periodical indexes covering both magazine and journal literature is extensive with new ones being created to accommodate recent subjects such as computers. With the impact of modern technology we are witnessing a revolution from the printed index to those available online or on an optical disk such as the CD-ROM version or ERIC or one known as INFOTRAC.

Frequently overlooked by many bibliographers are indexes to government publications. The federal government as well as state and local governments publish materials on almost every subject imaginable. Index sources such as the *Monthly Catalog of United States Government Publications* or the *CIS Index* (Congressional Information Service) offer a wealth of possible entries. There are, of course, other indexes covering government publications of a specialized nature.

The *Essay and General Literature Index*, which provides access to collections of articles in composite books, is often overlooked by bibliographers in their search for relevant bibliographic entries. Such sources are useful for identifying parts of larger, more encompassing works that might contain materials on a subject.

Of the less extensive sources are bibliographies at the ends of articles in encyclopedias, bibliographies in books or treatises, periodicals that are not yet included in periodical indexes, and cross-references for further and related items.

This, naturally, does not exhaust the list of possible sources for entries. One will doubtless discover more as the search progresses. The main point is that one must attempt to cover all bases, and not exclude some for whatever reason.

RECORDING BIBLIOGRAPHIC INFORMATION

As one consults the sources for entries, begin to record the bibliographical information immediately on cards according to the format established for the specific type of material identified by the style manual chosen for the project. It is important to remain consistent in the recording process in order to avoid confusion later on.

To illustrate some of the differences that exist in the various systems, listed below are two examples—one citing a book and the other a journal article—which contrast two different formats:[6]

Book Entry:

1. Turabian: McDougal, Walter A. The Heavens and the Earth: A Political History of the Space Age. New York: Basic Books, 1985.
2. Hurt: McDougal, Walter A. The Heavens and the Earth: A Political History of the Space Age. New York: Basic Books, 1985.

Article Entry:

1. Turabian: Jackson, Richard. ''Running Down the

Up-Escalator: Regional Inequality in Papua New Guinea.'' Australian Geographer 14 (May 1979): 175-84.

2. Hurt: Jackson, Richard. ''Running Down the Up-Escalator: Regional Inequality in Papua New Guinea,'' Australian Geographer, 14 (May, 1979), 175-84.

Notice there are minor differences in title underlining and punctuation. Again it is important to remain consistent. The style manual being used will establish the bibliographic format for other types of materials encountered in the search, such as government publications, parts of compendiums, possibly nonprint materials and the like.

There are also some basic principles to keep in mind when recording bibliographic information with respect to various elements of the citation. In some instances, full description is not important, however, in most it is vital. The subject will dictate, but one may not see the importance until further along into the project. It is safer, then, to begin with full information, full author's name, full imprint and collation, etc., until one is sure of all the uses that will be made of the entries. Eventually every item on the list will be examined. Compare the description copied from the sources with the material itself in order to make sure it is accurate.[7]

For author entries, provide the full name, if it can be found, or at least include initials if the author has more than one given name or full given name of only one. At least this latter is needed for positive identification. Taking the full name will familiarize one with authorities in the field. Also if there is an editor, translator, illustrator, co-author, etc., they are important and should be recorded as part of the citation.

As a general rule the full title of a work should always be given. A full title is necessary to properly identify the work cited and is often indicative of its contents. The *Readers' Guide to Periodical Literature* will mean nothing to the uninitiated if shortened to *Readers' Guide*. Very seldom is the beginning of a title abbreviated for that is the part by which it is alphabetized. However, if a title is cumbersome and includes unnecessary words, insert an ellipsis (. . .) to indicate the omission. If no author of a work is given, simply enter it under title. In such instances the title is given in the same place normally occupied by the author entry.

The edition should be noted if it is other than the first. First editions are noted in the typical bibliography only in the case of rare or otherwise very important books such as the first edition of John Steinbeck's *Tortilla Flat* (1935). A new edition indicates that new material has been added and often that old material has been deleted, so it is important to note which edition is indicated. Also, paging usually differs in editions so, a reference to one edition will not necessarily be correct for another.

The imprint (i.e., place of publication, publisher, and date of publication or copyright date) should be given in full. List the copyright date if it differs more than a year from the date on the title page. Decide whether the full designation for a publisher is to be used or a shortened form, e.g., Scarecrow or Scarecrow Press, Inc. When the decision has been made, it must be adhered to for every entry included in the bibliography. Pamphlets published for free distribution normally are listed with full address of the publisher if such can be located on the publication or elsewhere. It is well to include this in the imprint, because the user may need to obtain a copy.

For most bibliographies do not list the price of items unless the purpose of the bibliography demands its inclusion. Prices vary with time, locality, conditions of the book trade, etc., so to quote a definite price is risky at best.

The collation is the physical description of the material being cited and can include volumes or paging, illustrations, portraits, plates, maps, diagrams, etc. The use made of the bibliography will determine how extensive one will want to indicate physical features. In biography and history, portraits and maps are important; books on architecture or art depend on illustrations as a rule, and note if in color or black-and-white. The subject and the way it is handled will normally determine completeness of collation desirable, but this may not be realized until well into the project, and much additional time and effort will be wasted in retracing steps to record the missing details. Consequently it is better to begin with extensive collation data until all the uses to be made of the bibliography are determined.

If the item being cited is part of a series, particularly a numbered series, this should be noted in parentheses following the collation, since the identification of a book with a series often gives an idea of its importance. Unnumbered series are not as important and usually can be omitted without causing any problem with identification.

When notes or annotations are included they should be located approximately two spaces below the entry so that they may be easily found. Annotations will be discussed later on.

Indentions may vary; however, when one form has been selected and adopted you must use it consistently throughout the bibliography. Consistency in this instance will add to the appearance of the bibliography and make it easier to select the entry desired.

Most of these standard elements will be covered in the style manual adopted for the project, but it will be useful to have reviewed them here in case they were overlooked.

OBTAINING MATERIAL AND VERIFICATION OF INFORMATION

The secondary sources from which one is selecting entries are prone to error; consequently, every book, journal article, document, or item chosen for inclusion should be examined first hand if possible. Also do not decide from the title that an item is worthless for titles are deceiving. Compare the information on the card with the item itself to prevent errors. If one is annotating, examination is mandatory.

Standards for Descriptive Bibliographies

The descriptive bibliography is a development or further state in the evolution of the catalog and will therefore share some of the problems that arise in enumerative bibliography. A descriptive bibliography differs from an enumerative bibliography in the quantity and kind of detail that is included. It has as its goal the identification of books as physical objects, so that a person who has never seen a particular book before can recognize it from a written description presented in a systematic fashion. The essential fact of description is its concern with books as physical objects rather than intellectual products.

The techniques of description used in this type of bibliography include the following: a) transcriptions (or reproductions) of the title page or other part of the book, which both record information and provide identification, b) the collation or physical description of the book, which may or may not include a formula that analyzes its format in a conventional shorthand and, by explaining its construction, says something abouts its manufacture, c) details of the contents of the book, d) a description of the binding material and the lettering and other matter that appear on it, e) a list of any variations that occur in the binding or other elements of the book, and f) notes on any other information that may throw light on the book's history.[8]

Although a descriptive bibliography will normally contain information under all six headings, the weight that is attached to each of them will vary. For example, if the bibliography concerns books that are chiefly of interest for their texts, full details of contents will be needed, but it may be unnecessary to say much about typography or paper. On the other hand, if the subject of the bibliography is the work of a particular printer, the typography and paper of his or her book(s) will have to be fully described, while details of their contents may be largely omitted.

In deciding what and how much to include, consider the following questions for each entry: What is the purpose of the descriptions? Who really needs each item of information? Can anything be abbreviated? Only thus can one avoid burdensome and expensive superfluity and escape the ultimate absurdity of mistaking the means of descriptive bibliography for its end, of practicing bibliography for bibliography's sake.

The conventions of bibliographical description in simplified form are set out briefly in the following paragraphs. They have been derived largely from the work of Fredson Bowers, whose expertise in this area is recognized as authoritative.[9] No one, of course, would claim these conventions and rules are perfect in every respect, but they serve their purpose, and they are the common language of descriptive bibliography. Even though these conventions have been greatly simplified, references to more detailed treatments can be found in the suggested sources for further investigation at the end of this chapter. To illustrate each element in the descriptive process, a well-known novel by John Steinbeck is used.

Title Page

The bibliographic descriptive process normally begins with the title page. The best descriptive device is reproducing the title page in photographic facsimile. Failing that, you can transcribe a book's title page in full by the method known as "quasi-facsimile." This step is important for two reasons: first because it brings together in their original form all the necessary details of author, title, printer, publisher, and place and date of publication; and second because it provides a wealth of arbitrary but characteristic typographical detail that will usually serve to distinguish one setting of a title page from another.[10]

Here we come up against the question of whether different typefaces should be used to show that such differences occur in the original. On this point no definite rule can be made, for books of different periods call for different methods. Thus in early printed pages any or all of the following typefaces may be used: Roman, Italic, Gothic (or black letter), all of which may use capitals and/or lower-case letters. Down to the end of the eighteenth century and even later the long "s" may occur, and so on. Variant settings of the title page may indicate new issues or editions and so may be of prime importance.

Where these differences are significant they are best discussed in a footnote to the transliteration of the title page, thus avoiding a clumsy and, at best, inadequate method that often serves no useful purpose. In any case most modern books can be adequately dealt with by the use of ordinary Roman type. The following is an example of a transcribed title page of the first trade edition of John Steinbeck's *The Wayward Bus* (1947). Compare this with the photo-reproduction in Figure 10 (page 104).

> [*Enclosed within a rule*] The | Wayward | Bus | JOHN STEINBECK [row of fifteen ornaments] | THE VIKING PRESS · NEW YORK · 1947

Such a transcription shows everything that is contained on the title page and what is included on each line. The vertical strokes denote where each line of the title page ends. The underlined information contained within brackets or parentheses describes marking other than lettering that appear on the title page.

The Collation

In current practice the collation expresses the pagination of the item being described in the proper order. Also included is the size of the printed leaf, usually expressed in millimeters. The collation for this edition of *The Wayward Bus* is as follows:

> Collation: pp. [i]-[viii] [1] [2] 3-313; 202-135 mm.

In this illustration those preliminary page numbers that do not appear in type on any page are contained within brackets and are expressed in lower-case Roman numerals. Brackets are also used to show that certain pages of text do not appear in print. Descriptive bibliographies of books

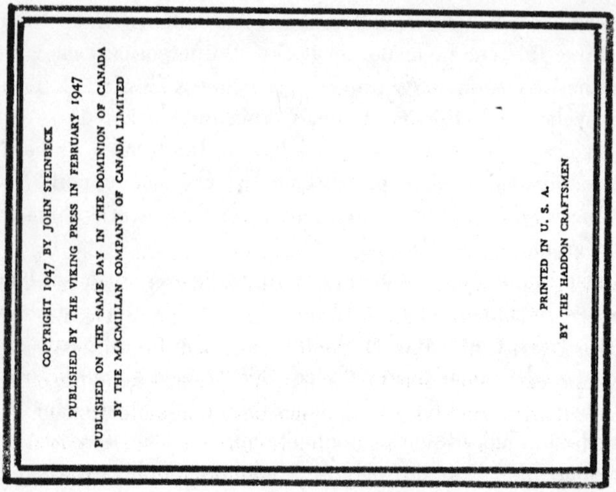

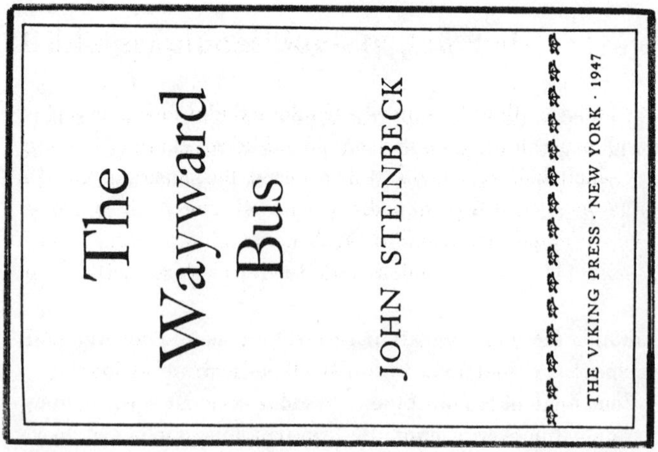

The
Wayward
Bus

JOHN STEINBECK

THE VIKING PRESS · NEW YORK · 1947

Figure No. 10.
Title Page

COPYRIGHT 1947 BY JOHN STEINBECK
PUBLISHED BY THE VIKING PRESS IN FEBRUARY 1947
PUBLISHED ON THE SAME DAY IN THE DOMINION OF CANADA
BY THE MACMILLAN COMPANY OF CANADA LIMITED

PRINTED IN U. S. A.
BY THE HADDON CRAFTSMEN

Figure No. 11.
Verso (Back) of Title Page

and other materials published around 1900 and earlier normally express the collation in terms of signatures by an elaborate formula. Most modern descriptive bibliographies do not employ this amount of detail in the collation. For further information on this form of usage consult either Bowers or Pearce.[11]

Statement of Contents

In the contents statement, all of the pages are accounted for in the order in which they appear. Each part is delineated with as much detail as is necessary to identify it. The statement of contents for *The Wayward Bus* is as follows:

> *Contents*: p. [i] half title. The Wayward Bus; [ii] blank; [iii] list of books by the same author; [iv] COPYRIGHT 1947 BY JOHN STEINBECK | PUBLISHED BY THE VIKING PRESS IN FEBRUARY 1947 | PUBLISHED ON THE SAME DAY IN THE DOMINION OF CANADA | BY THE MACMILLAN COMPANY OF CANADA LIMITED | PRINTED IN U.S.A. | BY THE HADDON CRAFTSMEN; [vii] *For* | GWYN; [viii] blank; [1] fly title The Wayward Bus; [2] blank; 3-312 text.

Note that, as in the collation, the page numbers that do not appear in print are within brackets. The information on the verso (that is, the back) of the title page is usually given in exact detail, which can be important in identifying various issues or printings of a particular work. The verso of the title page is very handy in its own right. It virtually always contains the (valuable) copyright information, Library of Congress Card Number, and sometimes notices of printing, binding, presswork, and printing history. Compare the above statement of contents with the illustration in Figure 11.

Exterior Description

Exterior description concerns the material in which the work being cited is contained, or bound, and its color. Sometimes other qualities of binding material needing description, such as the texture of the cloth—sand-grain, pebble-grain, and so on. The lettering on the front, back and spine of the binding should be fully described and transcribed in a manner similar to that used for the title page. If a book is issued in a box or casing of some kind, this should also be described in the same way as the binding. The description for the binding of *The Wayward Bus* is as follows:

> *Binding:* Dark reddish-orange cloth (Centroid 38). Front cover stamped in gilt. The Wayward Bus | BY JOHN STEINBECK | [blind-stamping of a bus on the front cover, showing up lighter than the rest of the binding]. Spine stamped in gilt: JOHN | STEINBECK | The | Wayward | Bus | [ornament] | THE VIKING PRESS. Top edges stained green, all edges trimmed. Colored pictorial dust jacket.

Included in the above is a description of the state of the edges of the book, whether trimmed, smooth, rough-trimmed, deckle edge, and, if so, gilded or with some other color. In some cases it may be necessary to describe the dust jacket in more detail, particularly if it is critical in delineating the priority of issues or editions. If there are any variants in the binding, these should be described. *The Wayward Bus* has several variants, and these are indicated as follows:

> *Variants:* 1. Browner than Centroid 38. Blind stamping of a bus on front cover is darker than rest of binding.
> 2. Pinker than Centroid 38. Blind stamping of bus on front cover is the same shade as the rest of the binding.

With all of the elements discussed above the physical description of the first trade edition of *The Wayward Bus* is complete, and one can now turn to things not covered and designate these as notes. There is no set rule as to what should be included as notes except that the information should aid the main function—that is, description. For example, notes for *The Wayward Bus* include the following:

> *Notes:* 100,000 copies published at $2.75, February 1947. A copy of unrevised galley proofs is in the Humanities Research Center at the University of Texas at Austin.

It is here that points or variations in issues can be described in appropriate detail.

Standards for Annotated Bibliographies

In a broad sense an annotated bibliography is a list of books, articles of other materials accompanied by explanatory notes which give some idea of either the content or value (or both) of the items listed. Annotated bibliographies must be distinguished from the related areas of descriptive and analytical bibliography, both of which are based primarily on the study of physical format. Bibliographers engaged in annotating are not concerned with describing the format of a text or with drawing conclusions from textual data about the origin of a book, but with the skills he or she must employ that are every bit as important and should be no less precise.[12]

A fact of life in the scholarly world today is that there are more and more annotated bibliographies being produced than ever before. The advantages of annotated bibliographies are obvious. The most prominent advantage is that annotations give the user an idea of content and also often provide some evaluation of its value with regard to the project at hand.

When contemplating the compilation of an annotated bibliography there are some general standards or guidelines one should follow. The most important requirement for a bibliography of this kind, and the factor that most influences its value, is usefulness—the ease with which accurate and complete information may be retrieved from its listings. The compiler's main responsibility is to ensure that the user will be able to locate dependable information quickly and efficiently. In order to do this effectively one must have a thorough knowledge of the subject and above all be a careful and accurate reader of scholarship and criticism.[13]

Like any other branch of bibliography, the field of annotated bibliography employs a wide range of formats, from checklists which include only brief parenthetical comments to "running commentary" bibliographic essays. Any specific suggestions cannot possibly address all the variations. Many of the standards or guidelines that follow are general and can apply to most annotated bibliographies.

Different bibliographies serve different purposes. One kind lists (and credits) the sources of an author's information; another lists comprehensively the books and articles of a single writer; a third kind lists works relevant to a specific subject area. The following steps can be used to prepare annotated bibliographies:

1. Obtain an overview of the project by examining the basic reference tools: almost all broad subject areas have basic guides. Narrow guides and current retrospective bibliographies treat the subfields of these subject areas. Therefore:

a. Consult the general bibliographies for information on guides to the literature.
b. Search the general guides for the bibliographies in your specific field.
c. In the specific bibliographies, note the references relevant to the subject area.
d. Check any author lists that may be available. If author X is known to have written in the area of interest, search appropriate indexes and abstracts under the author's name for more recent materials. The *Science Citation Index, Social Science Citation Index* and the *Arts and Humanities Citation Index* list authors whose papers cite work by X and the appropriate Source Index gives further information about the cited papers.
e. Institutional reports that list publications, such as the *Annual Report of Argonne National Laboratories for Isotope Research,* can be very useful.
f. Checking subject encyclopedias, handbooks, directories, and the like. Specific research guides, such as Tz-chung Li's *Social Science Reference Sources: A Practical Guide*. Westport, CT.: Greenwood Press, 1980. can help at this point.

2. Determine the scope of the bibliography: Will one include retrospective material, material in foreign languages, microforms, periodical articles, or manuscript material? Will the bibliography be comprehensive or selective? (Remember that the task here is to compile an annotated bibliography of a restricted subject).
3. Determine the arrangement whereby the material can most easily be found and understood. The usual methods of arrangement are: (a) alphabetical by author, (b) alphabetical by subject, (c) classified, and (d) chronological.
4. Choose a format for entries. The usual elements for bibliographical citation and attribution include (use of given name, initials, and internal punctuation should mirror the cited author's use); title; edition; imprint (place, publisher, date); collation (pages, illustrations, etc.); and, possibly series note. The entries must be consistent and complete so that the others can locate exactly the works cited.
5. In the annotations, distinguish fact, opinion, conclusions, judgment, inferences, and the like.
6. Use index cards or a file management program (if using a microcom-

puter) to collect citations; they are easy to manipulate and rearrange.[14]

An examination of several journals in a field of interest should convince one that there is no universal standard for bibliographic citation. Most subject fields have style manuals and one likely exists for a field of interest. If not, then there are many excellent style manuals of a general nature such as Turabian's *A Manual for Writers of Term Papers, Theses, and Dissertations* (1987) now in its 5th edition. Consistency of format is one hallmark of good bibliographic practice.[15] For a list of style manuals see Appendix B.

In conjunction with item 5 above, there are some further considerations that will be helpful in writing annotations. Bibliography users expect an annotation to be an accurate and complete summary of the contents of an item. Consider the following:

1. Explain the main purpose of the work.
2. Briefly describe the contents.
3. Indicate the possible audience for the work.
4. Note any special features.
5. Warn of any defect, weakness, or bias.[16]

Direct value judgments such as "a most important study" or "a worthless commentary" should be avoided; these often indicate much more about the prejudices of the bibliographer than about the work being annotated. The bibliographer should be willing to give each scholar his or her due. Each argument should be given objectively with a minimum of judgmental interpolation. If you feel incapable of paraphrasing or summarizing an item accurately, rely on direct quotation to capture the thrust of the argument. Annotation need not be completely neutral, however. One can indicate the value of a publication without an overt judgment. Take advantage of the connotation of 'annotation verbs.' For example, the verb "proves" (as in "Proves that Steinbeck knew the works of the minor British novelist. . . .") tells the reader that the argument is convincing. "Suggests" in the same context is equally demonstrative. There is a tendency to overuse "provides" and "argues," and the result is usually flat annotation. The language is rich in strongly connotative verbs—"contends," "asserts," "demonstrates," and in another vein, "supposes," and "speculates."[17]

Other things to remember include cross referencing of items that are derivative; avoid unnecessary detail; and attempt to capture the argument of a work from the author's point of view. Each work cited and annotated should have been read carefully and completely and the documentation checked to discover relevant citations. Annotations should be written cogently and lucidly. At times a clipped or telegraphed sentence style can be used effectively; however, it is preferable that annotations be written in complete and understandable sentences.[18]

The following are some examples of annotated entries:

1. *A Short Descriptive Annotation:*

Levant, Howard. "The Unity of *In Dubious Battle:* Violence and Dehumanization," *Modern Fiction Studies*, 11 (Spring 1965), pp. 21–33.
A discussion of interwoven images, themes, and the use of language in this Steinbeck novel.

2. *A Short Evaluative Annotation:*

Lisca, Peter. *The Wide World of John Steinbeck*. New Brunswick, NJ: Rutgers University Press, 1958.
For many years this has remained the major critical study on Steinbeck's fiction. Lisca's insights remain valid, and he couples textual notation with perceptive analysis.

3. *A Medium Length Descriptive and/or Analytical Annotation:*

Bendix, Reinhard. *Kings of People: Power and the Mandate to Rule*. Berkeley, CA: University of California Press, 1973.
A general study of the evolution of political authority and the idea of popular sovereignty. Uses a Weberian framework, and places a heavy emphasis on the role of bureaucratic (and patrimonial) officialdom in the process of historical transformation. Includes detailed analyses of Britain, France, Germany (Prussia), the Soviet Union, and Japan.

4. *A Medium Length Evaluative Annotation:*

Burhans, Clinton S., Jr. *The Would-Be Writer*. Lexington, MA: Xerox Corp., 1971.

This work assists students in writing courses to grasp the basic writing process, thereby making more meaningful their subsequent training in more advanced thinking and writing. The book helps one to think through a topic with pre-writing, writing, and re-writing steps.

Selected Related Writings

ENUMERATIVE BIBLIOGRAPHIES

Cole, George Watson. "Compiling a Bibliography," *Library Journal*, 26 (November/ December 1901), pp. 791–795, 859–863.

"Guidelines for the Preparation of a Bibliography," *RQ*, 22 (Fall 1982), pp. 31–32. Repeated in Krummel (pp. 143–146).

Guidelines for the Preparation of Bibliographies. Washington, DC: U.S. Department of Agriculture, National Agricultural Library, 1982.

Higgins, Marion Villers. *Bibliography: A Beginner's Guide to the Making, Evaluation and Use of Bibliographies*. New York: H. W. Wilson, 1941.

Krummel, Donald W. *Bibliographies: Their Aims and Methods*. London: Mansell, 1984.

________ and John B. Howell. "Bibliographic Standards and Style," *Scholarly Publishing*, 10 (April 1979), pp. 223–240.

Robinson, Anthony M. L. *Systematic Bibliography: A Practical Guide to the Work of Compilation*. 4th ed. New York: Saur, 1979.

Shaw, Ralph Robert. "Mechanical and Electronic Aids for Bibliography," *Library Trends*, 2 (April 1954), pp. 522–531.

DESCRIPTIVE BIBLIOGRAPHIES

Bowers, Fredson Thayer. *Principles of Bibliographical Description*. Princeton, NJ: Princeton University Press, 1949. (Reprinted in 1986)

Gaskell, Philip. *A New Introduction to Bibliography*. Corrected issue. New York: Oxford University Press, 1974.

Pearce, M. J. *A Workbook of Analytical & Descriptive Bibliography*. London: Bingley; Hamden, CT: Linnet, 1970.

ANNOTATED BIBLIOGRAPHIES

Colaianne, A. J. "The Aims and Methods of Annotated Bibliography," *Scholarly Publishing*, 11 (July 1980), pp. 321–331.

Fenner, Peter and Martha C. Armstrong. *Research: A Practical Guide to Finding Information*. Los Altos, CA: William Kaufman, Inc., 1981. Consult pp. 153–163.

Harner, James L. *On Compiling an Annotated Bibliography*. New York: The Modern Language Association of America, 1985.

Menapace, John. "Some Approaches to Annotation," *Scholarly Publishing*, 1 (January 1970), pp. 194–205.

Notes

1. D. W. Krummel & John Bruce Howell, "Bibliographic Standards and Style," *Scholarly Publishing*, 10 (April 1979), p. 223.

2. Gira Kumar and Kirshan Kumar, *Bibliography*. (New Delhi: Vikas Publishing House, 1976), p. 201.

3. Anthony M. L. Robinson, *Systematic Bibliography*. . . . 4th ed., rev. (New York: Saur, 1979), p. 19.

4. These general arrangements are covered in some detail by Donald W. Krummel in Chapter V of his book *Bibliographies: Their Aims and Methods*. (London: Mansell, 1984), pp. 85–95.

5. Ralph R. Shaw, "Mechanical and Electronic Aids for Bibliography," *Library Trends*, 2 (April 1954), p. 523.

6. The two approaches illustrated here were derived from Kate L. Turabian's *A Manual for Writers of Term Papers, Theses, and Dissertations*. 5th ed. Revised and expanded by Bonnie Birthwhistle Honigsblum. (Chicago: University of Chicago Press, 1987), and Payton Hurt's *Bibliography and Footnotes: A Style Manual for Students and Writers*. 3rd ed., Revised and enlarged by Mary L. Hurt Richmond. (Berkeley, CA: University of California Press, 1973, ©1968).

7. These basic principles are also covered in greater detail by Marion Villers Higgins in her practical guide entitled, *Bibliography: A Beginner's Guide to the Making, Evaluation and Use of Bibliographies*. (New York: H. W. Wilson, 1941), pp. 18–23.

8. Philip Gaskell, *A New Introduction to Bibliography*. Reprinted with corrections. (New York: Oxford University Press, 1974), p. 321.

9. Fredson Bowers, *Principles of Bibliographical Description*. (Princeton, NJ: Princeton University Press, 1949), p. 135.

10. Percival Horace Muir, *Book-Collecting, More Letters to Everyman*. (London: Cassell, 1949), p. 44.

11. Most of the works cited in the "Suggestions for Further Investigation" relating to descriptive bibliography explain the collation formula in considerable detail, especially Bowers. Pearce also provides some excellent examples for the enterprising student.

12. A. J. Colaianne, "The Aims and Methods of Annotated Bibliography," *Scholarly Publishing*, 11 (July 1980), p. 321.

13. Ibid., p. 324.

14. Peter Fenner and Martha C. Armstrong, *Research: A Practical Guide to Finding Information*. (Los Altos, CA: William Kaufmann, Inc., 1981), pp. 153, 158.

15. Ibid., p. 158.

16. James D. Lester, *Writing Research Papers: A Complete Guide*. (Glenview, IL: Scott, Foresman, 1984), p. 40.

17. See Colaianne, pp. 328–329.

18. Ibid., pp. 329–330.

Chapter Seven

EVALUATING BIBLIOGRAPHIES

Introduction

Within the study of bibliography the evaluation process takes place at different times and for different reasons, but it is always essential. Like any publication the evaluation process begins with an idea. An idea for a bibliography is conceived at the time one perceives a need. At this point a purpose is established and the bibliography is compiled with this in mind and culminates in the form of a manuscript. This manuscript is then usually presented to a publisher who in turn evaluates its marketability and decides either to publish or reject it. If rejected the process stops (unless the manuscript is submitted to another publisher), but if it is accepted and is published, a new level of evaluation takes place. Consumers then evaluate the bibliography to determine if it fulfills their needs. This latter process may be repeated many times before the bibliography becomes dated and little used or is revised or updated. It is this selective level of the evaluative process that we are concerned with in this chapter.

Anyone who is using a bibliography should ask four basic questions: What is its aim or objective? Its authority? Its scope? And its usability? These four questions also involve a number of interrelated ones that are an integral part of the evaluation process.

Aim or Objective

The aim or objective of a bibliography should be evident from the title or form. The user must determine if the author or compiler has fulfilled the aim or objective as stated in the text of the bibliography. If these have not been clearly stated, this is a good indication the bibliography's usefulness is questionable. Aims and objectives are often further indicated in a table of contents, introduction, preface, or in the index which will tell what subjects are covered.[1] A quick check of one or all of these will indicate the bibliography's possible utility.

Authority

Closely related to aims or objectives are a set of questions concerning the qualifications and expertise of authors or compilers. What are the compiler's qualifications for the fulfillment of his or her aims or objectives? If the author is a recognized scholar, there is usually little problem with authority. But how does one determine the qualifications of a bibliography's author? Most contemporary published works, including bibliographies, provide a brief statement either on the dust jacket or somewhere in the book about an author's background and present activities.[2] Of course you may rely on your own understanding and depth of knowledge. And finally there are numerous biographical sources available which might yield needed biographical information.

Another aspect of authority involves the sources used by the compiler. Did he or she utilize primary source materials, or rely on secondary material? If new sources were explored, were they well chosen and sufficient.[3] If secondary sources were used mainly in compiling the bibliography, then the chances for error are greatly increased and the resulting bibliographical information highly unreliable. Even if highly respected sources were used, one should be prepared to check the original source for accuracy.

A secondary but nevertheless important role, is the imprint of a publisher that may indicate the relative worth of a published bibliography. Some publishers have excellent reputations for issuing bibliographies, and other are known for their fair-to-untrustworthy titles.[4] Even such publishers as Scarecrow Press, Garland, Libraries Unlimited, G. K. Hall and others that specialize in bibliographic works cannot always maintain the quality of their publications at as high a level as they would like.

In the final analysis, authority is a matter of the reputation of the author and/or the publisher. But neither is infallible. Authority, in a sense, can also be measured, but only by careful scrutiny. In compiling bibliographies there is no excuse for poor presentation. Objectivity should be a prime goal even though it is not completely attainable.[5] When one detects sloppy or biased presentation in bibliographic works, they should be used only with great care.

Scope

The term scope can be misleading because of its various meanings. Here scope refers to the extent of a bibliography. For example if a bibliography claims to be comprehensive in its coverage of journal articles published on American literature from 1900 to 1950, and it includes only 2,000 entries, then one would be a little suspicious of its stated scope especially when compared to similar bibliographies. Since most bibliographies are selective in nature, there should be a clear statement by the compiler of what is and what is not included and what criteria were used to determine selection or rejection. And, do the selection criteria fit the audience claimed in the bibliography?

Other questions involving scope are almost as numerous as there are types of bibliographies. Users should study the scope of any bibliography in terms of number of entries, length, language, timeliness, access points, and so on. Currency is one of the most important features of many bibliographies, particularly if designed for ready reference. Undeniably one of the facts of life is that all bibliographies are dated before they are even off the presses. Always check when a bibliography was published and compare it with the most current date in its inclusive entries. This will provide a clue to currency if it is important in the selection of materials.

Usefulness

One of the major determinants of usefulness is the degree to which the bibliography in hand meets basic needs from the point of view of one member of its intended audience. This obviously includes what has already been discussed plus a number of other important elements.

Among these elements, arrangement is highly important. Entries should be organized in a manner suitable to the subject treated. This makes it easy to use without having to consult an index. It is essential, however, that multiple means of access be provided. Overall the arrangement for a classified bibliography should be logical and easy for users to understand.[6] The indexes should be sufficiently detailed to provide acceptable levels of recall and precision. Appropriate cross-references should provide guidance to additional sources. The entries should reflect standards established by a style system adopted for the subject matter and adhered to consistently. Accuracy is another element that is very important to usefulness. If frequent errors occur, the bibliography's usability becomes highly suspect. And finally, annotations render bibliographies very helpful in assisting users in selecting materials quickly and effectively to satisfy specific needs.

Evaluation Checklist

The following checklist outlines the essential features of bibliographies for evaluation purposes. Neither this outline nor the previous discussion is meant to prescribe a rigid order or procedure for evaluating a bibliography but rather to suggest some of the possible variations that can be found and might otherwise be overlooked. The essential elements of scope, entry, and arrangement are in fact inseparable, being mutually dependent and collectively influenced by the aims of the bibliographer. No single feature can be analyzed or evaluated in isolation; the characteristics of a bibliographical population are determined by the compiler's goals which in turn influence the choice of headings and entries; the internal organization is based on all of these factors; while the position of particular entries within each sequence depends on their form as well as on the filing rules and chosen arrangement.[7] The checklist below, coupled with the criteria already discussed, should assist in selecting the type of bibliography that will best suit the intended purpose.[8]

I. *Authority:*
   1. Subject and bibliographic competency of editor or compiler
   2. Reputation of publisher
   3. Use of primary or secondary sources in compilation

II. *Aim and Scope:*
   1. Purpose of bibliography: descriptive vs. enumerative
   2. Length of period covered
   3. Balance in selection and treatment
   4. Formal limitations: types of materials covered, etc.

III. *Arrangement and Organization:*
   1. Grouping of material: alphabetical, classified, chronological, geographical, etc.
   2. Quality of supplementary indexing
   3. Cross-References

IV. *Bibliographical Endures:*
   1. Bibliographical citations and their accuracy
   2. Annotations: descriptive, analytical, critical
   3. Additional information: location of materials, special features, etc.

V. *Format and Physical Makeup:*
   1. Typography: size and variations of type
   2. Page makeup
   3. General appearance of format.

Everyone who employs a bibliography to find information for whatever reason will need to evaluate one or more bibliographic instruments in terms of his or her needs. The criteria outlined above, if applied systematically, should provide the means to accomplish this quickly and effectively.

Selected Related Writings

"Criteria for Evaluating a Bibliography," *RQ*, 11 (Summer 1972), pp. 359–360.

Gratch, Bonnie. "Toward a Methodology for Evaluating Research Paper Bibliographies," *Research Strategies*, 3 (Fall 1986), pp. 170–177.

Lang, Jovian. "Evaluation of Reference Sources Published or to Be Published," *The Reference Librarian*, 15 (Fall 1986), pp. 55–64.

Stevens, Norman. "Evaluating Reference Books in Theory and Practice," *The Reference Librarian*, 15 (Fall 1986), pp. 9–19.

Whittaker, Kenneth. *Systematic Evaluation: Methods and Sources for Assessing Books*. London: Bingley, 1982.

Wynar, Bohdan S. *Introduction to Bibliography and Reference Work* . . . 4th ed. Littleton, CO: Libraries Unlimited, 1967. Consult pp. 59–60.

Notes

1. William A. Katz, *Introduction to Reference Work, Volume 1, Basic Information Sources*. 4th ed. (New York: McGraw-Hill, 1982), p. 22.

2. Kenneth Whittaker, *Systematic Evaluation: Methods and Sources for Assessing Books*. (London: Bingley, 1982), pp. 66–67.

3. See Katz, p. 23.

4. Ibid.

5. Jean Key Gates, *Guide to the Use of Libraries and Information Sources*. 5th ed. (New York: McGraw-Hill, 1983), p. 87.

6. See Katz, pp. 26–27.

7. Mary Whouley, "Guide for the Analysis and Evaluation of Bibliographical Instruments" (Unpublished paper prepared for Course L230, Bibliographical Organization, School of Librarianship, University of California, Berkeley, July 15, 1969), p. 27.

8. Bohdan S. Wynar, *Introduction to Bibliography and Reference Work. . . .* 4th ed., rev. (Littleton, CO: Libraries Unlimited, 1967), pp. 59–60.

Chapter Eight

ONLINE DATABASES AND BIBLIOGRAPHIC SEARCHING

Introduction

To say that the computer has profoundly affected the study of bibliography is to understate the case. The personal computer is almost as commonplace as the typewriter and its value in research is well established. Librarians, students, scholars, and others can now query databases containing millions of bibliographic records to published literature and extract those citations tailored to their specific requirements.[1] These databases—electronic files of information that can be stored, searched, transmitted, and manipulated—are changing the way bibliographers gather and disseminate bibliographic information.

What Is a Database?

A database is a machine-readable file of information that is accessed through a computer-telephone link called a modem. The electronic files contain a variety of information ranging from the complete texts of articles as they appeared in the *New York Times*, for example, to chemical equations and census data, to administrative rules, regulations, and court decisions.[2] Online services or compact disks (CD-ROMS) are available to the user through company libraries and local public or academic libraries. Individuals, through a contractual arrangement with a vendor, can subscribe to online services themselves. Librarians, however, usually have access in a number of ways. They may have a subscription with the actual producer of the database, as in the case of VuText. Or they may have a contract with a vendor such as DIALOG, BRS or ORBIT that might provide access to over 200 databases. In many libraries, the patron will have access to both types of services and hundreds of databases, for which there may be a charge.

Database producers or vendors become the "switching center" for patrons. The databases are loaded on the vendor's main computer. The vendors supply the central computer, searching software, and the telecommunication facilities to accommodate incoming calls from patrons' telephones and terminals. Any computer terminal equipped with a modem, or telephone communications device, can tap into a database system such as DIALOG or BRS. In the majority of cases the patron simply dials a telephone number that links the terminal on the patron's desk with a satellite-communication system, inputs a password accompanied by an established protocol, and the linkage is completed. The patron's terminal communicates with the producer's or vendor's central electronic files.[3]

Types of Databases

Currently there are three major types of databases. The most commonly used is the bibliographic file, which provides citations to materials such as magazine and newspaper articles, government reports, articles in scholarly journals, reports, conference proceedings, and the like. Citations can be arranged in a variety of formats, but most include the title of the article and the source of publication, the date and page numbers, the author's name, and the volume and issue numbers where appropriate. In some bibliographic databases, abstracts are also included for many of the citations. The abstract is usually short and outlines the salient contents of the article or report. In using these databases one can easily compile an extensive list of citations to articles and/or other materials, depending on the nature of the database.

There are other databases that are statistical in nature. Here the files contain number-based information, such as census data; demographic data; marketing and consumer data; information about circulation size; and the like.

The most extensive and complete type of databases are the full-text variety. These databases are most prevalent for newspapers, business, and law. Here the computer stores the complete text of every article, document, report, case, or item included. This eliminates the need for one to locate and photocopy the original article. Naturally full-text databases are more expensive to use than are the other types of services, but they do save time.[4]

Database Structure

In order to understand the basics of online bibliographic searching it is helpful to examine the structure of databases in general. As is the case with many other specialized information sources, databases have a structure and logic of their own. While overall the primary concepts are the same, the technical detail of information storage and retrieval may differ slightly from one database to another. At any rate users must be conversant with the conventions of the searching process to successfully retrieve meaningful information.

To store and retrieve information from electronic files, full-text and bibliographic database systems use a method of language matching. Users must provide the terms or concepts, which the computer then tries to locate among the millions of bits of information stored in the electronic memory. Each item in the database consists of words—either in the entire text of the articles stored or a brief citation and abstract. Items in the databases are also "tagged" with descriptors, identifiers, or keywords. These are terms that indexers, working for the database provider, think are likely to best describe the content of the particular article or item in the database. Figure 12 shows a sample citation or record from the ERIC database.

Some database producers publish thesauri, or guides that list all the descriptors, or keywords that the indexers may choose from when assigning those tags to items in the database.[5]

The Search Process[6]

In most cases, a topic is suitable for online searching when: 1) two or more concepts must be combined or coordinated (e.g. Information Retrieval and Online Systems); 2) subject headings in printed indexes or abstracts are inadequate because they are too broad or narrow, or because the topic is so current that a subject heading has not yet been devised for it (e.g. Automated Bibliographic Systems); 3) a comprehensive search is

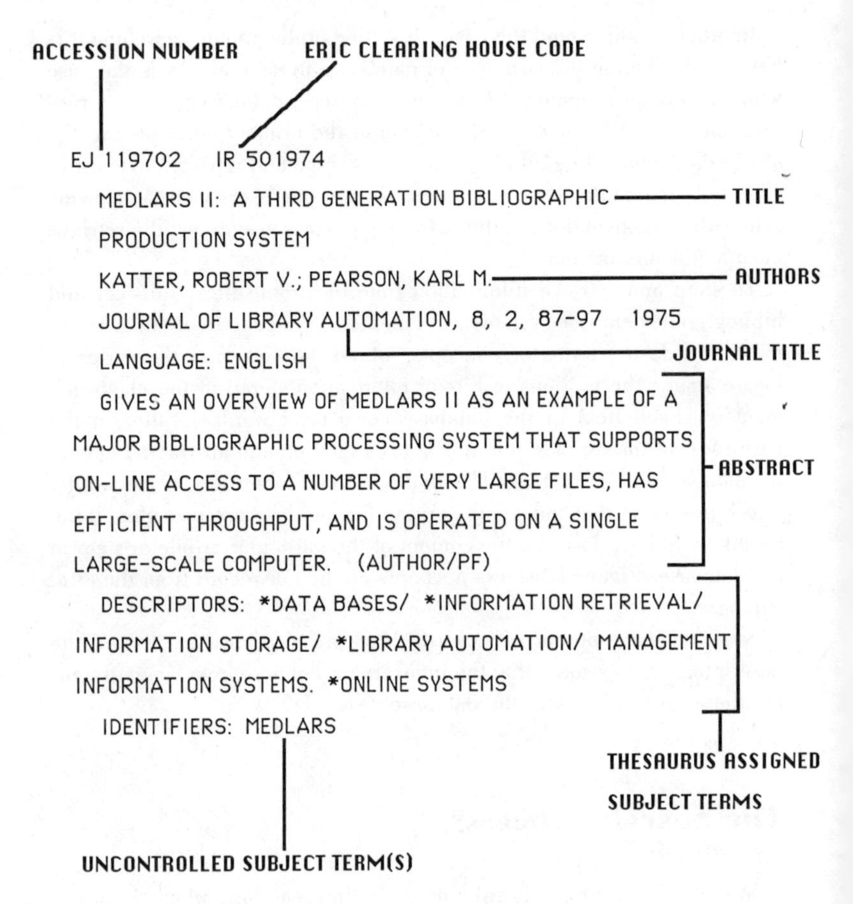
Below is a sample citation or record from the ERIC database:
ACCESSION NUMBER
ERIC CLEARING HOUSE CODE
EJ 119702 IR 501974
MEDLARS II: A THIRD GENERATION BIBLIOGRAPHIC
PRODUCTION SYSTEM
TITLE
KATTER, ROBERT V.; PEARSON, KARL M.
AUTHORS
JOURNAL OF LIBRARY AUTOMATION, 8, 2, 87-97 1975
JOURNAL TITLE
LANGUAGE: ENGLISH
GIVES AN OVERVIEW OF MEDLARS II AS AN EXAMPLE OF A
MAJOR BIBLIOGRAPHIC PROCESSING SYSTEM THAT SUPPORTS
ON-LINE ACCESS TO A NUMBER OF VERY LARGE FILES, HAS
EFFICIENT THROUGHPUT, AND IS OPERATED ON A SINGLE
LARGE-SCALE COMPUTER. (AUTHOR/PF)
ABSTRACT
DESCRIPTORS: *DATA BASES/ *INFORMATION RETRIEVAL/
INFORMATION STORAGE/ *LIBRARY AUTOMATION/ MANAGEMENT
INFORMATION SYSTEMS. *ONLINE SYSTEMS
IDENTIFIERS: MEDLARS
THESAURUS ASSIGNED
SUBJECT TERMS
UNCONTROLLED SUBJECT TERM(S)

necessary; or 4) the topic is interdisciplinary (e.g. Automated Bibliographic Systems in Biology).[7]

Usually searchers have a choice of how to instruct the computer to search through the items in the database. The records contained in the database may be searched by having the computer look at every word in a record, whether it be a bibliographic citation or a complete article. When the computer recognizes one of the requested search terms in the record, that word is identified as appropriate to the search. Or the searcher can instruct the computer to look through just the descriptors and keywords, the titles, the author part of the record, or any other combination of search logic.[8]

This process of communicating with the computer to retrieve information from an online bibliographic database can be broken down in to five basic steps:

1. *Formulate a search question or statement and identify the concepts.* The first step in the search process is to develop a concise, one-sentence statement of the research question. For example: What type of treatment is useful for helping older people who suffer from depression or melancholy? If the research problem involves more than three concepts, successive search questions and strategy will have to be considered.

Concepts can be identified by reexamining the research question and underlining those words or phrases that represent the searcher's main interests. A word of caution. Searches usually involve two or three concepts at most. If only one important concept is identified, a computer search is probably not necessary, as a manual search in a printed index will usually be equally successful and will only cost a little time.[9] There appears to be three concepts in the example above: What type of *treatment* is useful for helping *older people* who suffer from *depression* or *melancholy?* This search statement might produce a large number of records or might limit the results unnecessarily. The searcher must be prepared to broaden the search by reducing the number of concepts, or limiting the search through vocabulary or record element.

2. *From thesauri, indexes or other sources, select topics or subject terms that represent concepts evident in the search question or statement.* Subject descriptors or terms used in online searching correspond to the subject headings used when scanning printed indexes and abstracts. The *Thesaurus of Psychological Index Terms* (4th ed. 1985) for example is used to choose terms to be employed in searching the PsycINFO database online. Most online databases make available such a published list of

CONCEPTS FROM SEARCH TOPIC	CORRESPONDING TERMS FROM THESAURUS
A. Treatment	Treatment Treatment Outcomes
B. Older People	Aged Geriatrics Gerontology
C. Depression or Melancholy	Depression (Emotion) Reactive Depression Sadness

Figure No. 13. Concept and Thesaurus Terms

descriptors or subject headings. This list is known as a *controlled vocabulary*.[10]

When conducting any search, it is important at this point to examine carefully the relevant printed indexes, abstracts, and thesauri, if this has not been done previously. This step is necessary in choosing the proper subject terms. Often one discovers that the information being sought is readily available using manual searching methods. To research the example given, one might find that the most useful periodical indexes and abstracts are those from the social sciences, such as the *Social Sciences Index* and *Psychological Abstracts*.

List the subject headings used to search these tools on the subject headings list and search record cards. From the *Thesaurus of Psychological Index Terms* select the appropriate descriptors (see Figure 13). Notice that one can (and will often want to) select more than one descriptor to represent a particular concept.

Actually, a major advantage of searching online is that one is not limited to a controlled vocabulary. It is possible to use natural language to search most databases in what is called *free-text* mode, which is somewhat like being able to create your own subject headings. In this mode the searchable vocabulary can be expanded to include all words, names, or phrases that occur in any citation, abstract, or full-text document stored in the database. This capability to search for the occurrence of personal names and obscure, specialized, slang or newly coined terms is often useful. It is an important advantage of searching online databases.[11]

Of course free-text searching is also fraught with potential hazards as well as opportunities. Not only do the meanings of words change with their context, but many different terms, abbreviations, or phrases might be employed by different authors to express the identical concept (for example TV or video for television). And naturally, spelling and grammatical variations must also be taken into account. The degree of care with which possible free-text search terms are prepared will determine the completeness of the results obtained as well as how many *false drops* (irrelevant citations) are also retrieved. Computers, unfortunately, do not know what we "mean"; they can only locate exact matches of the particular characters we have entered (e.g., aged when used free text pulls up school aged children). The computer will only search for the terms requested.

Since the concepts in the example search are adequately represented by existing descriptors, there is no real need to use free-text searching. Suppose, however, that during our search we had become interested in a particular type of treatment for depressed elderly persons where a technique called "self enrichment" is used. A descriptor does not exist for self enrichment in the *Thesaurus of Psychological Index Terms* so a search of the PsycINFO database would require searching in free-text mode. To do this, it would be necessary to create a list of all the synonyms, spelling variants, grammatical forms, changes in word order, and the like, which might occur in natural language when this concept appears in an article title or abstract. Such a list might include: self-enrichment, self enrichment, selfenrichment, self enriching, and so on. Thus, creating an adequate list covering all contingencies can be tricky, but truncating as in "self enrich?" can help. It is generally preferable to use a controlled vocabulary to combine with the use of natural language when searching many topics. The combination can increase the number of relevant citations retrieved.

The precision of searches conducted in a free-text mode can be improved by the use of specifying the proximity of natural language terms to one another. For example it is possible to specify that we wish to retrieve only documents in which the words "self" and "enrichment" are directly adjacent to each other. On the other hand, we could specify that there could be a specific number of intervening words, or that the words occur within the same sentence or the same paragraph. The type of commands used are generally known as *proximity operators*. Their properties and use vary in different systems.

3. *Select a database or databases appropriate for the main topic*. During preliminary searching of printed indexes and thesauri for subject terms that database likely to provide the best results should be discovered. A librarian doing the search, will have current information on relevant databases and will be able to advise the researcher. However, if the user is conducting the search on an end user system, it definitely is advisable to discuss options with a librarian or qualified person in the field. More than one database is often used, particularly in a field such as psychology which involves many different aspects.[12]

4. *Coordinate terms and concepts, then run the search, evaluate the results and make any needed adjustments*. There are some special terms that searchers use to tell the computer how to coordinate, or combine, subject terms. This coordination or combining is accomplished by a process borrowed from the field of logic. Searchers use *Boolean logical operators* (so called because they were devised by an English mathematician named George Boole, 1815–1864) to do this. Two logical operators—*and* and *or*—are used most often in online bibliographic searching. The meaning of these coordinating terms is easily demonstrated by using *Venn diagrams* (named for the English logician John Venn, 1834–1923).[13]

In Figure #14, *treatment* and *depression* are terms contained in bibliographic records that the computer is searching. The computer is instructed to *and* the sets of records together or put them in an "and" relationship. The shaded area represents those records that the computer would retrieve. It includes only those records in which *both* treatment and depression appear.

When we *or* the sets of records (Figure #15) or put them in an "or" relationship, we retrieve all the records to which at least one of these descriptors has been assigned—either melancholy or depression. They need not necessarily both be assigned to the same document. Consequently many more records will be found with the "or" operator.

Most online searches are conducted by "or-ing" together all the synonyms and related terms that represent a concept. The resulting set of records, which tend to be many in number, are then "and-ed" to produce a much smaller set. Simply stated: Terms are "or-ed," then concepts are

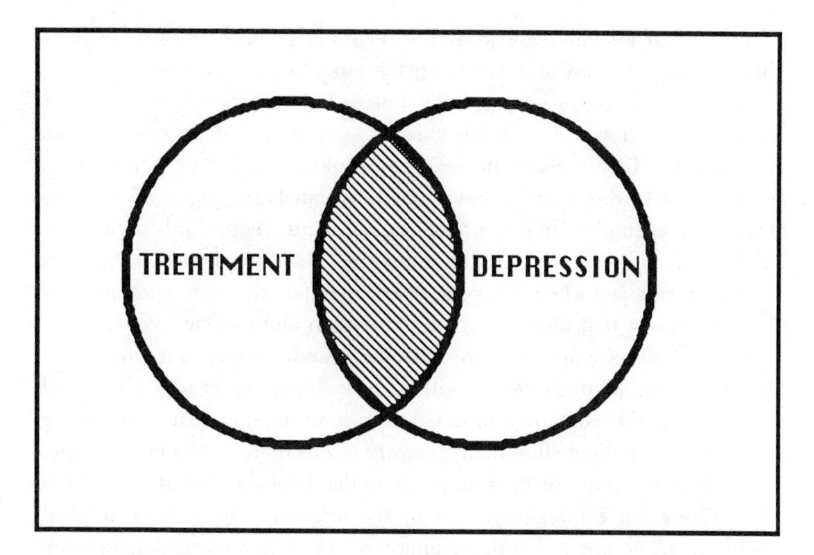

Figure No. 14. Treatment and Depression

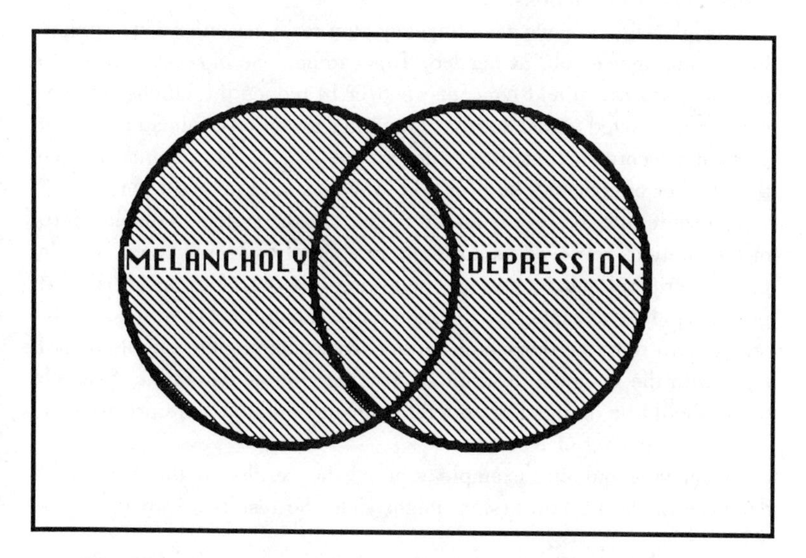

Figure No. 15. Melancholy or Depression

"and-ed." If all has gone well, the resulting group of records forms a bibliography of relevant sources on the topic being searched.

The third Boolean process, the *not* operator, is used to subtract a concept from a set. A searcher may be interested in depression but not melancholy. In this case the searcher could use the "not" operator to exclude all of the records that mention melancholy. Figure #16 illustrates this example. However, material containing both words depression and melancholy are not included in the final set of the search. Therefore, caution is advised when using the "not" operator. Relevant citations may have been lost that deal with both depression and melancholy.

Unless one is employing an end user search system like Knowledge Index, a search intermediary will actually input the search terms and strategy via the computer terminal or microcomputer. The computer's response will indicate how many *postings* or *hits* there are (in other words, how many document records there are in the database that fit the criteria that have been established). Often, the original search statement will yield either too few or too many citations to satisfy a particular research need. For example, the user would like to have more than 5 citations but would be overwhelmed with 100. Cost should also be considered, since most databases charge a fee for each citation printed on or off line. Along with this is an additional charge for the online time needed to retrieve a large number of citations.

It is advisable to have a contingency plan ready for either narrowing or broadening the search, as needed. This can be done in several ways. *To narrow a search:* a) add concepts; and/or b) reduce the number of synonyms and related terms; and/or c) limit to a specified publication year or parts of a record such as title or descriptor. *To broaden a search:* reduce the number of concepts, and/or add synonyms and related terms.[14]

To ensure that the results are on target, ask the system to display 5-10 of the citations retrieved as a sample in a simplified format such as title plus descriptors and identifiers. Following this procedure also makes it possible to take advantage of the interactive capabilities of online searching systems to refine the search further. By examining the sample record titles with the assigned descriptors, it is possible to determine if search terms should be dropped or added to enhance either a more precise or a more complete set of results.

In carrying out our example search, the results in the PsycINFO database in the DIALOG system might yield the results shown in Figure #17.

The final product of most online searches is a list of citations, printed

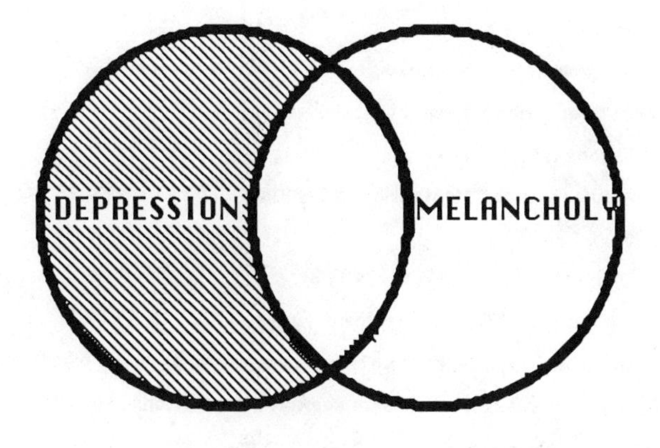

Figure No. 16. Depression not Melancholy

?SS Treatment and aged and depression (emotion)

Set #	# of Citations	Concept
S1	24987	TREATMENT
S2	8339	AGED
S3	10593	DEPRESSION (EMOTION)
S4	23	TREATMENT AND AGED AND DEPRESSION (EMOTION)

Figure No. 17. Search Strategy

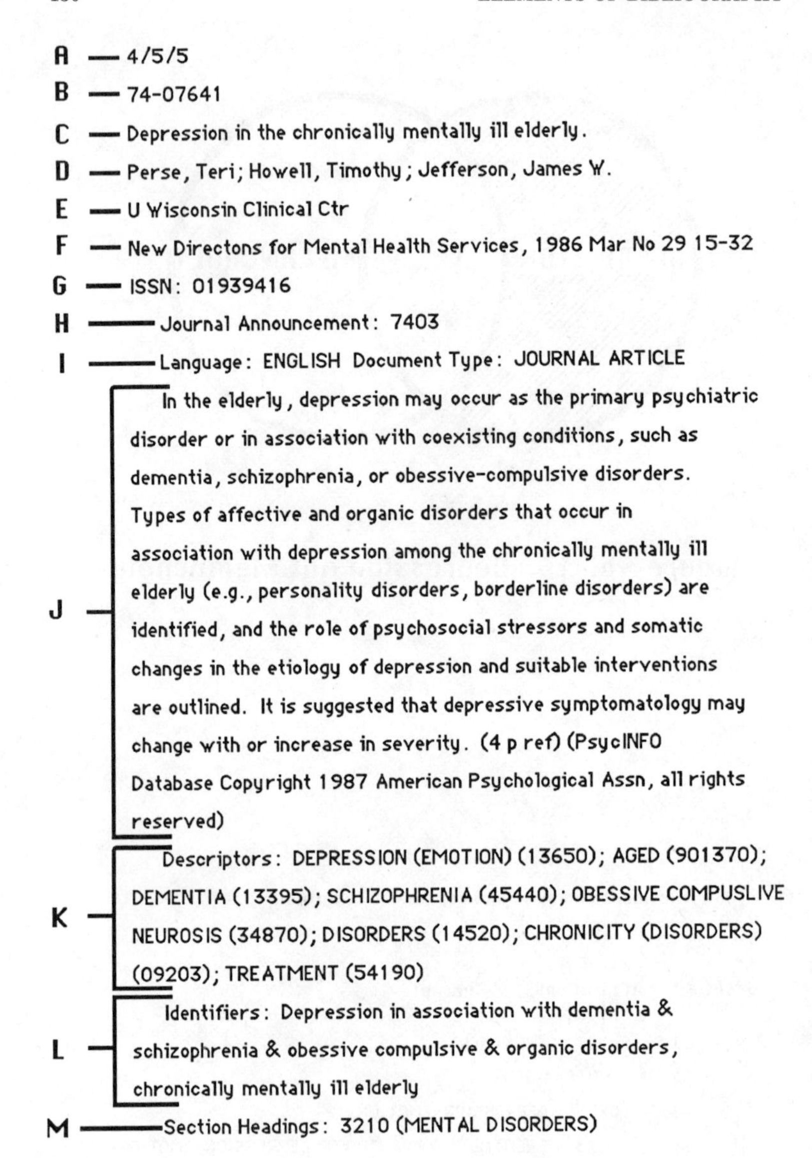

A — 4/5/5

B — 74-07641

C — Depression in the chronically mentally ill elderly.

D — Perse, Teri; Howell, Timothy; Jefferson, James W.

E — U Wisconsin Clinical Ctr

F — New Directons for Mental Health Services, 1986 Mar No 29 15-32

G — ISSN: 01939416

H — Journal Announcement: 7403

I — Language: ENGLISH Document Type: JOURNAL ARTICLE

J — In the elderly, depression may occur as the primary psychiatric disorder or in association with coexisting conditions, such as dementia, schizophrenia, or obessive-compulsive disorders. Types of affective and organic disorders that occur in association with depression among the chronically mentally ill elderly (e.g., personality disorders, borderline disorders) are identified, and the role of psychosocial stressors and somatic changes in the etiology of depression and suitable interventions are outlined. It is suggested that depressive symptomatology may change with or increase in severity. (4 p ref) (PsycINFO Database Copyright 1987 American Psychological Assn, all rights reserved)

K — Descriptors: DEPRESSION (EMOTION) (13650); AGED (901370); DEMENTIA (13395); SCHIZOPHRENIA (45440); OBESSIVE COMPUSLIVE NEUROSIS (34870); DISORDERS (14520); CHRONICITY (DISORDERS) (09203); TREATMENT (54190)

L — Identifiers: Depression in association with dementia & schizophrenia & obessive compulsive & organic disorders, chronically mentally ill elderly

M — Section Headings: 3210 (MENTAL DISORDERS)

Figure No. 18. Sample Record

either online with the bibliographic citation immediately available or printed offline at the vendor's headquarters and delivered by mail within a few days to a week. Figure #18 shows a sample record from the above strategy.

Key to Sample Record: A) Set number/Format number/Record number; B) Volume number-Abstract number in *Psychological Abstracts;* C) Title of article; D) Authors; E) Author's affiliation; F) Title of Journal, Date and page numbers; G) International Standard Serial Number; H) Date and issue of journal in which article is found, e.g. Vol. 74, Issue No. 3; I) Language and Type of document; J) Abstract; K) Descriptors; L) Identifiers; M) Main section headings.

If the search was done on a microcomputer, another option to receive the results is available. Microcomputers, using suitable communications software programs, are capable of capturing the results of a search in their internal memory so that the results may be downloaded to floppy disks for storage. With an appropriate database management software program, such as dBase III, the citations retrieved can be added to others and entered in the database, either manually or through downloading. In this way, a personal online database can be created.

The software program should allow the addition of personal descriptions and notes to individual records. And it should also allow sorting of records, selective retrieving and printing them, for use with a word processing program such as Microsoft Word, Word Star, MultiMate, WordPerfect, and so on. Of course, such downloading practices do have copyright implications, and database vendors and producers have varying policies and attitudes regarding downloading, which should be explored.[15]

5. *Locate and retrieve relevant documents*. As with any search for information, the final step in using a bibliographic database is locating and retrieving the appropriate documents from those found in the search.

After exploring the resources of local public or academic libraries to determine which publications are easily available, the library's interlibrary loan service can be used to obtain the materials needed. Many online vendors offer an additional service for securing publications. These *document delivery services,* allow publications to be ordered online for delivery through the mail. Charges for this service will vary from one supplier to another.

Generally computers can search and coordinate several terms at the same time, are not dependent on a controlled vocabulary, and are very fast. Remember that computers are "dumb" and can only find what has been asked for. A topic is suitable for an online search when: 1) two or more concepts must be combined or coordinated; 2) subject headings in printed indexes are inadequate because they are too narrow or too broad, or because the topic is so current that a subject heading has not yet been assigned; 3) a comprehensive search is necessary; or 4) the topic is interdisciplinary.

Searches must be carefully planned if they are to be effective. Before a database can be accessed the vendor protocols and telecommunications software must be learned. A manual search should also be conducted, appropriate thesauri consulted, and a written search plan or strategy developed. A trained librarian, who is familiar with online searching, should review the search strategy before going online.

Follow basic search procedures such as: 1) formulate a search question or statement and identify the concepts; 2) from thesauri, indexes or other sources select topics or subject terms that represent concepts evident in the search question or statement; 3) select a database or databases appropriate for the main topic; 4) run the search, coordinating concepts and terms, evaluate the results and make needed adjustments; and 5) locate and retrieve relevant documents.

End User Searching

An end user is a person for whom information is being retrieved, or for whom information is being processed. Actually in current usage this term means that the person receiving and using the information is also the person doing the searching and retrieving as well.[16]

For the most part online searching, until quite recently, has been performed by an experienced searcher acting as an intermediary between a computer and a researcher. The reason for this is not that the principles are difficult to understand and master but that the protocols and conventions used in the communication process are usually rather complicated and vary widely from one database vendor to another. In the past few years, however, database vendors have been attempting to simplify their searching techniques to make it possible for most persons, i.e., end users, to access at least some of their online databases directly. Coupled with this is a number of fairly new databases available via optical disk or CD-ROM players through dedicated offline terminals.

In 1983, services such as DIALOG'S *Knowledge Index* and *BRS/After Dark* were made available directly to end users. The main advantage of these services is that they offer a relatively easy-to-learn searching system and at significantly reduced rates.[17] They are available just in the evening and on weekends and offer only a selection of the databases available through the full services. BRKTHRU, a simplified searching system that retains most of BRS's regular features was added by BRS in 1985 for end users. It is, for example, available during daytime, evening and weekends, and includes all regular BRS databases. However, the reduced rates were eliminated. Another type of end user service, Easy Net, which began operation at the end of 1984, is designed to serve as a gateway to other database vendors by simplifying access procedures. This system automatically chooses a database appropriate for a topic. One feature common to most end user systems is that they make it easy for the consumer to pay by accepting major credit cards.

To make it more feasible for researchers to have direct access to databases, new software has been developed such as ProSearch. This type of software simplifies the searching process by serving as a programmed intermediary between the end user and the computer. Called *front-end* software, some of these programs are also designed to minimize expensive online time by allowing search statements or strategies to be entered in before going online.[18]

Since 1985 we have witnessed a new dimension in end user services with the introduction of systems on laser disks or compact disks, such as Silver Platter's ERIC and PsychLit, MEDLINE, etc. There are also numeric databases on CD-ROM such as Disclosure. These systems utilize databases stored, not on large computers at remote locations, but on players connected to the user's own personal computer. They are usually updated monthly or quarterly and provide varying methods of access. Also it is possible to attach printers so that patrons can obtain an immediate printout of their search.

Obviously end user systems and software vary a great deal in the amount of instruction they require for effective use. Although this situation is changing, there is presently a certain degree of trade-off between the amount of time required to learn a system and its capabilities. The general rule is—the more instruction required, the more sophisticated the searches that can be done. For example, many systems use a "menu" type interface that makes it easy for novices to start searching but may ultimately prove intrusive. Fortunately, some of these systems allow searchers to progress from a menu interface to a more direct one as the searchers become more proficient.[19] Also, many end user searchers never need the sophisticated capabilities of the original search systems.

Selected Related Writings

Alberico, Ralph. "Front End Games," *Small Computers in Libraries*, 6 (February 1986), pp. 10–15.

_________. "Justifying CD-ROM," *Small Computers in Libraries*, 7 (February 1987), pp. 18–20.

Arnold, Stephen E. "End-Users: Dreams or Dollars," *Online*, 11 (January 1987), pp. 71–81.

Brundage, Christina A. "End User Services and Training In the Academic Environment." In: *Virginia Conference on Online Searching in Community Colleges*. Annandale, VA: Northern Virginia Community College, Annandale Campus, March, 1986. pp. 51–56.

Cohen, David A. "Undergraduate On-Line Literature Searching," *Teaching Political Science*, 17 (Winter 1987), pp. 69–73.

Fenichel, Carol H. and Thomas H. Hogan. *Online Searching: A Primer*. 2nd ed. Medford, NJ: Learned Information, 1984.

Garman, Nancy. "Downloading . . . Still a Live Issue? A Survey of Database Producers Policies for Both Online Services and Laserdisks," *Online*, 10 (July 1980), pp. 15–25.

Janke, Richard V. "Online After Six: End User Searching Comes of Age," *Online*, 8 (November 1984), pp. 15–29.

Li, Tze-chung. *An Introduction to Online Searching*. Westport, CT: Greenwood Press, 1985.

Ojala, Marydee. "End User Searching and its Implications for Librarians," *Special Libraries*, 76 (Spring 1985), pp. 93–99.

Solomon, Kristine. "The Mechanics of Online Searching." In: *Online Technique and Management*. Edited by James J. Maloney. Chicago: American Library Association, 1983. pp. 57–71.

Vigil, Peter J. *Online Retrieval: Analysis and Strategy*. New York: Wiley, 1988.

Notes

1. Charles L. Gilreath, *Computerized Literature Searching: Research Strategies and Databases*. (Boulder, CO: Westview Press, 1984), p. xiii.

2. Carol H. Fenichel and Thomas H. Hogan, *Online Searching: A Primer*. 2nd ed. (Medford, NJ: Learned Information, 1984), p. 7.

3. Jean Ward and Kathleen A. Hansen, *Search Strategies in Mass Communication*. (New York: Longman, 1987), p. 125.

4. Rebecca B. Rubin, Alan M. Rubin, and Linda J. Piele, *Communication Research: Strategies and Sources*. (Belmont, CA: Wadsworth, 1986), pp. 79–80.

5. See Fenichel and Hogan, pp. 16–19.

6. There are many ways to conduct online searches. The approach suggested here has been devised from the studies contained in the "Selected Related Writings" at the conclusion of this chapter.

7. See Rubin, etc., p. 77.

8. Ching-chih Chen and Susanna Schweizer, *Online Bibliographic Searching: A Learning Manual*. (New York: Neal-Schuman, 1981), pp. 2–3.

9. See Gilreath, p. 20.

10. Bernard Houghton and John Convey, *On-Line Information Retrieval System: An Introductory Manual to Principles and Practice*. (London: Bingley & Hamden, CT: Linnet Books, 1977), p. 21.

11. Tze-chung Li, *An Introduction to Online Searching*. (Westport, CT: Greenwood Press, 1985). See particularly Chapter 3, pp. 25–36 for a good discussion of the pros and cons of free-text searching.

12. See Fenichel & Hogan, pp. 13–16.

13. Kristine Salomon, "The Mechanics of Online Searching," In: *Online Searching Techniques and Management*. Edited by James J. Maloney. (Chicago: American Library Association, 1983), pp. 61–64.

14. See Rubin, etc., pp. 89–90.

15. For a view of downloading practices see Nancy Garman's article "Downloading . . . Still a Live Issue? A Survey of Database Producer Policies for Both Online Services and Laserdisks," *Online*, 10 (July 1986), pp. 15–25.

16. Although mainly related to academic libraries, an excellent introductory overview of end user searching is provided by Christina A. Brundage in her article "End User Services and Training in the Academic Environment," In: *Virginia Conference on Online Searching in Community Colleges*. (Annandale, VA: Northern Virginia Community College, Annandale Campus, March, 1986), pp. 51–56. Also available as an ERIC document, see ED270124.

17. See Fenichel & Hogan, p. 42.

18. An enlightening discussion of front end services is given by Ralph Alberico in his article "Front End Games," in *Small Computers In Libraries*, 6 (February 1986), pp. 1–15.

19. Stephen E. Arnold, "End-Users: Dreams or Dollars," *Online*, 11 (January 1987), p. 81.

Chapter Nine

TRAINING IN THE FIELD OF BIBLIOGRAPHY

Introduction

Developments in bibliography are not new; they have been influencing institutions and bibliographers for some time. What is new is the speed with which technological developments are taking place. Currently, technological and other changes are taking place so rapidly that they must be dealt with continuously. Computer, communication, and reprographic technologies have significantly affected bibliographic services and management. In addition to the speed with which these technologies have grown, the synergistic effect due to the merging of these technologies has profoundly influenced the total information environment in most countries. Libraries and their bibliographic services are the backbone of the national information environment, and consequently have a special responsibility to take advantage of that influence and enhance their capability to provide more efficient and effective information service to their patrons.[1]

Technological developments have influenced virtually every facet of bibliographical activity. The computer has, in various ways, affected the acquisition of materials, technical processing of these materials; preparation of such bibliographic control tools as catalogs and union lists; such services as reference, circulation, and online searching that merge computer and communication technologies.[2]

Naturally these technological changes in bibliography have serious implications for bibliographic education and training. Library schools, where most bibliographers are trained, are under increasing pressure to provide a deeper and more diverse educational experience to prospective bibliographers so that their graduates can assume professional positions and function effectively in a highly competitive and technologically oriented environment.[3]

Traditionally the bibliographer has been one who compiles lists of books, periodical articles, and audiovisual materials, on specialized topics. This also applies to one who annotates bibliographies with physical description and analysis of subject content of materials and recommends acquisition of materials in specialized subject areas.[4] This role now has been expanded to include those who study the transmission of literary texts from author to printed format.

Training on bibliographic subjects in library schools today has changed dramatically from that provided before World War II, largely due to technological developments. Very few library schools currently offer courses labeled "bibliography" but subsume them under course offerings such as "Literature of Science and Technology," or "Social Science Bibliography." As Chris Needham observes, "library schools over the past few years have discarded bibliography—at least as a label."[5] Bibliography-related courses include, as a central element, the study of bibliographic tools of various kinds and a range of reference materials. Such courses have always reflected an awareness of a practical need for those who know information sources. This need has dominated the thinking of many of the teachers of bibliography.

Below is a listing of the more prominent areas of specialization within the study of bibliography. Under each section a brief statement outlines career possibilities along with an example of course content. This is followed by a list of institutions offering courses in this area. If an institution has an emphasis in a particular area it is so indicated by an asterisk (*).

Analytical or Critical Bibliography

Training in analytical bibliography is applicable to several areas of scholarly activity including librarianship, literary research, and the antiquarian book trade.

Sample Course Content

Introduction to the physical aspects of printed books and the methods of analytical and descriptive bibliography. The Hand-Press Period (1500–1800) is emphasized, but the problems of the Machine Press

Period (1800–1950) are also covered. Students study many sources of bibliographic information germane to the work of the rare book and special collections librarian. Topics include cannons of bibliographical description; study of watermarks; book collecting and the antiquarian book trade; and book catalogs.

Some schools have specialized related courses such as *Seminar in Foundations of Library and Information Studies: Codicology* which is being offered at the University of Texas at Austin. Description—The Archaeology of the manuscript book. Study of all elements involved in the production of medieval manuscripts. Organization of medieval manuscript production (monastic scripture, commercial workshops), medieval libraries, and the history of collections of medieval manuscripts. The transition from the techniques of the hand-produced manuscript to the printed book.

Institutions Listing Courses in This Area

Alabama, Alberta, *British Columbia, Catholic, California—Berkeley, *California—Los Angeles, *Columbia, Illinois, Indiana, Kentucky, Pittsburgh, Rutgers, Texas, Toronto.

Book Publishing

Many schools offer courses related to book publishing and in some cases publishing in the periodical and children's-literature fields. Employment opportunities in this field are expected to grow slowly during the next decade.

Sample Course Content

A survey of modern publishing practice with respect to the consideration and editing of the manuscript, the production of the printed book, its promotion, and its distribution. The economic, social, and literary factors that influence the writing, publishing, and reception of books and periodicals are examined.

Institutions Listing Courses in This Area

Alabama, Albany (SUNY), Alberta, Atlanta, British Columbia, *California—Berkeley, California—Los Angeles, *Chicago, Florida State, Hawaii, *Illinois, Kentucky, Louisiana State, Michigan, North Carolina, Oklahoma, Pittsburgh, Pratt, Rosary, St. John's, Simmons, South Carolina, Southern Mississippi, Texas, Texas Woman's, Toronto, Washington, Western Ontario.

Bookselling

Only one institution offers courses on bookselling although most offer related ones. For example, those on rare books and analytical bibliography are related to the antiquarian book trade, which has steadily expanded over the past decade and is expected to grow in the future.

Sample Course Content

Study of the organization and utilization of the antiquarian book trade. Includes administrative principles, techniques, and problems in antiquarian out-of-print materials; the organization and economics of the antiquarian book trade; valuation and prices.

Institution Offering Course in These Area

University of Texas at Austin.

Since 1977 the University of Denver in conjunction with the *A B Bookman's Weekly* has offered an Antiquarian Book Market Workshop-Seminar which offers courses to meet the current needs of veteran and new booksellers as well as bibliophiles, book collectors and librarians.

Enumerative or Systematic Bibliography

This area of bibliographic activity is associated most closely with librarianship. Although employment is expected to grow over the next decade, the field is likely to remain rather competitive. The best prospects for jobs are in school and public libraries away from large East and West Coast cities.

Sample Course Content

Primary bibliographies as the basic record of publication. General (national and international) bibliographies—and related tools serving as supplements or substitutes—are considered from the point of view of scope, arrangement, descriptive techniques, and historical development. Except for general aspects of theory or technique, the derivative secondary bibliographies drawn up for special subjects are excluded. Consideration is given to the principal substitutes for general bibliographies and to differing national solutions for common bibliographical problems.

Institutions Listing Courses in This Area

Albany (SUNY), Arizona, Chicago, British Columbia, Clarion, Columbia, Dalhousie, Florida State, Illinois, Indiana, Iowa, Kent State, Long Island, Missouri, North Carolina, North Carolina Central, North Carolina—Greensboro, Oklahoma, Pratt, Rosary, Rutgers, San Jose State, Simmons, South Carolina, Tennessee, Washington, Wisconsin—Madison, Wisconsin—Milwaukee.

Indexing and Abstracting

One of the appealing aspects of indexing and abstracting is that both full-time and part-time employment opportunities are available. Indexers are employed by publishers, abstracting and indexing services, special libraries, research organizations, and information-analysis centers. Indexers and abstractors may also be self-employed as freelance entrepreneurs.

Sample Course Content

In-depth survey of procedures used to abstract and index library materials. Includes vocabulary-control techniques, abstracting methods useful for specialized collections. State-of-the-art review of manual and computer-based abstracting and indexing services.

Institutions Listing Courses in This Area

Arizona, British Columbia, Buffalo (SUNY), *California—Los Angeles, Catholic, Chicago, Columbia, Dalhousie, Drexel, Emporia, Florida State, Hawaii, Louisiana State, McGill, Missouri, Montreal, North Carolina, North Carolina—Greensboro, Northern Illinois, North Texas State, Pratt, Queens (CUNY), Rosary, Rutgers, St. John's, Simmons, Syracuse, Texas, Texas Woman's, *Western Ontario, Wisconsin—Madison, Wisconsin—Milwaukee.

Printing Trades

Employment in the printing trades is expected to increase more slowly than the average for all occupations through the mid-1990s. Most job openings will arise as experienced workers retire, die, or change occupations. There are also those with graduate library degrees who establish their own shops. A fair number of courses related to the printing trades are taught in accredited institutions.

Sample Course Contents

Introduction to printing with movable type. This course is designed to give students some experience in designing and printing books and broadsides. Examination of paper, typefaces, composition work, and simple bookbinding are included.

Institutions Offering Courses in This Area

*Alabama, Albany (SUNY), Arizona, Brigham Young, *California—Berkeley, California—Los Angeles, Catholic, Clarion State, *Columbia, Dalhousie, Drexel, Emporia State, Florida State, Illinois, Indiana, Louisiana State, Long Island, Kentucky, McGill, Maryland, Michigan, Missouri, North Carolina, Northern Illinois, Pittsburgh, Pratt, Rutgers, *Queens (CUNY), St. John's, San Jose State, *South Carolina, South

Florida, Southern Connecticut, Southern Mississippi, Tennessee, Texas, Toronto, Wisconsin—Madison.

Rare Books and/or Special Collections

Other than in libraries that maintain rare-book or special collections there are career opportunities for persons with training in this area in the antiquarian or out-of-print bookselling field. Training in analytical bibliography is helpful for one desiring to enter this field.

Sample Course Content

Development, administration, and use of rare-book and special collections. Includes historical background, survey of resources of rare-book and special collections, acquisition and processing, housing and equipment, organization, preservation and restoration, and user access.

Institutions Offering Courses in This Area

McGill University; University of British Columbia; *University of Toronto; Catholic University of America; *University of Chicago; University of Missouri, Columbia; *Columbia University; State University of New York, Albany; Syracuse University; University of North Carolina; University of Oklahoma; Drexel University; University of Pittsburgh; University of Tennessee, Knoxville; North Texas State University; Texas Woman's University; University of Texas at Austin; University of Southern Mississippi; University of Maryland; University of Wisconsin, Madison; Kent State University; and University of Alabama.

For a number of years the School of Library Service at Columbia University has offered a Rare Book School during the summer. Various five-day non-credit courses on topics concerning rare and special collections are offered by specialists.

Selected Related Writings

The literature on training for bibliographic related careers tends to become dated quickly. Therefore always look for the most current available information. One good source is the *Occupational Outlook Handbook* which is published annually by the Bureau of Labor Statistics of the U.S.

Department of Labor. This handy compendium provides a survey of career fields including librarianship and related fields. It covers the nature of these fields, the qualifications and training required and projects future trends and needs. If a job or position description is needed, consult the *Dictionary of Occupational Titles*. 4th ed. (Washington, D.C.: U.S. Employment Service, U.S. Department of Labor, 1977).

LIBRARIANSHIP

Anderson, Lynn. *Exploring Careers in Librarianship*. New York: Rosen Publishing Group, 1985.

Dewey, Barbara J. *Library Jobs: How to Fill Them, How to Find Them*. Phoenix, AZ: Oryx Press, 1987.

Garoogian, Rhoda and Andran. *Careers in Other Fields for Librarians: Successful Strategies for Finding the Job*. Chicago: American Library Association, 1985.

Needham, Chris. "If Bibliography Is Out, What Is In?" In: *Bibliography and Reading: A Festschrift in Honor of Ronald Staveley*. Edited by Ia McIlwaine, John McIlwaine, and Peter G. New. Metuchen, NJ: Scarecrow Press, 1983. See pp. 106–117.

The New Information Professionals. Proceedings of the Singapore-Malaysia Congress of Librarian and Information Scientists: Singapore, 4–6 September 1986. Edited by Aijta Thuraisingham. Aldershot, Eng.: Gower, 1987.

Subramanyam, K. "Information Technology and Library Education," *Encyclopedia of Library and Information Science*, 41, Suppl. 6 (1986), pp. 161–193.

BOOKSELLING

Bohling, Curt. "Librarian to Bookseller: Reflections on Two Careers," *AB Bookman's Weekly*, 79 (June 22, 1987), pp. 2767–2772.

Gilbert, Dale L. *Complete Guide to Starting a Used Bookstore: Old Books into Gold*. Chicago: Chicago Review Press, 1986.

Manual on Bookselling: How to Open and Run Your Own Bookstore. 3rd ed. Edited for the American Booksellers Association by Robert D. Hale, Allan Marshall, and Jerry N. Showalter. New York: Harmony Books, 1980.

Smith, F. Seymour. *Bibliography in the Bookshop*. 2nd ed., rev. London: Andre Deutsch, 1972.

INDEXING

Borko, Harold and Charles L. Bernier. *Indexing Concepts and Methods*. New York: Academic Press, 1978. See Chapter 15, pp. 213–220.

Cleveland, Donald B. and Ana D. *Introduction to Indexing and Abstracting*. Littleton, CO: Libraries Unlimited, 1983. See pp. 173–174.

Neufeld, M. Lynne. *Abstracting and Indexing Career Guide*. Philadelphia: National Federation of Abstractors and Information Services, 1983.

Notes

1. K. Subramanyam, "Information Technology and Library Education," In: *Encyclopedia of Library and Information Science*. (New York: Dekker, 1986), Vol. 41, Suppl. 6, pp. 161–162.

2. Ibid., p. 162.
3. Ibid.
4. *Dictionary of Occupational Titles*. 4th ed. (Washington, DC: U.S. Employment Service, U.S. Department of Labor, 1977), p. 73.
5. Chris Needham, "If Bibliography is Out, What Is In?" In: *Bibliography and Reading: A Festschrift in Honour of Ronald Staveley*. Edited by Ia McIlwaine, John McIlwaine and Peter G. New. (Metuchen, NJ: Scarecrow Press, 1983), p. 106.

Chapter Ten

BIBLIOGRAPHY AND THE FUTURE

Introduction

When considering future prospects for both branches of bibliography, one cannot help but be impressed with the technological advances of the past thirty years. More than ever before technology is changing our way of doing many things and the study of bibliography is no exception. We have come a long way from the arduous and tedious labor of manual gathering and compiling to the optical disk systems that print out bibliographic citations or full-text articles right before our eyes. In proceeding toward the 1990s and a new century, technological developments will continue to improve information transfer.

Trends in Enumerative Bibliography

Throughout history the work of bibliographers consisted predominantly of arranging thousands of entries many times in different sequences manually. Obviously this method of compilation was extremely time-consuming and vulnerable to inaccuracies. The application of computer technology to this kind of activity opens up new and wide-ranging possibilities with respect to coverage, arrangement, speed, consistency, accuracy, and most importantly, accessibility. With the proliferation of extensive online and optical disk databases, it now becomes possible to scan and manipulate unit records that allow one to compile a bibliography that, in terms of its scope, can accommodate a required combination of characteristics and also provide various access points.

The earliest application of computers to information storage and retrieval occurred in the 1950s, but it was not until the early 1960s that they came into their own and were used by librarians, publishers, booksellers, scholars and many others. It was during this period that a number of major bibliographic systems were developed in the United States. The most notable of these were the Defense Documentation Center (then known as the Armed Services Technical Information Agency), the National Aeronautics and Space Administration, and the National Library of Medicine. The largest one was that developed by the National Library of Medicine—the Medical Literature Analysis and Retrieval System (MEDLARS)—which was implemented in 1964.[1]

Because so much of what librarians do is rooted in bibliographic practices which can, in turn, be facilitated by computer applications, we find that, more and more, computers are playing an increasing role in library operations. From cataloging, reference work, management and other operations, library automation is commonplace today. Sophisticated circulation systems now control what we check out from libraries and provide a wealth of data on library operations, which through analysis, improve library services. Large database networks such as OCLC and RLIN provide catalogers with important bibliographic information for cataloging collections and a large measure of elusive bibliographic control. These large databases also facilitate access to fugitive materials for scholars through interlibrary loan. Furthermore online catalogs are becoming more prevalent, especially in large academic libraries. These can be accessed by home personal computers equipped with modems.

Reference librarians are also using computer-oriented processes to assist patrons in finding needed information. Online bibliographic searching has already been covered in detail in Chapter Eight. New optical disk systems are rapidly taking the place of printed indexes. Also, individual databases such as ERIC. PsycLit, and COMPENDEX (the Engineering Index) are now available on CD-ROM. There are in addition other new and revolutionary data systems now being developed that will enhance reference service over the next decade and beyond.

With regard to the bookselling industry, in both antiquarian and trade sectors, automation is being widely utilized in a number of bibliographically-related areas. Computers are becoming essential in lessening the burdens of detailed work. They can keep accurate records, produce reports and catalogs. More specifically, computers in the bookselling industry are being used for: 1) cataloging books and printing lists and quotes allowing the bookseller to type a book record once and edit it when the copy is sold and get another with a slightly different description; 2) keep mailing and customer lists and printing mailing lists for one or more groups of customers; 3) allowing the bookseller to search for books in a database by author, title, or subjects; 4) keeping want lists and running a search service keeping track of sales, profit, losses, and other business-type information.[2] To assist booksellers important trade bibliographies such as *Books in Print* are also available on CD-ROM. Many services offered by booksellers to libraries in particular as well as to the general public are developing rapidly as an offshoot of the direct application of the new technology and show great promise for the future.

Other bibliographically-related professions such as the printing trades, indexing and abstracting services, and information brokerage firms are utilizing computerized systems in a big way. New and improved software packages have made these areas into highly automated ventures depending on computer-literate professionals. The application of bibliographically-oriented programs in these fields is well established.

Trends in Analytical Bibliography

Earlier we indicated that analytical or critical bibliographical scholarship involves the critical analysis of the text and its presentation. Generally analytical bibliographers inspect the physical form of a book (mainly codices, but also pamphlets, unbound tracts, broadsides, and placards) and all of its relations which purport to transmit the same text, in order to ascertain exact identification, confirm attributions, and determine changes that occurred as an author communicated with an audience. In other words, analytical bibliography is first and foremost concerned with the text in various stages of transmission.[3]

In the past this process was done basically with manual and visual comparison. Over the past few years new methodologies and techniques have been developed to aid the analytical bibliographer in the examination of text and in editing. The most important innovation is the Hinman collator, the first application of optics to textual studies. This device is used in over twenty research libraries, as well as several pharmaceutical firms and in the Central Intelligence Agency. Text comparison was made easier by the Lindstrand Comparator, and the possibility of improving the tedium of microfilm work lies in the Vinton Collating Machine. Recently I. N. Rothman has patented his Houston Editing Desk and Editing Frame for work with flat copy. Gordon Lindstrand speculates that the future of mechanical collation of texts will depend on how well computerized scanners will be capable of multi-edition collation.[4]

Lawrence McCrank insists that computer-assisted production of new editions is well developed in literary and historical editing, as well as in the design of enumerative bibliographies. Recent advances in text processing and availability of inexpensive package programs are slowly revolutionizing the world of bibliographical scholarship and text editing. The study of bibliographic items in minute detail by using computers has led to analyses that were unthinkable a few years ago. Scientific analysis of physical properties of graphic materials now makes it possible to identify their origins and history. Add to this the widespread use of the technical advances in reprography that aid in the preservation of materials and you have great promise for the advancement of bibliographical scholarship in future years.[5]

Toward a Paperless Society

Over the past several decades we have witnessed an information explosion unparalleled in the history of humankind. Although it had its origins in antiquity, the invention and development of the printing press added immensely to the movement up to the middle of the twentieth century. Much of recorded information to that point was contained on paper and disseminated in various forms, especially the book. Alternatives to traditional publishing have been sought more actively due to the steady and protracted increases in publishing costs.

With the advent of the computer we have entered, with ever-increasing speed, into what is termed the "information age." E. B. Parker[6] indicates that we are on the brink of a new social revolution—the information revolution—which will be just as important as the industrial revolution was to printing. This implies a transition from an industrial to an information society, in which information processing will dominate industrial production as a labor activity. He further predicts that future economic gains will be made through the information rather than the production sector and that governments in the long run have more to gain from investment in improved information processing than from further investment in industrial productivity.

The leading scholar in the conceptualization of the paperless society is Frederick Wilfrid Lancaster. His ideas and investigations of computer applications in the field of information retrieval are well documented in the literature. Lancaster cites the advances of electronics in the past thirty years in providing access to indexes and abstracts not only in urban areas but in small communities by means of personal computers with modems.

Another prospect for the paperless society is the availability of book and periodical material online instead of in printed form. For example, a library, rather than subscribing to a periodical, can pay to have access to the equivalent full-text database as the need arises. Lancaster points out that the text of some newspapers is now accessible online as is the text of some directories and the like. The full text of statutes and other legal materials has been accessible online for many years, and it appears only a matter of time before the full texts of scholarly journals, patents, reports, and many more reference books are available in this format. At the same time, other forms of electronic publications are emerging on the scene, including magazines on tape cassettes for use with home computers and bilingual dictionaries somewhat resembling pocket calculators.[7]

The effect of computers and telecommunications on libraries has been felt in two ways. In the first case, computers have been utilized for internal record keeping in such areas as acquisitions, receipt of serials, circulation systems, and cataloging. As a result we find a reduction in paper records, including the disappearance of the card catalog and the formation of networks to share and exchange records. The second effect is the use of computers and telecommunications to allow libraries to access outside databases. This permits libraries to increase greatly their capabilities for literature searching and question answering. Lancaster indicates that in a wide number of instances the librarian's role could be dramatically affected in situations where all of the information needs for a particular institution could be obtained online. Thus librarians could operate merely from an office with only a terminal, or they could freelance from the home or form themselves into group practices as doctors and attorneys do. These trends, of course, are already becoming well established within the profession.[8]

The views of those who write about the paperless society have not gone without criticism. Some people look at what is happening with a sense of marvel mingled with horrid fascination at the possible demise of libraries as we know them.[9] There are some rather large and sophisticated electronic networks that simply have not done the job for which they were designed. Billions of "bits" in a computer, says Edmund G. Hamann, retrievable by programs of marvelous intricacy, are no match for the serendipitous faculty of the human brain—ask any researcher for examples. Lancaster may be right, but only up to a point. So long as the process of people helping people gets the job done, librarians will be around.[10] And after all is said and done, what happens if someone pulls the plug? Another critic indicates that librarians are skeptical of yet another "scientific solution" to all of their problems and that the use of economic jargon is a little suspect in the light of current realities. This critic also points out that Lancaster's views apply mainly to scientific literature.[11]

Conclusion

It is evident that the application of computers to bibliographic work in some areas has been highly successful. Bibliographic data recorded on various types of storage devices can be constantly revised and updated and accessed in a number of ways. In effect the work can be accomplished promptly, accurately, and consistently. Additionally, it appears that there are many possibilities for cooperative ventures.

Through the use of online bibliographic services and optical storage devices we now have access to an ever-increasing and vast body of information that was not available just a few short years ago. Also, by the use of networks, libraries can within a short period of time locate and obtain materials from other libraries many miles away.

Lest one think that computers are the only thing in bibliographic work, please be reminded that, despite the great advantages of the computer, conventional published bibliographies will retain their own importance within the total sphere of bibliographic organization. Conventional bibliographic production, coupled with the new technology, offers exciting prospects for the future of the disciplines it supports.

Selected Related Writings

Cleveland, Donald B., and Ana D. *Introduction to Indexing and Abstracting*. Littleton, CO: Libraries Unlimited, Inc., 1983.

Guskin, Alan E., Carla J. Stoffle and Barbara E. Baruth. "Library Future Shock: The Microcomputer Revolution and the New Role of the Library," *College & Research Libraries*, 45 (May 1984), pp. 177–183.

Herron, Nancy L. "The Paperless Society," *Encyclopedia of Library and Information Science*, 41, Suppl., 6 (1986), pp. 227–289.

Lancaster, F. W. "The Future of the Librarian Lies Outside the Library, *Catholic Library World*, 51 (April 1980), pp. 388–391.

Lancaster, F. W. "The Paperless Society Revisited," *American Libraries*, 16 (September 1985), pp. 553–555.

Lodder, N. Margaret. "The Application of Computers to Systematic Bibliography." In: *Systematic Bibliography*. By Anthony M. L. Robinson, 4th ed. New York: Saur, 1979. See pp. 83–95.

McCrank, Lawrence J. "Analytical and Historical Bibliography: A State of the Art Review." In: *Annual Report of the American Rare, Antiquarian and Out-of-Print Book Trade, 1978/1979*. Edited by Denis Carbonneau. New York: BCAR Publications, 1979. See pp. 175–185.

Wilkinson, John. "Beyond the Computer," *Canadian Library Journal*, 41 (October 1984), pp. 243–247.

Notes

1. Frederick Wilfrid Lancaster, *The Dissemination of Scientific and Technical Information: Toward a Paperless System*. (Urbana, IL: Graduate School of Library Science, University of Illinois, 1977), p. 4.

2. Richard M. Weatherford, "Computers in the Antiquarian Book Trade," *AB Bookman's Weekly*, 77 (January 6, 1986), p. 14.

3. Lawrence J. McCrank, Analytical and Historical Bibliography: A State of the Art Review." In: *Annual Report of the American Rare, Antiquarian and Out-of-Print Book Trade, 1978; 1979*. Edited by Denis Carbonneau. (New York: BCAR Publications, 1979), p. 176.

4. Ibid, p. 180.

5. Ibid, p. 181.

6. E. B. Parker, "Background Report." In: *Proceedings of the OECD Conference on Computer Telecommunications Policy*, February 4–6, 1975. (Paris: OECD, 1976), pp. 87–129. As cited in Frederick W. Lancaster, "The Future of the Librarian Lies Outside the Library," *Catholic Library World*, 51 (April 1980), p. 388.

7. See Lancaster, p. 389.

8. Ibid., p. 390. Lancaster reports progress toward the paperless society in his article, "The Paperless Society Revisited," *American Libraries*, 16 (September 1985), pp. 553–555.

9. Edmund G. Hamann, "Whither Libraries?" *College & Research Libraries*, 40 (May 1979), p. 267.

10. Ibid.

11. Gabriel Austin, "To the Editor," *College & Research Libraries*, 40 (May 1979), pp. 267–268.

Chapter Eleven

REFERENCE SOURCES IN BIBLIOGRAPHY

Introduction

Reference materials related to the study of bibliography fall into two broad classifications: 1) *basic reference works* such as a general encyclopedia that provides bibliographical and factual information on a variety of subjects within the field; and 2) *specific reference works* such as a dictionary that includes definitions for a specific area within the field. Both areas are examined below with representative examples from each area accompanied by a discussion of their relevance to the study of bibliography.[1]

Abstracting Services

Abstracting services publish summaries of original articles, books, and so on, and are more explicit guides to bibliographic literature than indexes. Since the gist of an article or book is given along with a complete reference, one may quickly gather a bibliography on a particular subject and eliminate unsuitable material without having to refer to the original publications.

A good abstracting service often provides the author's address or research location in the event that personal communication is desired. It gives the name of the journal that published the article or the title of the book, including the number of pages should photocopying be needed. If the article or book abstracted is of an experimental nature, information is supplied on the methods of the investigation, the data it uncovered, the final results, and the conclusions it reached. The quality of abstracts varies greatly, and the user must appraise each one carefully.[2] There are two abstracting services related to bibliography that are excellent sources of information.

Information Science Abstracts. New York: Plenum Publishing Corp., etc., 1966— v.1— Monthly.

Provides abstracts of journal literature, books, and reports focusing on the information science aspect of the library and information science fields. Entries are arranged in a classified scheme with author and subject indexes in each issue that are cumulated annually. Coverage of bibliographic literature is difficult to evaluate, but examination of random volumes reveals a reasonable number of related entries on various aspects of the field. Title varies: 1966–67, *Documentation Abstracts;* 1968 *Documentation Abstracts and Information Science Abstracts*. Also available online since 1983 as File 202 on the DIALOG system covering records back to 1966.

Library and Information Science Abstracts. London: Library Association, 1969— v.1— Monthly.

Supersedes *Library Science Abstracts*, 1950–1968. Entries are provided within a classified arrangement. All abstracts are in the English language. The monthly author and subject indexes are cumulated annually. Coverage is international in scope and second only to *Library Literature* in importance to bibliographers. Types of materials scanned for abstracting includes a large number of journals, as well as books, theses, conferences and other reports. LISA is also available as File 61 on DIALOG and Derwent-SDC ORBIT covering records back to 1969.

Bibliographies

Bibliography serves to broaden the contact between users of information and the masses of information available to them. To date no comprehensive bibliography on the study of bibliography has been compiled. The works cited below provide some access to several aspects of the field.[3]

Annual Bibliography of the History of the Printed Book and Libraries. The

Hague: Nijhoff, 1973— . Coverage from 1970— v.1— .
Attempts to record "all books and articles of scholarly value which relate to the history of the printed book, to the history of the arts, crafts, techniques, and equipment, and of the economic, social, and cultural environment involved in its production, distribution, conservation, and description."—*Pref*. Each volume contains over 2,000 entries in a classified arrangement. Includes relevant doctoral dissertations and book reviews but excludes writings on modern technical processes. Major access is provided by a name index only. There is a large gap between publication date and date of coverage (e.g., v. 9 covering 1978 was published in 1982). There are no annotations.

Besterman, Theodore. *Bibliography, Library Science, and Reference Books: A Bibliography of Bibliographies*. Totowa, NJ: Rowman and Littlefield, 1971. 271p.
Extracted from Besterman's monumental *World Bibliography of Bibliographies*, this work includes many relevant items related to the study of bibliography. Some entries have brief comments.

Breslauer, Bernard H. *The Uses of Bookbinding Literature*. New York: Book Arts Press, School of Library Service, Columbia University, 1986. 44p.
From the perspective of an experienced antiquarian bookseller who has had a long relationship with historic book bindings, this guide discusses the best literature of bookbinding covering both English and foreign titles. The author's critical evaluations are accompanied by an alphabetical section entitled "Lists of Books and Articles Mentioned in the Text," compiled by Martin Antonetti. This work will be particularly valuable for historians of the book, especially those whose research leads them into the study of early international fields of bookbindings.

Winckler, Paul A. *History of Books and Printing: A Guide to Information Sources*. Detroit, MI: Gale, 1979. 209p.
Since the study of bibliography has been enormously affected by the development of printing and books a bibliography of this kind is valuable. Includes 776 entries (mostly annotated) under nine broad

sections. Most sections have more specific subdivisions. Separate author, title, and subject indexes are provided.

Dictionaries

The correct use of words is the basis of communication in any field of knowledge. Bibliography is no exception, and the need for a thorough knowledge of terminology is important. A good dictionary serves as a guide to the correct use of words within a certain time frame. A dictionary published in 1987 differs considerably from one compiled ten, twenty, or a hundred years ago. Since you will undoubtedly encounter some new terminology when you study the field of bibliography, the dictionaries listed below should be of assistance to you.[4]

The ALA Glossary of Library and Information Science. Heartsill Young, ed. Chicago: American Library Association, 1983. 245p.
Compiled with the assistance of area specialists. Contributes "toward the development of standard terminology, or a set of terms, which will enable librarians and other information scientists better to communicate with each other and with specialists in related fields" such as bibliography. Includes many terms related to the study of bibliography.

The Bookman's Glossary. 6th ed., rev. and enl. Edited by Jean Peters. New York: Bowker, 1983. 223p.
Defines some 1,800 terms "used in book publishing, book manufacturing, bookselling, the antiquarian trade, and librarianship."—*Pref*. Many of these terms relate to the study of bibliography. Also included are brief biographical sketches of persons of note in the fields of bibliography, the graphic arts, and book publishing.

Feather, John. *A Dictionary of Book History*. New York: Oxford University Press, 1986. 278p.
Here, in a single alphabetical sequence, is provided not only a glossary of the technical terms of printing and bibliography, but also details of private presses, illustrators, collectors and libraries, the history of the book trade and of book production. It gives

information which in combination cannot be found in any other single volume. This, coupled with up-to-date notes for further reading, is its greatest strength. There, are of course, exclusions and some errors that are unavoidable in a work of this nature.

Glaister, Geoffrey Ashall. *Glaister's Glossary of the Book: Terms Used in Papermaking, Printing, Bookbinding, and Publishing with notes on Illuminated Manuscripts and Private Presses*. 2nd ed. Completely revised. Berkeley, CA: University of California Press, 1979. 551p.
Serving primarily as an encyclopedic dictionary, this work covers 2,000 years of book-production history, explaining the terms used in papermaking, printing, bookbinding, and the book trade, etc. Also included are biographical entries for prominent craftspeople, notes on schools of illumination, famous manuscripts, private presses, printing societies, literary prizes, and well-known book collectors. Many terms defined are related to the study of bibliography.

Harrod, Leonard Montague. *Harrod's Librarian's Glossary of Terms Used in Librarianship, Documentation and the Book Crafts, and Reference Books*. 6th ed., compiled by Ray Prytherch. Brookfield, VT: Gower, 1987. 855p.
Provides definitions of "standard librarianship terms, printing and publishing terms, archival terms and terms in related fields" such as bibliography. One of the most useful sources for definitions in the field. Although largely oriented toward British usage, this work gives much attention to American practice and terminology.

Moth, Axel Fredrik Carl Mathias. *Technical Terms Used in Bibliographies and by the Book and Printing Trade*. Boston: Longwood, 1977, ©1917. 263p.
Polyglot in nature this dictionary includes many terms related to bibliography in English, Danish, Dutch, French, German, Italian, Latin, Spanish, and Swedish.

Roberts, Matt T., and Don Etherington. *Bookbinding and the Conservation of Books: A Dictionary of Descriptive Terminology*. Washington, DC: Library of Congress, 1982. 296p.
The terms contained in this compilation cover all aspects of the book as a physical entity including papermaking, printing, binding,

and conservation. Non-specialists will find the entries well written and concise, but with enough detail to make them useful to the specialist. For some definitions there are helpful line drawings, and there are extensive cross references to guide the user to appropriate entries. This work will be useful to librarians, conservators, and students of bibliography.

Vitale, Philip H. *Bibliography, Historical and Bibliothecal; A Handbook of Terms and Names*. Chicago: Loyola University Press, 1971. 251p.
Includes definitions and brief biographical sketches of terms significantly connected to the history of writing, publishing, bibliography and other related fields. Entries are arranged under two broad areas. Part one is a glossary of terms and Part Two contains the biographical sketches.

Directories

When one is looking for names, addresses, phone numbers, or other factual information on individuals or organizations related to bibliography, directories then become a most useful source. Naturally one should check the source in hand for currency otherwise the information provided will most likely be out-of-date; directories, in general, tend to become outdated quickly. For directory type information in the field of bibliography there is no single source. There are, however, a number of specialized directories, issued annually or kept reasonably current, that one will find useful. Some of these are published by bibliographical societies and others by commercial presses covering the book trade, book collecting, librarians, etc. Below are some representative examples.[5]

American Book Trade Directory. New York: Bowker, 1915—
Biennial (formerly triennial).
Listings cover retailers, wholesalers, antiquarian booksellers etc., both in the United States and Canada. Well indexed.

American Library Association. *ALA Handbook of Organization and Membership Directory*. Chicago: American Library Association, 1980/81— . Annual.

Individual and institutional members are listed with addresses. The handbook section is also published separately.

Bibliographical Society, London. *List of Members—Bibliographical Society*. London: The Society, n.d.
Lists names and addresses. Frequency not indicated, but probably it is issued to members annually.

Bibliographical Society of America. *List of Members*. New York: The Society, 1904— .
Members are listed alphabetically by surname along with addresses. Institutional members are listed separately at the end of the main alphabet. Issued annually as a supplement to the *Papers of the Bibliographical Society of America*.

Directory of Specialized American Bookdealers 1984–1985. Prepared by the Staff of the *American Book Collector*. New York: Moretus Press, 1984. 344p.
Geographically arranged by state or Canadian province, this compilation lists each store, its hours, and brief comments about its special interests or offerings. Provided is an index of dealer specialties unfortunately without cross-references.

International Directory of Book Collectors 1985–87: A Directory of Book Collectors in Britain, Ireland, America, Canada and the Rest of the World. 4th ed. Roger Sheppard and Judith Sheppard, comps. Beckenham, Eng.: Trigon Press; distr. New York: Bowker, 1985. 340p.
Within the regions of the United Kingdom and Ireland, America and Canada, and the rest of the world, collectors are listed alphabetically, with each entry providing the collector's name, address, subjects or authors collected, and book club or book society membership (if any). A subject index and an author and illustrator index provide access to the collectors and their specialty interests. Includes many known bibliographers.

Encyclopedias

An encyclopedia is a work of one or more volumes with information on all branches of knowledge, topically arranged in alphabetical order.

There are general encyclopedias as well as those on a subject or group of related subjects. Editors and contributors of a good encyclopedia will be specialists in their respective fields. The knowledge will be evident in their choice of subject and in the bibliography that follows each article. No encyclopedic work exists for the subject of bibliography alone, but those cited below provide much useful information related to the study of bibliography.[6]

ALA World Encyclopedia of Library and Information Services. 2nd ed. Chicago: American Library Association, 1986. 895p.
Although one would expect the subject of bibliography to be covered extensively in a work of this type, there is surprisingly little, and most of that is included in articles on other subjects. There are, however, some articles on such noted bibliographers as Conrad Gesner, Charles Evans, Alfred William Pollard, Ralph R. Shaw, and others which makes this volume useful.

Encyclopedia of Library and Information Science. Allen Kent and Harold Lancour, eds. New York: Dekker, 1968— v.1— .
Rather lengthy signed articles by specialists make this set extremely valuable. Within each volume the articles are organized in a dictionary arrangement usually with extensive bibliographies appended to them. Many of these articles cover specific aspects of bibliography in considerable detail. Also includes some biographical sketches of deceased bibliographers. Now issued with updating supplements.

Landau, Thomas, ed. *Encyclopedia of Librarianship*. 3rd ed., rev. London: Bowes and Bowes; New York: Hafner, 1966. 484p.
Articles, presented alphabetically, range from a few words to signed pieces covering several pages. Slanted toward British usage; some articles have bibliographies appended to them.

Guides to the Literature

Broadly defined this term refers to any work that assists someone in their use of other books, periodicals, etc. In a narrower sense it can refer to the type of source designed to chart or map one's way through the literature of a reasonably extensive area of knowledge and in the process help the user to evaluate, organize, and introduce the literature. This distinguishes it from either a bibliographical list or an introductory treatise. By nature it is much more versatile, more informative than the one, and, unlike the other it introduces the literature, not the content or the subject. There is no guide to the literature of bibliography per se, except for this guide and possibly D. W. Krummel's work. The guides to reference books discussed below relate to the field of bibliography because they list numerous types of bibliographical instruments. There are many materials related to bibliography, however, that they do not cover.[7]

Guide to Reference Books. 10th ed. By Eugene Sheehey and others. Chicago: American Library Association, 1986. 1560p.

Over the years under different editors this work has been the premier guide with international coverage of reference materials. The general arrangement is by subject chapters with many subdivisions. Annotations are mostly descriptive and there is excellent index access.

Walford's Guide to Reference Material. 4th ed., edited by Albert John Walford. London: Library Association, 1980— v.1— (In progress).

Each volume covers a broad subject such as Science and Technology along with more specific subject chapters with many subdivisions. Emphasis is on English-language publications. Each volume has its own index of authors, titles, and subjects. To be issued in three main volumes.

Indexes

An index is a list arranged in some useful order. We have long since learned that information is lost without indexing. Ancient book lists have been discovered on stone tablets from long before the Christian era. Monasteries of the Middle Ages maintained elaborate book lists and information inventories. As the volume and complexity of information has increased, we have been compelled to devise progressively better and more sophisticated machine-readable systems. The published indexes cited below are perhaps most closely related to the study of bibliography.[8]

Bibliographic Index; A Cumulative Bibliography of Bibliographies. New York: H. W. Wilson, 1937— v.1— .
Issued twice a year with annual cumulations this index includes bibliographies found in the periodicals scanned for the various Wilson indexes, as well as significant books and pamphlets. In order to be included a bibliography must contain at least 50 entries. Subjects and authors are organized in a single alphabetical sequence.

Index to Reviews of Bibliographical Publications: An International Annual. Troy, NY: The Whitston Publishing Co., etc., 1976— v.1— .
Designed especially for graduate students, professional librarians, and teaching faculty in the fields of English and American literary bibliography, this publication provides an extensive listing of reviews of significant bibliographical publications in English, French, and German language journals.

Library Literature. New York: H. W. Wilson, 1921/32— v.1— .
For students of librarianship in general and bibliography in particular, this is perhaps the most extensive listing of materials related to the study of bibliography. Arrangement of entries is alphabetical by author and subject. Materials scanned for inclusion are books, pamphlets, theses, etc., as well as professional journals.

Yearbooks

A yearbook is usually an annual publication that appears under the same editorship and contains the information that is current in a particular field of knowledge. Several of the works cited below, while not yearbooks in a strict sense, do fulfill the role of presenting new research on subjects related to the study and practice of bibliography.[9]

The ALA Yearbook of Library and Information Services. Chicago: American Library Association, 1976— v.1— Annual.
Each volume includes an article on "Bibliographies and Indexes." Reviewed here are a number of published bibliographies, the pro-

gress toward bibliographic control, and the status of bibliographic services. From time to time articles relating to some aspect of bibliography are included, especially the subject of national bibliographies.

Proof: The Yearbook of American And Textual Studies. Edited by Joseph Katz. Columbia, SC, etc.: Faust, etc., 1971–1977. v.1–5.
No longer published. During its short life the publisher and place of publication has varied. The extant volumes contain a number of excellent articles on various aspects of textual criticism, plus some bibliographical surveys.

Virginia. University. Bibliographical Society. *Studies in Bibliography; Papers*. Charlottesville, VA: The Society, 1948/49— v.1— .
For the student interested in the theory and history of bibliography this well-known series is indispensable. For many years it has been edited by Fredson Bowers, possibly the most outstanding analytical bibliographer of the twentieth century. The articles are of exceptionally high quality written by experts in the field and they collectively contribute to the expansion of bibliographic research.

Selected Related Writings

Since there are no guides to the literature for the study of bibliography one must consult general sources for reference materials related to the field.

Galin, Saul. *Reference Books: How to Select and Use Them*. New York: Random House, 1969.

Katz, William A. *Introduction to Reference Work*. 5th ed. 2 vols. New York: McGraw-Hill, 1987.

Shores, Louis. *Basic Reference Sources: An Introduction to Materials and Methods*. Chicago: American Library Association, 1954.

Notes

1. For an excellent discussion of the different types of reference sources see, *Basic Reference Sources: An Introduction to Materials and Methods*. By Louis Shores. (Chicago: American Library Association, 1954), pp. 1–226.

2. Basic functions and uses of abstracting services is discussed in *Writer's Research Handbook: The Research Bible for Freelance Writers*. By Keith M. Cottam and Robert W. Pelton. (New York: Barnes & Noble, 1977), p. 25.

3. Primary types of bibliographies are covered in *Guide to Reference Books*. 10th ed. By Eugene P. Sheehey and others. (Chicago: American Library Association, 1986), p. 1.

4. An excellent explanation of dictionaries and their uses is provided by William A.

Katz in his book, *Your Library: A Reference Guide*. (New York: Holt, Rinehart and Winston, 1979), pp. 78–81.

5. As a reference tool, the functions of directories are discussed by Malcolm J. Campbell in, *Printed Reference Material*. 2nd ed. Edited by Gavin L. Higgens. (London: The Library Association, 1984), pp. 165–195.

6. For a brief explanation of encyclopedias and their uses see *Information in the Social Sciences*. 3rd ed. Revised by William H. Webb and associates. (Chicago: American Library Association, 1986), p. 15.

7. Ibid., p. 14.

8. Basic functions of periodical indexes are covered by Cottam & Pelton, pp. 20–28.

9. See Webb and associates, p. 15 for a short explanation of Yearbooks and their uses.

Chapter Twelve

PERIODICALS RELATED TO THE STUDY OF BIBLIOGRAPHY

Introduction

Today new research in most fields of knowledge is first reported in the periodical literature and only later consolidated into books or monographs. This situation is particularly true in the study of bibliography. Given the nature of the discipline, many contributions inevitably consist of brief notes or articles on individual copies of a book, providing facts that supplement a previously published bibliography or that augment the accumulated evidence about a given printing, binding, or publishing practice. With the passage of time a sizable body of information develops, and a new book, drawing the scattered material together, may be called for; but until that time those periodical pieces represent the current state of knowledge.[1] Older volumes of periodicals are never entirely obsolete, since they provide contemporary opinions and judgments of persons, events, subjects, and books, and can be used to trace the historical development of a subject.

Obviously the degree of access to the periodical literature of bibliography depends largely on the quality of the indexing and abstracting services available to the user. Up to about the middle of the twentieth century these types of services were, at best, sporadic and fragmented.[2] Currently the picture is much brighter. Access to the periodical literature has been increased greatly with the creation of cumulating indexes, such as *Library Literature*, which is a good example of the subject approach. This index can be contrasted with such standard general periodical indexes as the *Readers' Guide to Periodical Literature*, which are based on fixed groups of journals. Abstracting services are particularly useful because they summarize the article cited. Of major significance to bibliography are *Library and Information Science Abstracts* (1969—), formerly *Library Science Abstracts* (1950–1968), and *Information Science Abstracts* (1966—). Both of these abstracting services have a classified arrangement and cover periodicals containing articles related to various aspects of the study of bibliography. Add to this both the LISA and Information Science Abstracts databases available online and there is fairly reasonable coverage of the literature. There will naturally be fugitive materials not covered by indexing sources which are only known through personal contact between bibliographers and scholars.[3]

Periodicals relevant to the study of bibliography fall into the following divisions: General Periodicals, Antiquarian and Book Trade Periodicals, Bibliographical Society Journals, Book Collecting Journals, Library Journals, and Online Searching Journals. The periodicals for this list were selected on the basis of their applicability to the aspects of bibliography covered in the body of this guide. Current bibliographical information is provided for each title including the indexing or abstracting service in which it is covered (if any). The annotations are largely descriptive and attempt to provide enough information to evaluate a title's usefulness.

General Periodicals

Those periodicals cited in this section constitute the broader spectrum of the discipline. They cover both scholarly research and things of importance to bibliographers including conferences, new publications, and bibliographies of various kinds.

AEB, *Analytical & Enumerative Bibliography*. DeKalb, IL: Bibliographical Society of Northern Illinois, 1977— v.1— . Quarterly.

This journal is the official publication of the society established in 1971. It contains articles and notes on many bibliographical subjects, including both enumerative and analytical bibliography, textual criticism, manuscripts and paleography, printing history, book-trade history, libraries and/or collections, and the general state of bibliography or bibliographies. Also included are book reviews and a section listing books received. The first and third issues publish one of the series of *English Political Dialogues, 1646–1651*, critical old-spelling editions of this collection of twenty-one dialogue dramas. The EPD dramas are skits, or reviews, of a satirical and political nature that were written and perhaps performed during the English Civil War. Indexed in *Modern Language Association International Bibliography*.

American Antiquarian Society. *Proceedings*. Worcester, MA: The Society, 1812— v.1— . (Semi-Annual).

This venerable journal reports on the twice-yearly meetings of The Society and provides three or four scholarly papers dealing with the history of printing and binding in America or some phase of American literary or cultural history. Special features include signed obituaries of recently deceased members, providing valuable biographical information on those distinguished individuals, and some issues include "American Bibliographical Notes," covering recent acquisitions, additions and corrections to standard bibliographies, and other items of bibliographical importance. Indexed in: *Bibliographical Index*, *Biography Index*, *American History and Life*, *Essay and General Literature Index*, and the *Arts & Humanities Citation Index*.

Bibliography Newsletter. New York: Terry Belanger, 1973— v.1— . Frequency varies. 12 numbers comprise each volume.

Each issue usually contains two or more numbers. As the title suggests, various paragraphs consider American and English exhibitions, conferences, manuscripts and special collections, rare books, libraries, printing, computers, preservation—just about everything of interest to the bibliographer. Particularly valuable for book collectors are the current notes on "remainders" (i.e. best buys from various presses and stores). Has a cumulated annual index.

Bibliography, Documentation, Terminology. Paris: Unesco, 1960— v.1— . Bimonthly.

This publication can be classified as an alerting service for bibliographic information. Each issue consists of a forty-five to fifty-page bulletin of reports on new bibliographic activities. The newsletter serves as a good source for ordering new material, and special information is provided about available titles. Designed primarily for large academic and public libraries, special libraries, and scientific and technical information centers. This publication is available in English, French, Spanish, and Russian. Indexed in *Library Literature*.

Bulletin of Bibliography & Magazine Notes. Westwood, MA: F. W. Faxon Co., 1897— v.1— . Quarterly.
Each issue features three to four bibliographies that begin with short introductory statements about the subject and with an overview of the status of bibliographic coverage of the area. Of particular value (especially to libraries) is the column "Births, Deaths and Magazine Notes," found in each issue and listing new, changed, and discontinued titles. Has a cumulative index covering 1897–1975. Indexed in *America: History and Life; Bibliographic Index; Modern Language Abstracts, Historical Abstracts, Biography Index, and Bibliography of English Language and Literature*.

Pages. Detroit, MI: Gale, 1976— v.1— . Annual.
Well illustrated and designed for the nonprofessional bibliophile. Includes new and highly professional material. Features book-collecting fantasies—from auctions and illustrators to publishing and literary comment. Has excellent format with sepia drawings, prints, and photography on every page. [No longer published?]

Antiquarian and Book Trade Periodicals

The periodicals cited in this section are only representative of the large number that fall within this category. They do, however, provide an excellent sample of those that are particularly useful to bibliographers. Quite frequently they carry articles by specialists on such topics as typography, bookbinding, papermaking, and others related to the study of bibliography.

AB Bookman's Weekly for the Specialist Book World. Clifton, NJ: Jacob Chernofsky, 1948— v.1— . Weekly.
Designed mainly for the book trade and those who purchase books. Divided into three sections: a) introductory pages, which include articles, news notes, book reviews, obituaries, and materials on everything from auctions to letters to the editor; b) the largest

section, listing books wanted by dealers and libraries; and c) a listing of books for sale. Of particular value to the bibliographer is the first section. Indexed in *Library Literature*.

Antiquarian Book Monthly Review. Oxford, Eng.: ABMR Publications, Ltd., 1974— v.1— . Monthly.
Considered a basic journal for book dealers, librarians, and private collectors as well as bibliographers. Each issue features three or four articles, which vary from historical and bibliographical pieces to reports on book fairs, libraries, and individual authors. Includes some useful features: "Book Chat," "In Perspective," "Bibliographical Notes," "Auction," "Trade Notes," as well as news of book dealers and their catalogs. Excellently written articles, often documented and illustrated, along with timely news items of interest to bibliographers.

Bar Quarterly. Kent, Eng.: William Dawson & Sons, 1977— v.11— . Quarterly.
Actually this periodical is an extension of the annual *Book Auction Records*. Books sold at auction are listed alphabetically by author or title. Price and relatively complete bibliographical data are supplied in each citation. Every issue contains one or two articles along with listings of books sold at auction. Of particular value for the analytical bibliographer or specialist.

Bibliographical Society Journals

The organs of bibliographical societies naturally constitute the central group of journals for bibliographical study, both because they are scholarly in approach and because they are not usually limited to any one aspect of the book. Because of their nature these journals will be of limited interest to the enumerative bibliographer but of immense interest to analytical or descriptive bibliographers.

Bibliographical Society of America. Papers. New York: Bibliographical Society of America, 1904— v.1— . Quarterly.
Perhaps the most scholarly publication of its kind published in the United States. Each issue contains several articles by experts on

aspects of bibliography, both analytical and historical. Although the contributions tend to be somewhat esoteric, there are usually one or two items of interest to anyone even remotely involved with books and publishing. The book reviews are excellent, and following lengthy critical remarks there are extensive notes by the review editor. Indexed in *Humanities Index*, *Library Literature*, and *Modern Language Association International Bibliography* and abstracted in *Library and Information Science Abstracts*.

Bibliographical Society of Canada. Bulletin. Toronto, Ont.: The Society, 1973— v.1— . Semiannual.
Carries general articles and items related to bibliographical activities in Canada.

Cambridge Bibliographical Society. Transactions. London: Cambridge University Press, 1949— v.1— . Annual.
Issued in five parts and cumulated every fifth year. Contains highly specialized bibliographic research, usually in literature and history. Emphasis is on English, with detailed articles by subject experts. Indexed in *British Humanities Index*.

The Library. London: Oxford University Press, 1899— v.1— . Quarterly.
This journal is in many ways the British equivalent of the *Papers of the Bibliographical Society of America*. It consists of the transactions of the Bibliographical Society, London. The primary focus is on all aspects of the history of books, publishing, printing, libraries, and book collecting. The articles are scholarly yet written in a simple, clear style. The book reviews, while limited in number, are excellent. Generally most useful to the analytical or descriptive bibliographer. Indexed in *Library Literature* and *Modern Language Association International Bibliography* and abstracted in *Library and Information Science Abstracts*.

Book Collecting Journals

Including book collecting journals among those associated with the study of bibliography should not be surprising. They are not necessarily less scholarly than those issued by bibliographical societies, and indeed many of them are notable for their learned commentary. Consequently the dividing line between this group and the previous one is not distinct, but it makes some sense, for purposes of classification, to separate those journals associated with book collecting—by virtue of their title, their content, or their sponsoring organization—from those journals associated with bibliographical societies.

American Book Collector. Arlington Hts., IL: The American Book Collector, 1950–1976. v.1–26. Bimonthly.

For the twenty-six years of its existence this publication chronicled trends and interests of American book collectors, both in authors and types of materials collected. The nature of its articles was relaxed yet authoritative. Among the regular features were excellent book reviews, bibliographies of authors or illustrators or forms, summary reviews of auction sales, lists of dealers' catalogs recently published, and so on. Also it contained many excellent illustrations and photographs in each issue. Was incorporated into the *Book Collector's Market* for three issues: v.4, nos. 4–6, July/August 1979–November/December 1979. First issued as *The Amateur Book Collector,* September 1950 to December 1955, v.1–6, no. 4. Has the following cumulative indexes: v.1–5 (September 1950–June 1955); v.6–10 (September 1955–June 1960); v.11–15 (September 1960–June 1965); v.16–20 (September 1965–June 1970); v. 21–25 (September 1970–April 1975). A cumulative index for the entire set is in preparation. Was indexed in the *Modern Language Association International Bibliography*.

American Book Collector—New Series. New York: The Moretus Press, Inc., 1980— v.1— . Monthly.

This publication has changed title four times: a) *Bibliognost: The Book Collector's Little Magazine,* v.1, no. 1, February 1975–v.2, no. 2, May 1976; b) *Book Collector's Market,* v.2, no. 3, August 1976–v.3, no. 6, November/December 1978; c) incorporated *American Book Collector* into its title for three issues, v.4, nos. 4–6, July/August 1979–November/December 1979; d) became the *American Book Collector,* v.1, no. 1, January/February 1980. The aim of this new series is to provide news, articles, interviews, and reviews about book collecting to all book collectors. The articles are well written, and many should be of great interest to bibliographers.

Includes bibliographical checklist of leading authors in a new series. Indexed in *Modern Language Association International Bibliography, Book Review Index, ARTbibliographies Modern, Reference Sources,* and *Reference Services Review*.

The Book Collector. London: The Collector Ltd., 1952— v.1— . Quarterly.

William A. Katz in the current edition of *Magazines for Libraries* indicated that this journal is somewhat of a British cross between the *Papers of the Bibliographical Society of America* and the *American Book Collector*. It attempts to cater to both the sophisticated bibliographer and the amateur. The articles range from detailed research on various aspects of analytical bibliography to general comment on collectors and libraries. Introductory remarks by the editor are always informative. Contains excellent book reviews concerning bibliography, printing, and publishing. Indexed in *British Humanities Index, Library Literature,* and *Modern Language Association International Bibliography* and abstracted in *Library and Information Science Abstracts*.

Library Journals

The broad field of library-oriented publications—including general studies of librarianship as well as accounts of individual libraries—is immense and, since any material dealing with books may potentially be of significance to bibliographers, cannot be ignored. It is true that most of the general journals deal almost exclusively with matters of library administration, but they occasionally have articles of a historical nature, and they frequently review books of bibliographical interest.

Aldus. Houston, TX: University of Houston, 1963— v.1— . Semiannual.

Designed as a bibliographical view of holdings of the University of Houston. Has a handsome format and usually a lead article that features a recent acquisition, with detailed bibliographical data, along with illustrations, then one or two shorter pieces on various editions, collectors, authors, and research activities. Each issue contains exhibits and news of the sponsoring group. Of value to bibliographers because of the bibliographical data included on published works.

The British Library Journal. London: Oxford University Press, 1975— v.1— . Five issues per year.

Each issue includes an analysis by a well-known scholar of some item or collection of the British Library. This analysis covers such bibliographically related topics as special collections, bookbindings, and recent acquisitions. Well illustrated and designed. Indexed in *Library Literature*.

Bulletin of Research in the Humanities. New York: Readex Books, 1978— v.1— . Quarterly.

This title supersedes the *New York Public Library Bulletin, 1897–1977*. A major library publication considered to be a leader in the field of bibliography. Includes articles by renowned scholars who discuss all aspects of literature (primarily British and American) from history to the novel. This bulletin is particularly useful for the numerous bibliographies, checklists, and notes on recent exhibitions. Indexed in *Library Literature*.

Colby Library Quarterly. Waterville, ME: Colby College Library, 1943— v.1— . Quarterly.

Generally a bibliographical approach to literature in English, with a special interest in Maine authors and historians. The articles are largely literary criticism but often dwell on topics related to the study of bibliography. Indexed in the *Modern Language Association International Bibliography*.

Columbia Library Columns. New York: Friends of Columbia Library, Butler Library, Columbia University, 1951— v.1— . Three issues per year.

Has an excellent format, with illustrations. Articles are of high quality and are related to the collections of the Butler Library. These articles tend to be bibliographic and literary in nature. Some short notes from the sponsoring organization are included. Indexed in *Library Literature*.

Harvard Library Bulletin. Cambridge, MA: Harvard University Press, 1947— v.1— . Quarterly.

A well-designed scholarly publication that combines literature and bibliography with history and other disciplines. Each issue usually contains five to eight articles, sometimes on a central theme, by leading scholars in the fields covered. Indexed in *Library Literature* and *Modern Language Association International Bibliography*.

Huntington Library Quarterly. San Marino, CA: Huntington Library and Art Gallery, 1937— v.1— . Quarterly.
Includes coverage on a wide variety of scholarly topics, from literature to history. Articles are by scholars and include much bibliographically related information. Indexed in *Modern Language Association International Bibliography* and abstracted in *Abstracts of English Studies* and *Historical Abstracts*.

ICarbS. Carbondale, IL: Morris Library, Southern Illinois University, 1973— v.1— . Semiannual.
Emphasis is placed on research studies, based upon special collections of the Morris Library. Covers a wide variety of materials, from bibliographical to articles on intellectual freedom to reports on authors. Approach and format are of excellent quality. Indexed in the *Modern Language Association International Bibliography* and abstracted in *Abstracts of English Studies*.

John Rylands Library. Bulletin. Manchester, Eng.: John Rylands University Library, 1902— . Semiannual.
Consists of a scholarly series of monographs. The bulk of the material deals with the more esoteric aspects of English literature and bibliography. On occasion monographs on history and linguistics are included.

Library Chronicle. Austin, TX: Humanities Research Center, University of Texas, 1944—1970, v.1— ; New Series: 1971— v.1— . Semiannual.
One of the more elaborate, if not luxurious, of the library-oriented bibliography periodicals. Includes well-researched articles along with some news notes and sketches. At times the publication schedule is irregular. Indexed in *Library Literature*, and the *Modern Language Association International Bibliography* and abstracted in *Library and Information Science Abstracts*.

Library Quarterly; A Journal of Investigation and Discussion in the Field of Library Science. Chicago: University of Chicago Press, 1931— v.1— . Quarterly.

This periodical is considered by many to be the most prestigious and scholarly journal in the field of librarianship. The articles concentrate on current research in a wide spectrum of the discipline. The quality of the critical reviews by librarians is excellent. The bibliographer will find much here that is thought-provoking and informative.

Library Trends. Urbana, IL: Graduate School of Library Science, University of Illinois, 1952— v.1— . Quarterly.

This publication is actually an excellent monographic series. Each issue usually contains six to eight articles written by specialists, along with an introduction by the editor, giving in-depth information on a specific topic. Since its inception many of these studies have focused on aspects of bibliography.

Literary Research Newsletter. College Park, MD: Dept. of English, University of Maryland, etc., 1976— v.1— . Quarterly.

Directed toward instructors of and students engaged in literary research. Includes short articles, notes on bibliographic aids, and brief reviews and comments on new reference tools for literary students. This newsletter is not a report of research in progress for the most part. By its nature this journal will be of great interest to bibliographers. Along with reviews of bibliographic aids it includes from time to time articles related to the study of bibliography. Indexed in the *Modern Language Association International Bibliography*.

Princeton University Library Chronicle. Princeton, NJ: Friends of the Princeton University Library, 1939— v.1— . Quarterly.

Each issue contains two or three bibliographical articles on history, art, literature, and related subjects. At times there are special issues that cover the work of a single writer or artist. Excellent illustrations, and each issue includes library notes, news, and information of the sponsoring group. Indexed in *Library Literature*.

Private Library. Middlesex, Eng.: Private Libraries Association, 1957— v.1— . Quarterly.

Tends to be a more popular version of the *Book Collector*. Generally the articles are less esoteric, more inclined to emphasize the joys of book collecting without too much stress on bibliographical detail. Focuses on the work of private presses, both in England and elsewhere. Indexed in *Library Literature* and *Library and Information Science Abstracts*.

Serials Librarian. New York: Haworth Press, 1976— v.1— . Quarterly.
Articles cover copyright, indexing, and bibliographic control as well as topics related to serials. Indexed in *Library Literature*.

U.S. Library of Congress Quarterly Journal. Washington, DC: Library of Congress, 1943— v.1— . Quarterly.
This journal is not only beautifully designed and illustrated but covers a broad expanse of interests as reflected by the activities of the Library of Congress. The articles by scholars and members of the Library of Congress staff cover almost every subject. Certain issues focus mostly on a particular field. A special feature, "Some Recent Publications of the Library of Congress," is a valued checklist for the bibliographer-librarian. Indexed in *Library Literature* and abstracted in *Library and Information Science Abstracts*.

Yale University Library Gazette. New Haven, CT: Yale University Library, 1926— v.1— . Quarterly.
This publication is a major journal for the field of bibliography. Each issue usually has four to five articles based on materials located in the Yale University libraries. These articles are written by scholars, librarians, and instructional faculty at Yale. Also included in each issue is a recent acquisitions list. Indexed in *Library Literature*.

Online Searching Journals

Periodicals dealing with various aspects of bibliographic searching are now beginning to grow in number and are providing online searchers with valuable information on developing technologies and new searching techniques.

Database: The Magazine of Database Reference and Review. Weston, CT: Online, Inc., 1978— v.1— . BiMonthly.
Provides extensive in-depth articles on database usage, accompanied by comparisons and evaluations. Articles are well documented and there are valuable additional features related to database developments and book reviews. Indexed in: *Library Literature* and *Information Science Abstracts*.

Database Searcher: The Magazine for Online Database Users. (Formerly, *Database End User*). Westport, CT: Meckler, 1984— v.1— . Monthly.
Covers many areas of online searching with brief information sections emphasizing developments, new products, search strategies and techniques. Includes addresses of providers covered in the text of the reports. Indexed in: *Library and Information Science Abstracts* and *Computer Database* (Online).

Online: The Magazine of Online Information Systems. Weston, CT: Online, 1977— v.1— . Quarterly.
Articles contained in this journal place emphasis on the practical aspects of online searching. There is a broad focus along with material related to total library integrated automation and strategies for training managers. Includes well-documented and illustrated articles long with informative additional features. Indexed in: *Current Contents*, *ERIC*, *Library Literature*, and *Library Science Abstracts*.

Online Review: The International Journal of Online & Videotext Information Systems. Medford, NJ: Learned Information, 1977— v.1— . BiMonthly.
Articles in this journal are mostly written by instructional professionals and therefore tend to be more theoretical and critical in nature. News sections report on broad worldwide activities related to online searching. Includes an extensive bibliography on online information retrieval which is updated annually. Indexed in: *Library Literature*.

Periodicals Lists

Several of the major periodical lists are helpful in a number of ways. They provide information for ordering subscriptions, supply complete bibliographical data, and indicate where a periodical is indexed.

Now in its fifth edition is William A. Katz's *Magazines for Libraries* (New York: Bowker, 1986), 1057p. This guide to magazine selection for public, school, and college librarians gives descriptive and critical annotations of the editorial content, point of view, and other significant features of approximately 6,500 periodicals. Arrangement is by subject, and each entry provides full bibliographical data. One must be careful, however, as some of the periodicals listed have ceased publication, and many of the subscription prices have increased.

The largest and most detailed source for periodical information is *Ulrich's International Periodicals Directory*. (New York: Bowker, 1932–). In-depth information is provided on thousands of periodicals from all over the world. They are arranged alphabetically under 250 subject headings. Coverage of publications on microfilm, along with abstracting and indexing information, has been expanded. International Standard Serial Number (ISSN) with country code and Dewey Decimal Classification numbers are noted in the main entries, together with subscription price, frequency of issue, name and address of publisher, circulation, languages used in text, year first published, and whether advertisements, reviews, bibliographies, illustrations, etc., are carried. Periodicals that have changed name since the last edition of *Ulrich's* are listed under old and new names. Separate listings are provided for ceased publications since the last edition and for new periodicals launched since 1975. *Ulrich's* includes separate listings of publications available from international organizations, congresses, and the United Nations. It is revised annually. Also published in the interim is *Ulrich's Quarterly*, with much the same information as the parent volume. Now available on CD-ROM.

Of a similar nature to the above is *The Standard Periodical Directory*, 8th ed. (New York: Oxbridge, 1986). It duplicates *Ulrich* but includes more elusive titles, house organs, yearbooks, and government publications and more descriptions of content.

The newest entry into this market is *The Serials Directory*. (Birmingham, AL: EBSCO Publishing, 1986), 3v. It lists over 114,000 periodicals giving full bibliographic and ordering information.

Selected Related Writings

Bobinski, George S. "An Analysis of 105 Major U.S. Journals in Library and Information Science." In: *Library Science Annual*. Littleton, CO: Libraries Unlimited, 1985, Vol. 1, pp. 29–41.

Budd, John. "Publication in Library & Information Science: The State of the Literature," *Library Journal*, 113 (September 1, 1988), pp. 125–131.

Tanselle, G. Thomas. "The Periodical Literature of English and American Bibliography," *Studies in Bibliography*, 26 (1973), pp. 167–191.

Notes

1. G. Thomas Tanselle, "The Periodical Literature of English and American Bibliography," *Studies in Bibliography*, 26 (1973), p. 167.

2. Jacquelyn M. Morris and Elizabeth A. Elkins. *Library Searching: Resources and Strategies*. (New York: Jeffrey Norton, 1978), pp. 45–46.

3. An annual review of the library press is provided in *The A L A Yearbook of Library and Information Services*. Chicago: American Library Association, 1976–to date, as a continuous feature. Outlines new developments and provides a general analysis.

Appendix A

EDUCATIONAL INSTITUTIONS

There are approximately sixty educational institutions within the United States and Canada with masters programs in library and information studies accredited by the American Library Association. Some have doctoral programs as well. These institutions are listed below in alphabetical order within each state. Since this list is always changing, consult the *Bowker Annual* or any current issue of the *Journal of Education for Library and Information Science* for an up-to-date listing with addresses.

ALABAMA	Graduate School of Library Service, University of Alabama, Tuscaloosa, Alabama 35487 (Degree: Master of Library Service)
ARIZONA	Graduate Library School, University of Arizona, Tucson, Arizona 85719 (Degree: Master of Library Science)
CALIFORNIA	Division of Library and Information Science, San Jose State University, San Jose, California 95192-0029 (Degree: Master of Library Science)
	School of Library and Information Studies, University of California, Berkeley, Berkeley, California 94720 (Degrees: Master of Library and Information Studies; Ph.D.)
	Graduate School of Library and Information Science, University of California, Los Angeles, Los Angeles, California 90024 (Degrees: Master of Library Science; Ph.D.)
CANADA	School of Library and Information Studies, Dalhousie University, Halifax, Nova Scotia, CANADA B3H 4H8 (Degree: Master of Library and Information Studies)

Graduate School of Library and Information Studies, McGill University, Montreal, Québec, CANADA H3A 1Y1 (Degree: Master of Library and Information Studies)

Ecole de bibliothèconomie et sciences de l'information, Université de Montreal, Montreal, Québec, CANADA H3C 3J7 (Degree: Maitrise en bibliothèconomie et sciences de l'information)

Faculty of Library Science, University of Alberta, Edmonton, Alberta, CANADA T6G 2J4 (Degree: Master of Library Science)

School of Library, Archival and Information Studies, University of British Columbia, Vancouver, British Columbia, CANADA V6T 1W5 (Degree: Master of Library Science)

Faculty of Library and Information Science, University of Toronto, Toronto, Ontario, CANADA M5S 1A1 (Degrees: Master of Library Science; Ph.D.)

School of Library and Information Science, University of Western Ontario, London, Ontario, CANADA N6G 1H1 (Degrees: Master of Library and Information Science; Ph.D.)

CONNECTICUT

School of Library Science and Instructional Technology, Southern Connecticut State University, New Haven, Connecticut 06515 (Degree: Master of Library Science)

DISTRICT OF COLUMBIA

School of Library and Information Science, Catholic University of America, Washington, D.C. 20064 (Degree: Master of Science in Library Science)

FLORIDA

School of Library and Information Studies, Florida State University, Tallahassee, Florida 32306-2048 (Degrees: Master of Science; Master of Arts; Ph.D.)

School of Library and Information Science, University of South Florida, Tampa, Florida 33620 (Degree: Master of Arts)

GEORGIA

School of Library and Information Studies, Atlanta University, Atlanta, Georgia 30314 (Degree: Master of Science in Library Science)

HAWAII

School of Library and Information Studies, University of Hawaii at Manoa, Honolulu, Hawaii 96822 (Degrees: Master of Library and Information Studies; Ph.D.)

ILLINOIS

Department of Library and Information Studies, Northern Illinois University, DeKalb, Illinois 60115-2854 (Degree: Master of Arts)

Graduate School of Library and Information Science, Rosary College, River Forest, Illinois 60305 (Degree: Master of Arts in Library and Information Science)

Graduate Library School, University of Chicago, Chicago, Illinois 60637 (Degrees: Master of Arts; Ph.D.)

Graduate School of Library and Information Science, University of Illinois, 1407 West Gregory, 410 DKH, Urbana, Illinois 61801-3680 (Degrees: Master of Science; Ph.D.)

INDIANA

School of Library and Information Science, Indiana University, Bloomington, Indiana 47405 (Degrees: Master of Library Science; Ph.D.)

IOWA

School of Library and Information Science, University of Iowa, Iowa City, Iowa 52242 (Degree: Master of Arts)

KANSAS

School of Library and Information Management, Emporia State University, Emporia, Kansas 66801-5087 (Degree: Master of Library Science)

KENTUCKY

College of Library and Information Science, University of Kentucky, Lexington, Kentucky 40506-0039 (Degrees:

Master of Science in Library Science; Master of Arts)

LOUISIANA

School of Library and Information Science, Louisiana State University, Baton Rouge, Louisiana 70803 (Degree: Master of Library and Information Science)

MARYLAND

College of Library and Information Services, University of Maryland, College Park, Maryland 20742 (Degrees: Master of Library Science; Ph.D.)

MASSACHUSETTS

Graduate School of Library and Information Science, Simmons College, Boston, Massachusetts 02115 (Degrees: Master of Science; Doctor of Arts)

MICHIGAN

School of Information and Library Studies, University of Michigan, Ann Arbor, Michigan 48109-1346 (Degrees: Master of Information and Library Studies; Ph.D.)

Library Science Program, Wayne State University, Detroit, Michigan 48202 (Degree: Master of Science in Library Science)

MISSISSIPPI

School of Library Science, University of Southern Mississippi, Hattiesburg, Mississippi 39406-5146 (Degree: Master of Library Science)

MISSOURI

School of Library and Information Science, University of Missouri, Columbia, Columbia, Missouri 65211 (Degree: Master of Arts)

NEW JERSEY

School of Communication, Information and Library Studies, Rutgers University, New Brunswick, New Jersey 08903 (Degrees: Master of Library Service; Ph.D.)

NEW YORK

School of Library Service, Columbia University, New York, New York 10027 (Degrees: Master of Science; D.L.S.)

Palmer School of Library and Information Science, Long Island University, Greenvale, New York 11548 (Degree: Master of Science in Library Science)

School of Computer, Information and Library Sciences, Pratt Institute, Brooklyn, New York 11205 (Degree: Master of Science)

Graduate School of Library and Information Studies, Queens College, City University of New York, Flushing, New York 11367-0904 (Degree: Master of Library Science)

Division of Library and Information Science, St. John's University, Jamaica, New York 11439 (Degree: Master of Library Science)

School of Information Science and Policy, State University of New York, Albany, Albany, New York 12222 (Degree: Master of Library Science)

School of Information and Library Studies, State University of New York at Buffalo, Buffalo, New York 14260 (Degrees: Master of Library and Information Science; Ph.D.)

School of Information Studies, Syracuse University, Syracuse, New York 13244-2340 (Degrees: Master of Library Science; Ph.D.)

NORTH CAROLINA

School of Library and Information Sciences, North Carolina Central University, Durham, North Carolina 27707 (Degree: Master of Library Science)

School of Information and Library Science, University of North Carolina, Chapel Hill, North Carolina 27599-3360 (Degrees: Master of Science in Library Science; Ph.D.)

Department of Library Science/Educational Technology, University of North Carolina at Greensboro, Greensboro, North Carolina 27412 (Degree: Master of Library Science)

OHIO

School of Library Science, Kent State University, Kent, Ohio 44242 (Degree: Master of Library Science)

OKLAHOMA	School of Library and Information Studies, University of Oklahoma, Norman, Oklahoma 73019 (Degree: Master of Library and Information Studies)
PENNSYLVANIA	College of Library Science, Clarion University of Pennsylvania, Clarion, Pennsylvania 16214 (Degree: Master of Science in Library Science)
	College of Information Studies, Drexel University, Philadelphia, Pennsylvania 19104 (Degrees: Master of Science; Ph.D.)
	School of Library and Information Science, University of Pittsburgh, Pittsburgh, Pennsylvania 15260 (Degrees: Master of Library Science; Ph.D.)
RHODE ISLAND	Graduate School of Library and Information Studies, University of Rhode Island, Kingston, Rhode Island 02881 (Degree: Master of Library and Information Science)
SOUTH CAROLINA	College of Library and Information Science, University of South Carolina, Columbia, South Carolina 29208 (Degree: Master of Librarianship)
TENNESSEE	Graduate School of Library and Information Science, University of Tennessee, Knoxville, Knoxville, Tennessee 37996-4330 (Degree: Master of Science in Library Science)
TEXAS	School of Library and Information Sciences, University of North Texas, Denton, Texas 76203 (Degree: Master of Science)
	School of Library and Information Studies, Texas Woman's University, Denton, Texas 76204 (Degrees: Master of Arts; Master of Library Science; Ph.D.)
	Graduate School of Library and Information Science, University of Texas at Austin, Austin, Texas 78712-1276 (Degrees: Master of Library and Information Science; Ph.D.)

UTAH

School of Library and Information Sciences, Brigham Young University, Provo, Utah 84602 (Degree: Master of Library and Information Science)

WASHINGTON

School of Library and Information Science, University of Washington, Seattle, Washington 98195 (Degrees: Master of Librarianship)

WISCONSIN

School of Library and Information Studies, University of Wisconsin-Madison, Madison, Wisconsin 53706 (Degrees: Master of Arts; Ph.D.)

School of Library and Information Science, University of Wisconsin-Milwaukee, Milwaukee, Wisconsin 53201 (Degrees: Master of Library and Information Science; Ph.D.)

Appendix B

MAJOR BIBLIOGRAPHICAL STYLE MANUALS

When compiling a bibliography, the bibliographer must decide upon an entry format and use it consistently throughout. For this purpose style manuals have been developed for specific disciplines as well as for general application. Many style manuals reflecting the wide range of format practice are covered in Mary R. Kinney's *Bibliographical Style Manuals: A Guide to their Use in Documentation and Research* (Chicago: Association of College and Research Libraries, 1953; ACRL Monograph 8), and John B. Howell's *Style Manuals of the English-Speaking World: A Guide* (Phoenix, AZ: Oryx Press, 1983). The selected list of style manuals which follows includes specifications for the bibliographic forms most frequently used in the world of scholarship.

GENERAL MANUALS

American National Standards Institute. *American National Standard for Bibliographic References*. New York: American National Standards Institute, 1977. 92p.
The attempt here is to "provide sufficient rules and guidelines for preparation of bibliographic references to both print and nonprint works."

Campbell, William Giles. *Form and Style: Theses, Reports, Term Papers*. With Stephen V. Ballou and Carole Slade. 7th ed. Boston: Houghton Mifflin, ©1986. 226p.
This manual is well designed, easy to use and contains many helpful examples.

Hoffman, Herbert H. *Bibliography Without Footnotes*. Santa Ana, CA: Headway Publications, 1977. 103p.
A rather unorthodox presentation of concepts for the place of footnotes and the compilation of bibliographies.

Manheimer, Martha L. *Style Manual: A Guide for the Preparation of Reports and Dissertations*. New York: Dekker, 1973. 161p.
A detailed treatment with bibliographic format based on *The Chicago Manual of Style*.

Miller, Joan I. *The Thesis Writer's Handbook: A Complete One-Source Guide for Writers of*

Research Papers. With Bruce J. Taylor. West Linn, OR: Alcove Pub. Co., ©1987. 135p.
A basic approach to documenting theses and research papers.

Turabian, Kate L. *A Manual for Writers of Term Papers, Theses, and Dissertations*. 5th ed. Revised and expanded by Bonnie Birtwistle Honigsblum. Chicago: University of Chicago Press, 1987. 300p.
A new and updated version of a widely used style manual derived from *The Chicago Manual of Style*.

University of Chicago Press. *The Chicago Manual of Style for Authors, Editors, and Copywriters*. 13th ed., rev. and expanded. Chicago: University of Chicago Press, 1982. 737p.
Noted for its exhaustive treatment of the publishing process and its many examples this work is probably the most widely used style manual available.

Webster's Standard American Style Manual. Springfield, MA: Merriam-Webster, Inc., Publishers, 1985. 464p.
Chapter Eight "Notes and Documentation of Sources" (pp. 179–212) provides a bibliographical style based on the *MLA Handbook*.

SUBJECT MANUALS

Agriculture

Guidelines for the Preparation of Bibliographies. Beltsville, MD: U.S. Department of Agriculture, National Agricultural Library, 1982. 64p.
Bibliographical style varies widely from CBE (see next item) and other major related subject areas but adhears mostly to the *GPO Style Manual*.

Biology

CBE Style Manual Committee. *CBE Style Manual: A Guide for Authors, Editors, and Publishers in the Biological Sciences*. 5th ed., rev. and expanded. Bethesda, MD: Council of Biology Editors, ©1983. 324p.
The bibliographical style used in this manual is based on the *American National Standard for Bibliographic References* with some modifications.

Chemistry

The ACS Style Guide: A Manual for Authors and Editors. Janet S. Dodd, editor; Marianne C. Brogan, advisory editor. Washington, DC: American Chemical Society, 1986. 264p.
Updates previous editions and recommends use of the *American National Standard for Bibliographic References* with a few modifications.

Education

National Education Association of the United States. *Style Manual: NEA Style Manual for Writers and Editors*. Washington, DC: National Education Association, 1974. 92p.
Presents a unique bibliographic style but relies heavily on *The Chicago Manual of Style*.

Government Publications

Brightbill, George D. *Citation Manual for United States Government Publications*. With Wayne C. Maxson. Philadelphia, PA: Center for the Study of Federalism, Temple University, 1974. 52p.
Provides a simplified bibliographic style for the non specialist. Citation formats conform mainly to *The Chicago Manual of Style* with some modifications.

Garner, Diane L. *The Complete Guide to Citing Government Documents: A Manual for Writers & Librarians*. With Diane H. Smith. Bethesda, MD: Congressional Information Service, ©1984. 142p.
Bibliographic style conforms to ANSI standards with some unique modifications.

United Nations. Dag Hammarskjöld Library. *Bibliographical Style Manual*. New York: United Nations, 1963. 62p.
Provides a general style for citing United Nations publications.

United States. Government Printing Office. *Style Manual/United States Government Printing Office*. Washington, DC: The Office, 1984. 479p.
Presents a bibliographic style unique to the United States Government Printing Office.

History

Lackey, Richard S. *Cite Your Sources: A Manual for Documenting Family Histories and Genealogical Records*. Jackson, MS: University Press of Mississippi, 1985, ©1980. 122p.
Covers the general sources for family history and genealogy with a basic bibliographical style.

Wilson, John R. M. *Research Guide in History*. Morristown, NJ: General Learning Press, 1974. 187p.
For a brief but adequate treatment for bibliographical citations see "Footnotes and Bibliography" on pages 19–44. The bibliographic style is based on *The Chicago Manual of Style*.

Journalism

Anderson, Peter Joseph. *Research Guide in Journalism*. Morristown, NJ: General Learning Press, 1974. 229p.
A rather brief but adequate system for bibliographic citation based on *The Chicago Manual of Style* is covered in a section entitled "Footnotes and Bibliography" on pages 63–84.

Law

Maier, Elaine C. *How to Prepare a Legal Citation*. Woodbury, NY: Barron's, ©1986. 228p.
A detailed guide for citing legal sources, replete with illustrations. Extremely useful.

Powers, Marion, D. *The Legal Citation Directory*. West Mantoloking, NJ: Franas Press, 1971. 302p.
In a dictionary arrangement this work provides a simple and direct approach to the problems involving the identification and implementation of legal citations.

Telply, Larry L. *Programmed Materials on Legal Research and Citation* 2nd ed. St. Paul, MN: West, 1986. 358p.
Provides a basic understanding of legal research and the application of citations.

A Uniform System of Citation. 13th ed. Cambridge, MA: Harvard Law Association, 1982, ©1981. 237p.
A valuable guide to citations for works predominately legal. Particularly useful for its extended list of periodical abbreviations and numerous examples.

Literature

Achtert, Walter S. *The MLA Style Manual*. With Joseph Gibaldi. New York: Modern Language Association of America, 1985. 271p.
This work sets the basic format for citing literary works. Also widely useful for other fields especially in the humanities.

The McGraw-Hill Style Manual: A Concise Guide for Writers and Editors. Edited by Marie Longyear. New York: McGraw-Hill, ©1983. 333p.
This detailed manual is a good example of a publisher's manual for the authors of its publications. Bibliographical style mostly conforms to the *MLA Style Manual*.

Seeber, Edward D. *A Style Manual for Students: For the Preparation of Term Papers, Essays, and Theses*. 3rd ed., rev. Bloomington, IN: Indiana University Press, 1976, ©1967. 94p.
Bibliographic style follows closely that of the *MLA Style Manual*.

Winkler, Anthony C. *Writing the Research Paper: A Handbook with the 1984 MLA Documentation Style*. With Jo Ray McCuen. 2nd ed. San Diego, CA: Harcourt Brace Jovanovich, ©1985. 284p.
As the title indicates bibliographical style followed in this manual conforms to the *MLA Style Manual* which is the standard for the field.

Mathematics

Swanson, Ellen. *Mathematics Into Type: Copy Editing and Proofreading of Mathematics for Editorial Assistants and Authors*. Rev. ed. Providence, RI: American Mathematics Society, 1979. 90p.
Provides a unique but flexible bibliographic style for publications in mathematics.

Medicine

Barclay, William R. *Manual for Authors & Editors: Editorial Style & Manuscript Preparation*. Compiled for the American Medical Association by William R. Barclay, M. Therese Southgate, and Robert W. Mayo. 7th ed. Los Altos, CA: Lange Medical Publications, ©1981. 184p.
Sets the basic bibliographic style for medical literature unique to *The Journal of the American Medical Association*.

Huth, Edward J. *Medical Style & Format: An International Manual for Authors, Editors, and Publishers*. Philadelphia, PA: ISI Press, ©1987. 355p.
Bibliographical style follows closely the Barclay manual.

Nonprint Materials

Fleischer, Eugene B. *A Style Manual for Citing Microform and Nonprint Media*. Chicago: American Library Association, 1978. 66p.
Provides a simplified bibliographic style for nonprint materials.

Shields, Nancy E. *Where Credit is Due: A Guide to Proper Citing of Sources, Print and Nonprint*. With Mary E. Uhle. Metuchen, NJ: Scarecrow Press, 1985. 252p.
An extensive and detailed manual covering a bibliographic style for nonprint materials.

Physics

American Institute of Physics. Publication Board. *Style Manual for Guidance in the Preparation of Papers for Journals Published by the American Institute of Physics*. 3rd ed. New York: The Institute, 1978. 56p.
Does not provide bibliographical style but the section on footnotes and references is well illustrated with various types of citations.

Political Science

Kalvelage, Carl. *Bridges to Knowledge in Political Science: A Handbook for Research*. With Albert P. Melone and Morley Segal. Pacific Palisades, CA: Palisades Publishers, ©1984. 153p.
Chapter Five (pp. 113–136) includes a system for footnotes and bibliographic citations based on *The Chicago Manual of Style*.

Psychology

Publication Manual of the American Psychological Association. 3rd ed. Arlington, VA: The Association, 1983. 208p.
This is probably one of the major style manuals in use today. It is, however, difficult to use.

Social Sciences

Appel, Livia. *Bibliographical Citation in the Social Sciences and the Humanities: A Handbook of Style for Authors, Editors and Students*. 3rd ed. Madison, WI: University of Wisconsin Press, ©1949. 32p.
A general guide with bibliographical style that follows the *MLA Style Manual*.

Hurt, Peyton. *Bibliography and Footnotes: A Style Manual for Students and Writers*. 3rd ed., rev. and enl. by Mary L. Hurt Richmond. Berkeley, CA: University of California Press, 1968. 163p.
Although concise, this work is very useful especially for social scientists because of its extensive treatment of related literature and government publications.

Mullins, Carolyn J. *A Guide to Writing and Publishing in the Social and Behavioral Sciences*. New York: Wiley-Interscience, 1977. 431p.
A general comparison of bibliographic style used in *The Chicago Manual of Style* and the manual published by the American Psychological Association.

Technical Publications

Mohrbacher, Robert D. *Style Guide for Technical Publications*. With Marilyn J. Cochran. Denver, CO: Engineering and Research Center, Technical Publications Branch, Division of Management Support, U.S. Department of the Interior, Bureau of Reclamantion, 1984. 208p.
Provides a basic bibliographic style for technical literature.

Reisman, S. J. *A Style Manual for Technical Writers and Editors*. New York: Macmillan, 1963, ©1962. 1v. (unpaged)
Although somewhat dated, this manual is still useful.

Appendix C

ABBREVIATIONS USED IN BIBLIOGRAPHY

There are many abbreviations used in all aspects of bibliography. The following list includes those used most frequently.

abr	abridged
Acs	autograph card, signed
ad, adv	advertisement
AD	autograph document, not signed
ADs	autograph document, signed
Adds	additions
a. e. g.	all edges gilt
AL	autograph letter, not signed
ALs	autograph letter, signed
AMs s	autograph manuscript, signed
anon	anonymous
anr	another
ANs	autograph note, signed
ap	author's proof
b	born; or back of page (verso)
bd	bound
bdg	binding
bds	boards
bev	beveled
bf	bold face (type)
bib	bibliography
bkrm	buckram
bkstrp	backstrip
bl	black letter
b/w	black and white
bxd	boxed, as it came from the publisher
c	copyright; or circa
ca	circa (about, approximately)

cap	collated and perfect
capt	caption
cat	catalog
cent	century
cf	calf
chpd	chipped
cl	cloth
cm	centimeter (approx. ⅖)
coa	cash on arrival
cod	cash on delivery
col	color or colored; column; colophon
cond	condition
cont	contemporary (*not* continued)
cor	corrected or cash on receipt
cov	cover(s)
cpl	complete
cr	crown octavo (a book size)
cvr	cover(s)
cwo	cash with order
D°	duodecimo (12mo) (a book size)
d	died
dec	decorated
dj, dw (d/w)	dust jacket, dust wrapper
doc	document
Ds	document, signed
dup	duplicate
ed	edition, editor
ed dl	de luxe edition
ee	edges
eg	edges gilt
...	ellipsis (omission)
eng	engraved or engraving
ep	endpaper(s)
est	established
ex	exchange allowed
ex-ill	extra-illustrated
ex-lib	ex-library copy
F	folio (a book size)
f	in fine condition (*not* fair)
facs	facsimile(s)
fcp	foolscap (a British book size)
fdc	first-day cover
fe	fore-edge
ff	folios (leaves); or following
fg	fine-grain (leather)

fig	figure(s)
fly	flyleaf
fo	folio
fp or front(is)	frontispiece
fs	facsimile
fx	foxed or foxing
g	gilt; or in good condition
gb	gilt back
gbe	gilt beveled back
ge	gilt edge
gl	gothic letter
glo	glossary
gr	grain
gt	gilt top
hc	hardcover
hf bd	half bound in leather
hf cf	half bound in calf
hm	handmade
id	idem (the same)
IFT	indexed, folio'd, and titled
ihm	imitation handmade (paper)
ill	illustrated or illustration(s)
imit	imitation
imp	imperfect (a book condition)
Imp	Imperial (a British book size)
impr	imprint
insc	inscribed or inscription
intro	introduction
IPT	indexed, paged, and titled
ital	italics or italic letter
JP	Japanese vellum
l	leaf; or lower
ll	leaves
le	limited edition
lea	leather
lev	levant morocco (a type of bookbinding)
lg	large (as in large-paper copy)
litho	lithographed
loc	located
lp	large paper
Ls	letter, signed
ltd	limited

m	marbled
mco, mor	morocco
me	marbled edge(s)
mps	marbled paper sides
ms(s)	manuscript(s)
mtd	mounted
nb	nota bene (mark well)
nd	no date given
nep	new edition in preparation; also NE/nd.
np	no place, publisher, or printer given, as the case may be
nu	name unknown
nv	new version
ny	no year indicated
O°	Octavo (8vo) (a book size)
ob	oblong
op	out of print
opp	out of print, at present
orig	original
os	out of stock
o/w	otherwise
p (or pp)	page (or pages)
p	paper; or post (after); or a poor copy
pdp	paste-down endpaper(s)
pict	pictorial
pl	plate
pol	polished (leather)
port	portrait(s)
pp	printed pages
p p	privately printed; or private press; also postpaid
pref	preface
prelims	preliminary leaves
pres	presentation copy
prtg	printing or printed
pseud	pseudonym
pt	part or in parts
ptd	printed
pub	published, publisher, or publication
Q	quarto (4to) (a book size)
qto	quarto
rb	rubbed; or rebound or rebinding
ref	reference

rev	revision or revised
rpt	reprint or reprinted
s	signed; or sprinkled
sa	sine anno (no date)
SASE	self-addressed stamped envelope (to be included for reply)
ser	series
sg or sgd	signed or signature
sig	signature
sm	small
s n	sine nomine (no publisher indicated)
spec bdg	special binding
spr	sprinkled
sq	square book
stns	stains
stp	stamped
swd	sewed
t	title page; or translated
teg	top edge gilt
thk	thick (volume)
TLs	typed letter, signed
t p	title page
tpd	tipped in
trans	translator
ts	typescript
u c	upper cover (top, in British use); or upper case
unb	unbound
up	university press
vd	various dates, years
vg	a very good (copy or condition)
vol	volume
vp	various places
w/	with
w a f	with all faults; as is
wrps	wrappers
x	Christian
xc	excellent condition
x-lib	ex-library copy
xr	no returns permitted
ye	yellow edges

ABBREVIATIONS: BOOK SIZE

American

F	Folio	13 inches or taller
4to	quarto	between 11 and 13 inches
8vo	octavo	8 to 9 inches
12mo	duodecimo	around 7 inches or slightly taller
16mo	septodecimo	6 to 7 inches
24mo	vigesimoquarto	5 to 6 inches
32mo	trigesimosecundo	4 to 5 inches
48mo	fortyeightmo	less than 4 inches tall
64mo	sixtyfourmo	about 3 inches tall

British

Im Fol	Imperial Folio	22 × 15½
Ry Fol	Royal Folio	20 × 12½
Cr Fol	Crown Folio	15 × 10
Fo Fol	Foolscap Folio	13½ × 10
Imp 4to	Imperial Quarto	15 × 11
Ry 4to	Royal Quarto	12½ × 10
Med 4to	Medium Quarto	12 × 9½
Dy 4to	Demy Quarto	11½ × 8¾
Cr 4to	Crown Quarto	10 × 7½
F 4to	Foolscap Quarto	8½ × 6¾
Imp 8vo	Imperial Octavo	11 × 7½
Ry 8vo	Royal Octavo	10 × 6½
M 8vo	Medium Octavo	9½ × 6
Dy 8vo	Demy Octavo	8¾ × 5⅝
L Cr 8vo	Large Crown Octavo	8 × 5½
Cr 8vo	Crown Octavo	7½ × 5
F 8vo	Foolscap Octavo	6½ × 4½

Appendix D

A GLOSSARY OF BIBLIOGRAPHIC TERMS

This glossary includes a list of common terms and expressions used in bibliography and bibliographic searching.

Abridgment: A shortened form of a work retaining the general sense and unity of the original.

Abstract: A brief summary that gives the essential points of a book, pamphlet, or article.

Abstract Bulletin: A printed or mimeographed bulletin containing abstracts of currently published periodical articles, pamphlets, etc., issued by special libraries and distributed monthly, weekly, or daily to their clientele.

Abstract Journal or Periodical: A periodical consisting of abstracts of current materials in books, pamphlets, and periodicals.

Abstracting Service: Abstracts in a particular field or on a particular subject prepared by an individual or a company and supplied regularly to subscribers or on request.

Access point: A data element (part of a record) used to retrieve a particular file or record. For example, a keyword assigned to a record by an indexer is one *access point,* among several others, to that record in the file.

Acronym: A word formed from the initial letter or letters of each of the name of an organization, group, or term, e.g., Unesco is the acronym for United Nations Educational, Scientific and Cultural Organization.

Almanac: 1) An annual publication containing a calendar, frequently accompanied by astronomical data and other information. 2) An annual yearbook of statistics and other information, sometimes in a particular field.

Analytical Bibliography: Analytical, or critical, bibliography involves the critical analysis of the text and its presentation. As such it is vitally concerned with the text in various stages of transmission.

Analytical Entry: The entry of some part of a work or of some article contained in a collection (volume of essays, serial, etc.) including a reference to the publication that contains the article or work entered.

Annals: 1) A periodical publication recording events of a year, transactions of an organization, or progress in special fields. 2) Earlier, a record of events arranged in chronological order. 3) In a general sense, only historical narrative.

Annotation: A note accompanying an entry in a bibliography or catalog, intended to describe or evaluate the work cited.

Annual: A serial publication, e.g., a report, yearbook, or directory issued once a year.

Anonymous: Authorship unknown or unavowed.

Anthology: A collection of extracts from the works of authors, sometimes limited to poetry or to a particular subject.

Appendix: Matter that follows the text of a book, which it usually illustrates, enlarges on, or supports by statistics.

Archives: 1) A collective noun used properly only in the plural. The organized body of records made or received in connection with the transaction of its affairs by a government or a governmental agency, an institution, organization, or establishment, or a family or individual, and preserved for record purposes in its custody or that of its legal successors. 2) An institution for the preservation and servicing of noncurrent archival material.

Author: The original writer or composer of a book, treatise, or document, as distinguished from an editor, compiler, or translator.

Author Bibliography: A bibliography that lists the works by and about an author.

Author/Title Catalog: Card catalog that has cards interfiled under authors' names and under titles.

Baud Rate: A standard measure for rating the speed of data communications. For example, a terminal operating at 1200 baud (generally equivalent to 1200 bits-per-second) can send or receive data at roughly 120 characters per second or about 1200 words per minute.

Bibliographer: 1) A person who is able to describe the physical characteristics of books by recognized methods. 2) One able to prepare bibliographies by recognized principles.

Bibliographic Control: The uniform identification of items or recorded information in various media and the mechanism for gaining subsequent access to such information.

Bibliographic Database: A database in which the records contain information *about* a document (title, author, subject headings, source) rather than the document itself. A bibliographic record is sometimes called a "document surrogate," especially if it contains an abstract.

Bibliographic Form: The style used for arranging information in a citation or a bibliography.

Bibliographic Organization: This is concerned with the pattern of effective arrangement achieved by means of a systematic listing of recorded knowledge.

Bibliographies of Bibliographies: Bibliographies that list useful bibliographies normally by subject, by place, or by individual.

Bibliography: The study of bibliography deals with the art or science of the description and history of books, including their physical makeup, authorship, editions, printing, publication, etc. On the other hand a bibliography is an intermediary instrument or device that assists in the transmission of information from the producer to the ultimate consumer.

Bibliophilic Bibliography: A listing of materials related to and for book collectors.

Binding: The process of folding, trimming, and assembling various elements of a printed folder, brochure, or book.

Book: A number of sheets of paper, parchment, etc. with writing or printing on them, fastened together along one edge, usually between protective covers.

Boolean Logic: A method of logic developed by George Boole, an English mathematician, which uses the logical operators—AND, OR, and NOT—to show relationships between sets or terms. Most online systems (but not all) allow the searcher the use of Boolean logic in developing search strategies.

Call Number: Letters, figures, and symbols, separate or in combination, assigned to a book to indicate its location on shelves. It usually consists of a class number and book number. Sometimes known as Call Mark.

Card Catalog: An index to the contents of a library's collection. Each entry is in a standardized format on cards of uniform size. These cards are filed alphabetically in drawers. See also *Dictionary Catalog, Divided Catalog, Author/Title Catalog* and *Subject Catalog*.

Catalog: A list or enumeration of names, titles, or articles arranged methodically, often in alphabetical order and usually with descriptive details, number or price accompanying each item; also, a book or pamphlet containing such a list, together with other information, as a university, library, or museum catalog.

Catalog Card: 1) One of the cards composing a card catalog. 2) A plain or a ruled card, generally of a standard size to be used for entries in a catalog or some other record.

Citation: References in a publication which refer the reader to another source.

Citation Index: A list of articles that, subsequent to the appearance of the original article, refer to, or cite, that article.

Classification: A systematic scheme of arrangement of books and other material according to a subject or form.

Classified Catalog: A catalog arranged by a numeric or alphabetic notation according to subject content. Also called classed catalog or class catalog.

Codex: A manuscript in book form.

Codicology: As a counterpart of analytical bibliography, codicology is concerned mainly with literary texts and narrative history, sometimes with liturgical texts, but less with discrete documents even when these are bound in codex form.

Collation: The technical description of a book, including pagination, format, signatures, and plates; that is, the examination of the sheets of a book that is to be bound in order to ensure that the pages, plates, indexes, etc. are in proper order; the act of comparing a book or set of sheets or signatures.

Colophon: A statement given in a book at the end of the text proper (common in early printed works though only occasionally in modern) giving some or all of the following particulars: the title or subject of the work, the name of the author, the name or the printer or the publisher (or both), the place and date of printing, and often the typeface and paper used. In addition there may be the device of the printer or the publisher, which alone would not constitute a colophon.

Command Language: The set of instructions used by the searcher to communicate with the computer in a particular search system.

Concordance: An alphabetical index of words showing the places in the text of a book or an author's complete works where each may be found.

Connect Time: The amount of time the remote terminal is connected to the host computer. This measure is usually one of the major elements in the costs associated with online searching.

Coordinate Index: An index that links references in such a way as to relate all references pertinent to a particular subject. The index allows a user to find those references that share two or more common characteristics of interest for a given search.

Copyright: The exclusive privilege of publishing and selling a work, granted by a government to an author, composer, artist, etc.

Corporate Entry: Catalog or index entry under the name of an organization or an institution, rather than an individual.

Cradle Books see *Incunabula*

Critical Bibliography see *Analytical Bibliography*

Cross-Reference: A reference made from one part of a book to another, or from one catalog entry to another.

Cumulate: To combine material in earlier issues, sometimes with the addition of new material, to form a new, unified list. See also *Cumulative Index*.

Cumulative Index: An index in periodical form, which combines successively the entries of earlier issues or volumes into a single index.

Data Element: A category of information within a record. For example, the title of an article is a standard data element in a bibliographic record.

Database: A collection of information items—facts, observations, bibliographic references, abstracts, etc.—organized for future access. In most of the systems now available for library research a "database" corresponds to all or part of an already existing indexing service such as *United States Political Science Documents*. The database may have more, the same, or less information than its print equivalent, but it almost always is organized for computer searching in such a way as to provide a greater number of access points than the print version.

Descriptive Bibliography: This branch of analytical bibliography is concerned with the precise description of books as physical objects.

Descriptor: A term (one or more words) which is assigned to describe the content of an item in a database. Although often used interchangeably with *identifier*, *descriptor* has come to mean a term chosen from a controlled vocabulary list or thesaurus, whereas *identifier* is a "natural-language" term; i.e., it is assigned by the indexer but not chosen from a controlled vocabulary list.

Dictionary: A book of alphabetically listed words in a language, with definitions, etymologies, pronunciation, and other information.

Dictionary Catalog: A catalog, usually on cards, in which all the entries (author, title, subject, series, etc.) and their related references are arranged together in one general alphabet. The subarrangement frequently varies from the strictly alphabetical.

Directory: A list of persons or organizations, systematically arranged, usually in alphabetic or classed order, giving address, affiliations, etc. for individuals, and address, officers, functions, and similar data for organizations.

Dissertation: A substantial paper (usually based on original research) presented by a candidate in partial fulfillment of the requirements for an academic degree or diploma.

Divided Catalog: A card catalog separated for convenience in use into two or more units, as an author and title catalog plus a subject catalog.

Document: An original or official paper relied upon as the basis of proof or support of something else; also, any writing, book, or other instrument conveying information.

Documentation: 1) The systematic collection, classification, recording, storage, and dissemination of specialized information, generally of a technical or scientific nature. 2) Written description of a computerized system's operating programs and facilities. A full and complete documentation is very important to a system's maintenance and often is the only means of finding out how to change the system when it becomes desirable to do so after its installation.

Downloading: The process of copying part of all of a database stored in one computer into another computer via online telecommunications. In the context of online searching, a search is performed and the results *downloaded* and stored in the searcher's own computer, generally a microcomputer.

Edition: All copies of a book, magazine, or newspaper produced from one setting of type.

Editor: One who prepares for publication a work or collection of works or articles by another person.

Elective Bibliography see *Selective or Elective Bibliography*

Encyclopedia: A book or set of books giving information on all branches of knowledge, generally in articles alphabetically arranged.

End User: The individual who ultimately uses the information retrieved in a search. This person may or may not be the terminal operator.

Entry: A record of a book in a catalog or list.

Enumerative Bibliography: One of the main branches of the study of bibliography that deals with graphic materials as intellectual entities. An enumerative bibliography is a listing of materials with some recognized relationship to one another.

False Drop see *False Hit*

False Hit: A citation retrieved in a computer search that meets the requirements of the stated logic, yet is irrelevant because of semantic or syntactic variations that were either unanticipated in the original profile or were unavoidable. Sometimes called *false drops*.

Field: A set of characters in a database treated as a unit which denotes a particular kind of data (e.g., author field, title field). This term is often used interchangeably with *data element*.

File: A database. A collection of related records. Some computer specialists refer to a database as a group of files, but in the online field these terms have become virtually synonymous.

Free-Text Searching: Searching without the use of a thesaurus or controlled vocabulary. Words in an abstract, for example, are often searchable in an online system, but successful retrieval of an item using free or full-text searching of the abstract would depend on a) the presence of the term in the abstract and b) the thoughtfulness of the searcher in choosing that term for searching.

Full Text: Refers to databases containing the entire text of articles, cases, or other original information sources. These files are distinguished from bibliographic databases, which contain only bibliographic references and perhaps summaries.

Full-Text Searching see *Free-Text Searching*.

General, or Universal, Bibliography: A bibliography that is not necessarily limited by time, geographical area, language, subject, or form.

Glossary: A list of terms with definitions or explanations; usually restricted to a particular subject.

Guide to the Literature: Lists and annotates sources of information for the literature of a specific discipline or subject area.

Handbook: A small reference book; a manual.

Heading: The word, name, or phrase at the top of a catalog card to indicate some special aspect of the work (authorship, subject, content, series, title, etc.) and to bring together in the catalog related materials and materials by a single author. Entries in the card catalog are alphabetized according to their headings. See also *Subject Headings*.

Historical Bibliography: This branch of analytical bibliography largely focuses on the origin of the book, first printings, printers of the exemplary works, and the historical background of literary works.

Hits see *Postings*

Host Computer: Online vendor's computer to which terminals are connected through the communications network.

Identifiers: Keywords added to a bibliographic citation to improve its retrievability. Identifiers differ from *descriptors* in that they are terms usually drawn from the original text and do not conform to a standard or controlled vocabulary list. In many databases identifiers are used to highlight either new concepts for which no commonly agreed upon subject terms exist or specific names (e.g., of tests) for which a general subject term has been deemed inappropriate.

Illustration: A pictorial or other representation in or belonging to a book or other publication, as issued; usually designed to elucidate the text.

Imprint: The name of a publisher, usually with the place and date of issue, generally placed at the bottom of the title page; occasionally, the name of the publisher's subsidiary or division under which a book is issued.

Incunabula: Books printed before 1501, or roughly, during the first fifty years following the invention of printing and publication of the Gutenberg Bible, in 1455. The word means cradle or swaddling clothes, indicating works produced during the infancy period of printing with moveable type.

Index: A table or list, usually alphabetical, of topics, names, etc. in a book, giving the number of the page or pages where each subject is treated, commonly placed at the end of the work; also a list of periodicals or books, or a guide to them.

Interactive System: An online system which allows the user to input instructions, receive a response, and then modify or manipulate the retrieved results. All online database systems currently are considered to be interactive systems. They are also referred to as conversational systems.

Intermediary: A specialist who performs searches on behalf of the actual user (often called the end user) of the information thereby retrieved.

Introduction: A preliminary portion of a book leading up to the main subject matter. An *introduction* is usually an attempt to define the organization and limits of a work; a *preface,* by contrast, may explain the author's reason for undertaking the work, his qualifications, his indebtedness to other authorities, etc.

Inverted Index (*Inverted File*): The computer index containing each access point in a machine-readable record on which a search can be made. Inverted indexes are central to online computer systems, allowing them to search vast numbers of terms without having to scan long strings of textual matter.

Issue: A distinct group of copies of an edition. A single part of a volume such as an issue of a journal.

Joint Author: A person who writes a book in collaboration with one or more associates.

Journal: A periodical or a newspaper.

Keyboarding: A process by which information is transcribed into computer-readable form, usually through a typewriter-like console.

Keyword: A significant word that expresses a subject, under which entries for all publications on a subject are filed in a catalog, bibliography, or index.

Leaf: A sheet of paper, usually in a book, having a page on each side.

Literature: A body of writings having to do with a given subject. The record of earlier work in any field is known as its *literature*. Examples would be records of observations and experiments.

Location Symbol: An identifying mark, such as a combination of letters, used in a bibliography, union list, or union catalog to indicate a library of collection where a copy of a given work may be found.

Logical Operators see *Boolean Logic*

Logging Off: The procedure used to end an online search session.

Logging On: The procedure used to begin an online search session.

Machine-Readable: Information recorded in a form which the computer or other electronic device can read and process.

Magazine: A periodical for general reading.

Main Entry: In a card catalog or index, the entry under which full information is given, usually the author entry.

Manual see *Handbook*

Microcomputer: A complete computing system which utilizes a microprocessor as its central processing unit and which also includes memory, circuitry for input and output and other functions, a power supply, and a keyboard or control panel.

Microprocessor: A central processing unit using LSI technology (large-scale integration). Often referred to as a "Computer on a chip."

Modem: A telecommunications device linking computer terminals and computer systems through telephone circuits.

Monograph: A systematic and complete treatise on a particular subject, usually detailed in treatment but not extensive in scope. It need not be bibliographically independent.

National Bibliography: A bibliography that is limited to materials published within a given country.

Non-Bibliographic Database: A collection of data which is numeric, full-text, or directorial in nature rather than bibliographic.

Note: Additional information about a book or its contents on a catalog card; for example, information indicating that a book has a bibliography.

Numeric Database: A database primarily consisting of numbers and other related data of a factual nature.

OCLC see *Online Computer Library Center, Inc.*

Offline: A method of data processing in which all search requirements are processed without interaction between the computer and the user; also referred to as batch mode processing since it is most economical to process large numbers of computer jobs together in this manner.

Online: A method of processing information in which the user is able to interact with the computer during the searching process, that is, while the equipment is on the line to the computer.

Online Computer Library Center, Inc. (OCLC): Formerly known as the Ohio College Library Center established in the mid-1970s, this bibliographic utility provides computer-based services organized by and for libraries whereby members contribute to and modify the resource databases as needed to provide various library and information services.

Online Searching: Searching wherein the search is processed while the user is connected to the computer, thereby allowing the user to interact with the computer and adapt the search according to the computer's responses.

Open Entry: A catalog entry that provides for the addition of information concerning a work of which the library does not have a complete set, or about which complete information is lacking.

Pagination: The numbering of the pages of a book. In electronic composition systems, pagination includes most or all functions of page makeup.

Pamphlet: A nonperiodical publication of at least five but not more than forty-eight pages, exclusive of cover pages. It usually is an independent entity, not being a serial, but it may be one of a series of publications having a similarity of format and subject matter.

Password: A unique identification code, usually a set of letters and numbers, which gives individual users access to the online system and which the online vendors use to charge their users.

Periodical: A publication with a distinctive title intended to appear in successive (usually unbound) numbers or parts at stated or regular intervals and, as a rule, for an indefinite time. Each part generally contains articles by several contributors.

Permuterm Index: A subject index of keywords aligned alphabetically, providing multiple indexing points for significant words in the title.

Postings: This term is used almost interchangeably with *hits* and *items* to mean the group of unique records in a given set of search results.

Preface: A short explanatory note by the author preceding the text of a book and usually touching on the purpose of the book, its sources, extent, etc.

Primary Literature: Manuscripts, records, or documents of original research. Also called source material or original sources.

Printout: A record on paper of the results of a computer's computations and processing.

Proceedings: The published record of a meeting of a society or other organization, frequently accompanied by abstracts or reports of papers presented.

Pseudonym: A name used by an author, which is not his real name. Also called a "pen name" or "nom de plume."

Publisher: Person, firm, or corporate body responsible for the issuing of a book or other printed matter.

Query see *Search*

RLIN see *Research Libraries Information Network*

Random Access: A term used in computer storage systems which means a method of retrieval, used in virtually all online systems, wherein the time required to access a piece of information is independent of its physical location on the storage medium. Previous to random access technology, a database would be searched in a sequential fashion (i.e., each item in a file would have to be examined in order and in turn).

Record: A unit of related information in a database. In a bibliographic database a record generally refers to all of the information stored in one document (e.g., journal article or a book).

Reference: The information (e.g., author, title, journal title, page) which identifies a source document.

Reprint: 1) A new printing of a book. 2) A term used for an edition in cheaper form than the original and often issued by another publisher specializing in such popular editions.

Research Libraries Information Network (*RLIN*): Founded in 1974 by the Research Libraries Group (RLG), this major bibliographic utility, like OCLC, provides computer-based services to member libraries.

Response Time: The amount of time it takes the computer to respond to the user's query.

Résumé: A summary of the chief points of a work.

Retrospective Search: A search that traces literature of a subject backward in time.

Revised Edition: A book that has been reissued with changes from the original or previous edition.

Scope Note: A brief statement, often added to an index term or subject heading, that clarifies the range of meaning.

Scroll: 1) A roll of papyrus or parchment, and also, later, of paper. 2) A writing formed into a roll, such as the engrossed proceedings of a public body or court.

Search: The act of requesting the computer to respond to a specific information need.

Search Analyst see *Searcher*.

Search Key see *Access Point*

Search Strategy: The method selected in using a retrieval system for a particular search.

Search Term: Subject heading or keyword used to locate material in indexes or the card catalog.

Searcher: The individual who analyzes the reference question, formulates the search strategy, and operates the terminal. This person may or may not be the ultimate user of the search results.

Secondary Literature: Sources that contain worked-over information (textbooks, encyclopedias, reviews, indexes, abstracts) and can help lead to primary (original) literature.

"See Also" Reference: A direction in a catalog from a term or name under which entries are listed to another term or name under which additional or allied information may be found.

"See" Reference: A direction in a catalog from a term or name under which no entries are listed to a term or name under which entries are listed.

Selective, or Elective, Bibliography: Examples are special reading lists issued by a library and books devoted to the "best" works for adults, children, students, businesspeople, and others.

Serial: A publication issued in successive parts, usually at regular intervals and generally intended to be continued indefinitely (serials include magazines, periodicals, annuals, proceedings, transactions, etc.).

Series: Separate and successive publications on a given subject, having a collective series title and uniform format, and usually all issued by the same publisher.

Series Statement: The name of a series to which a book belongs, enclosed in parentheses on the catalog card.

Set: The group of records which is retrieved at any one step in the search process. (See also: *Postings*)

Software: The set of programs, procedures, and languages used in a computer system. The term often connotes the availability of the programs for purchase or lease.

Source Documents: The journal articles, monographs, or other original or "primary" material which is indexed by or accessed through the database.

Style Manual: A manual that ensures consistency in spelling, capitalization, punctuation, abbreviations, footnoting, and bibliographic form.

Subheading: A secondary heading or title, usually set in less prominent type than a main heading, to divide the entries under a subject.

Subject Bibliography: A bibliography that is restricted to one subject or to one subject field.

Subject Catalog: A card catalog in which entries are arranged alphabetically according to assigned subject headings.

Subject Heading: A word, or group of words, under which all materials dealing with a given subject is entered in an index, catalog, or bibliography.

Subtitle: An additional, or second, title to a book.

Systematic Bibliography see *Enumerative Bibliography*.

Table of Contents: A list of preliminary sections, chapter titles, and other parts of a book, or of articles in a periodical, with references to pages on which they begin. Also called contents.

Terminal: The data communications device which enters data into and receives data from the computer.

Tertiary Literature: Provides access to secondary and primary literature.

Text: The main matter, as distinguished from the display matter, front matter, notes, appendix, and index.

Textual Bibliography: This is the application of the principles of analytical bibliography to the correction and interpretation of a text. It is much the same as textual criticism and is most often applied in editing literary works.

Thesaurus: A list of controlled vocabulary terms, usually cross-referenced and often showing relationships among terms.

Thesis: A substantial paper (usually based on original research) presented by a candidate in partial fulfillment of the requirements for an academic degree or diploma.

Title Entry: A catalog or index filed under the title of a work.

Title Page: A page at the beginning of a book, usually on the right, giving its title, its author (if acknowledged), and usually its publisher, with place and date of publication.

Tracing: In a card catalog, the record on the main entry card of all the additional headings under which the work is represented in the catalog. Also, the record on a main entry card or on an authority card of all the related references made. The tracing may be on the face or on the back of the card, or on an accompanying card.

Trade Bibliography: This term is often used as a synonym for "national bibliography." It refers to a bibliography issued for, and usually by, the booksellers and publishers of a particular nation.

Transactions: Published papers and abstracts of papers presented at a meeting of a learned society. The distinction between transactions and proceedings is that generally transactions are the papers of a meeting and proceedings are the deliberations and results of the meeting.

Truncation: The shortening of a word being searched for rather than using the whole word. For example, it may be beneficial to truncate the word "microcomputer" into "microcomput" in order to retrieve items with the terms "microcomputers" and "microcomputing" as well as the original term.

Union List: A complete record of the holdings for a group of libraries of material of a given type, in a certain field, or on a subject, sometimes known as a Union Finding List.

Unit Record see *Record*.

Update: The material most recently added to a database. Also the process of adding material to a database: e.g., the database is updated monthly.

Uploading: The process of transmitting a file stored locally (usually on a microcomputer) to a remote computer (usually a large mainframe). In the context of information storage and retrieval, this usually means a private database is created on an in-house computer and then is transmitted via telecommunications to an online vendor (*uploaded*) for storage and future retrieval.

Western Libraries Network (*WLN*): Formerly known as the Washington Library Network this bibliographic utility provides services on a regional basis. There are a number of these networks in the United States.

Yearbook: 1) An annual volume of current information in descriptive and/or statistical form, sometimes limited to a special field. 2) One of a series of annual reports of cases judged in Early law courts.

Appendix E

MAJOR BIBLIOGRAPHIC ORGANIZATIONS

Most bibliographic organizations are groups of professional scholars and others engaged in gathering information about literary works. Some specialize in promoting literary criticism, the art of bookmaking, or book collecting. Many promote historical research on books and publish studies containing the results of such research. Below is a selected list of major organizations.

American Antiquarian Society, 185 Salisbury Street, Worcester, MA 01609
Founded in 1812 this organization attempts to gather, present, and promote serious study of the materials of early American history and life. As part of its publishing program, The Society issues bibliographic works of great value relating to early American publishing and its impact on American Civilization. The Society's *Proceedings* are published semiannually

American Society of Indexers, 235 Park Avenue, South, 8th Floor, New York, NY 10003
Founded in 1968 this organization seeks to improve the quality of indexing and secure useful standards for the field.

Association for the Bibliography of History, c/o G. H. Davis, Department of History, Georgia State University, Atlanta, GA 30303-3083
Founded in 1978 this organization is composed of historians, bibliographers, librarians, and others promoting the development of bibliographical skills and tools to facilitate the study of history. It publishes a newsletter.

Bibliographical Society, British Library, Humanities and Social Sciences Division, Great Russell Street, London WC1B 3DG, ENGLAND
Founded in 1892 this prestigious bibliographic society seeks to further bibliographical research and publishing. It publishes a well known periodical *The Library*.

Bibliographical Society of America, P.O. Box 397, Grand Central Station, New York, NY 10163
The oldest American bibliographic group founded in 1904 includes scholars, collectors, librarians, rare book dealers, and others interested in books and bibliographies. It encourages bibliographical research and issues bibliographical publications including its quarterly *Papers*.

Bibliographical Society of Australia and New Zealand, c/o Rose Smith, 76 Warners Avenue, Bondi Beach, NSW 2026, AUSTRALIA
Founded in 1969 to promote research in bibliography. Publishes a quarterly *Bulletin* and occasional bibliographic works.

Bibliographical Society of Canada, Victoria College, University of Toronto, Toronto, Ontario, M5S 1K7, CANADA
Founded in 1946 to encourage bibliographical studies especially with respect to Canadian literature. Publishes an occasional newsletter and an annual cumulation of *Papers*.

Bibliographical Society of Northern Illinois, c/o Department of English, Northern Illinois University, DeKalb, IL 60115
Founded in 1971 to promote bibliographic projects on literary works. Publishes the quarterly *AEB Analytical & Enumerative Bibliography* (1977–).

Bibliographical Society of the University of Virginia, c/o University of Virginia Library, Charlottesville, VA 22903.
Founded in 1947 it includes amateur and professional persons interested in bibliographical studies. Publishes various works in the field as well as the annual *Studies in Bibliography*.

Cambridge Bibliographical Society, University Library, Cambridge, CB3 9DR, ENGLAND
Founded in 1949 to promote historical bibliography and the history of the book trade. Publishes occasional monographs and annual *Transactions*.

Edinburgh Bibliographical Society, c/o National Library of Scotland, George IV Bridge, Edinburgh, EH1 1EW, SCOTLAND

The Grolier Club, 47 East 60th Street, New York, NY 10022
Founded in 1884 to promote the study of literature, book collecting, and the study of the art of bookmaking. Publishes various catalogs and scholarly studies.

Institute for Bibliography & Editing, Kent State University, Kent, OH 44242
Founded in 1966 to promote "bibliographical and textual studies of English and American literature, including edition and publication, computer collation, and text processing of major works of William Shakespeare, Charles Brockden Brown, Robert Browning, and Joseph Conrad. Provides space, a Hinman collator, and a Lindstrand comparator to anyone qualified to do bibliographical and textual work."

Inter-American Bibliographical and Library Association, P.O. Box 600583, North Miami Beach, FL 33160
Founded in 1930 to promote bibliographical activities related to Latin American publications. Published the quarterly *Doors to Latin America*.

International Federation for Documentation (FID), Prins Willem-Alexanderhof 5, Postbus 90402, NL-2509 LK The Hague, NETHERLANDS
Founded in 1895 "to promote the study, organization, and practice of documentation

and to coordinate efforts of organizations and individuals interested in the problems of documentation. Issues a variety of publications including a newsletter.

Oxford Bibliographical Society, Bodleian Library, Oxford, OX1 3BG, ENGLAND
Founded in 1923 to encourage bibliographical research. Issues a variety of publications including *Proceedings and Papers*.

Society for Textual Scholarship, c/o David C. Greetham, Graduate Center, 33 West 42nd Street, New York, NY 10036
Founded in 1980 for scholars interested in interdisciplinary discussion of textual theory and practice, and literary documentary editors. Issues an annual publication entitled *Text*.

ANNOTATED BIBLIOGRAPHY

The entries in the annotated bibliography below are selected major writings associated with the study of bibliography. They are arranged alphabetically by author or title if no author is given. The annotations vary in length and style to illustrate representative types. Indicated at the end of each entry are the chapters to which they apply.

1. Aboyade, Bimpe. "The Librarian as Bibliographer," *UNESCO Bulletin for Libraries*, 25 (November/December 1971), pp. 344–347.

The author indicates that the librarian's role should be more than that of the enumerative bibliographer who produces and knows how to use finding lists. He also covers other aspects of bibliographical scholarship that are usually left to experts in other disciplines. Aboyade then attempts to define the needs of such scholars and how librarians might help them to make full use of their collections and possibly participate in some of these bibliographical activities. [Chapter One]

2. Alberico, Ralph. "Front End Games," *Small Computers In Libraries*, 6 (February 1986), pp. 10–15.

Front end or search assistance software systems are reviewed and evaluated. [Chapter Eight]

3. ________. "Justifying CD-ROM," *Small Computers in Libraries*, 7 (February 1987), pp. 18–20.

The author concludes that optical media will eventually become the primary means by which persons are provided direct access to large machine-readable stores of information. [Chapter Eight]

4. Amory, Hugh. "Physical Bibliography, Cultural History, and the Disappearance of the Book," *Papers of the Bibliographical Society of America*, 78 (September 1984), pp. 341–347.

A review essay covering the proceedings of a conference dealing with physical bibliography and the history of the book. Discusses various aspects of analytical bibliography. [Chapters Three and Five]

5. Anderson, Glenn A. "The Emergence of the Book," *College and Research Libraries*, 49 (March 1988), pp. 111–116.

A survey and comparison of the roll to the codex as the earliest forms of the book based on archaeological discoveries. [Chapter Three]

6. Arlt, Gustive O. "Bibliography—An Essential Piece of Equipment," *Library Journal*, 86 (April 16, 1961), pp. 1539–1541.
Arlt regards bibliography as an important aspect of research and scholarly communication. [Chapter One]

7. Arnold, Stephen E. "End-Users: Dreams or Dollars," *Online*, 11 (January 1987), pp. 71–81.
Examines the role of end users and new intermediaries in the use of online services and concludes that it will be some time before they become fully comfortable in using online services in their normal work activities. [Chapter Eight]

8. Atkinson, Ross. "An Application of Semiotics to the Definition of Bibliography," *Studies in Bibliography*, 33 (1980), pp. 54–73.
Semiotics basically refers to the science of signs. Atkinson applies semiotics to the definitions of bibliography. [Chapter One]

9. Barnes, Warner. "Training for Rare Book Librarians." In: *AB Bookman's Yearbook*. Clifton, NJ: Bookman's Weekly, 1980, pp. 57–63.
Summarizes the problem of attracting people to the field and details what is needed to find qualified persons and train them. [Chapter Nine]

10. Bates, Marcia J. "Rigorous Systematic Bibliography," *RQ*, 16 (Fall 1976), pp. 7–26.
Drawing heavily upon the work of Patrick Wilson, Bates sets out to provide a theoretical foundation and framework for the enumerative branch of the discipline, which she claims is just as technical, complex, and important as the analytical branch. This study makes an important contribution to the understanding of enumerative bibliography and how bibliographies should be compiled. [Chapters One, Four, and Six]

11. Bay, Jens Christian. "Conrad Gesner (1516–1565) the Father of Bibliography: An Appreciation," *Papers of the Bibliographical Society of America* (Chicago), 10 (April 1916), pp. 53–86.
Gesner's life and works are examined against the backdrop of a developing discipline yet in its infancy. His contribution was truly instrumental in making an accurate record of graphic materials during his lifetime. [Chapter One]

12. Beard, Jonathan. "How Medieval Printers Put Bibles Together," *New Scientist*, 114 (April 16, 1987), p. 15.
Modern chemical analysis of Gutenberg's printing ink makes it possible to determine how his masterpiece was created. [Chapter Three]

13. Belanger, Terry. "Descriptive Bibliography." In: *Book Collecting, A Modern Guide*. Edited by Jean Peters. New York: Bowker, 1977, pp. 97–115.
A brief but effective discussion of the functions and applications of descriptive bibliography especially related to book collecting. Also Belanger provides a very good overview of analytical bibliography. [Chapter Five]

14. Bell, Barbara L. *An Annotated Guide to Current National Bibliographies*. Alexandria, VA: Chadwyck-Healey, 1986. 407p.

Arranged in two basic divisions, the first includes regional bibliographies and the second an alphabetical listing by country. There is an extensive bibliography of source materials but sadly no index. This is the most extensive current listing available, which makes it extremely valuable. [Chapter Four]

15. Besterman, Theodore. *The Beginnings of Systematic Bibliography*. 2nd ed. New York: Burt Franklin, 1968, ©1936. 81p.

Provides an authoritative historical account of bibliographic beginnings up through the seventeenth century. Starting with Galen in the second century A.D., Besterman shows the gradual development of book lists in terms of successive classifications, which he supports with notable examples. He lists and tabulates the earliest printed bibliographies to demonstrate the intellectual interest of the fifteenth and sixteenth centuries. He covers the activities and accomplishments of Tritheim, the earliest medical and legal bibliographers, Gesner, Bale, and others. [Chapters One and Two]

16. *The Bibliographical Society of America, 1904–79: A Retrospective Collection*. Charlottesville, VA: Published for the Bibliographical Society of America by the University Press of Virginia, 1980. 557p.

A collection of thirty-nine essays that are excellent in themselves and influential in the development of the bibliographical art. Although the range of subject matter is wide there is a tendency to emphasize analytical bibliography. [Chapter Five]

17. *Bibliographica: Quarterly Review of Bibliographical Studies*. Westport, CT: Greenwood Reprint Corp., 1970. 3v.

A series of "papers on books, their history and art." Originally issued in twelve quarterly numbers from 1895 to 1897. These are scholarly articles on such subjects as illuminated manuscripts, woodcuts, bindings, provincial presses, and the early book trade, all by leading experts of the time. The issues were printed in lavish typography and binding. "This reprint edition reproduces all of the craftsmanship of the original, including 35 full color illustrations." [Chapter Three]

18. *Bibliographical Essays: A Tribute to Wilberforce Eames*. New York: Burt Franklin, 1968, ©1924. 440p. (Reprint)

A collection of scholarly essays in tribute to Eames dealing mostly with American bibliographic subjects such as printing, literary works and the like. [Chapter One]

19. *Bibliography and the Historian*. Edited by Dagmar Horna Perman. Santa Barbara, CA: Clio, 1968. 176p.

Contained in this work are papers based on studies prepared for the Joint Committee on Bibliographical Service to History held in May of 1967. These papers cover new technologies, services and systems up to the date of publication related to the capabilities of the computer in the storage, retrieval, and dissemination of bibliographical information associated with history. [Chapters Five and Eight]

20. Bibliographical Society, London. *The Bibliographical Society, 1892–1942, Studies in Retrospect*. London: The Society, 1949. 215p.

The studies of which this collection is comprised were written to celebrate the fiftieth anniversary of the founding of the Bibliographical Society. Contributors include W. W. Greg, Michael Sadleir, and other well known bibliographers. [Chapter Five]

21. Biggs, John R. *Basic Typography*. London: Faber and Faber, 1973. 176p.
This work is an "attempt to examine some of the fundamentals of typographic design that endure through all the vagaries of fashion in the hope that the student will develop first an analytic approach to design and second create solutions that grow out of the nature of the problem instead of trying to impose a preconceived formula." Biggs covers the basic principles, mechanics, and practice of typographic design. Includes many illustrations. [Chapter Three]

22. Binns, Norman E. *An Introduction to Historical Bibliography*. 2nd ed., rev. and enl. London: Association of Assistant Librarians, 1962. 387p.
A broad basic survey of historical bibliography and its origins. It covers the invention and spread of printing, along with a discussion of the processes used in making books. [Chapter Five]

23. Bloy, Colin H. *A History of Printing Ink, Balls and Rollers, 1440–1850*. London: Wynkyn de Worde Society; New York: Sandstone Press, 1980, ©1967. 147p.
Traces the history of printing inks from the invention of printing to the 19th century. Bloy's study, although not comprehensive, is authoritative and well written. An interesting feature is his inclusion of ink recipes on pages 99–125. [Chapter Three]

24. Blum, Andre. *On the Origin of Paper*. Translated from the French by Harry Miller Lydenberg. New York: Bowker, 1954. 79p.
A short but careful study of paper and its effect on the spread of printing from China through Europe and elsewhere up to the present time. The author also discusses the paper industry, and watermarks as a means of dating paper. [Chapter Three]

25. Blum, Rudolf. *Bibliographia: An Inquiry into its Definition and Designations*. London: Dawson; Chicago: American Library Association, 1980. 251p.
A translation from the German by Mathilde V. Rovelstad of his 1969 work *Bibliografia: eine Wort und begriffsgeschichtliche Untersuchung*. Blum traces the use of the term "Bibliographie" and its vernacular derivations from antiquity, and relates the terminology to changing concepts of bibliography. [Chapters One and Two]

26. Bobinski, George S. "An Analysis of 105 Major U.S. Journals in Library and Information Science." In: *Library Science Annual*. Edited by Bohdan S. Wynar. Littleton, CO: Libraries Unlimited, 1985, pp. 29–41.
Analyses the periodical literature in terms of its indexing (access), distribution, etc. Also discusses the state of the literature. [Chapter Twelve]

27. Boehm, Eric H. "On the Second Knowledge, A Manifesto for the Humanities," *Libri*, 22 (1972), pp. 312–323.
Stresses the need for bibliographic resources in the humanities and for improved access through refined indexing methods. [Chapter One]

28. Boghardt, Martin. *Analytische Druckforschung: Ein methodischer Beitrag au Buchkunde und Textkritik*. Hamburg: Dr. Ernst Hauswedell & Co. Verlag, 1977. 172p.

A study of analytical bibliography, printing history, and textual criticism accompanied by examples from German language sources. [Chapter Five]

29. Bohling, Curt. "Librarian to Bookseller: Reflections on Two Careers," *AB Bookman's Weekly*, 79 (June 22, 1987), pp. 2767–2772.

Bohling recounts the reasons for his changing careers. Some elements of bibliographic practice are discussed. [Chapter Nine]

30. Bond, William H. "Bibliography and Bibliographers," *AB Bookman's Weekly*, 47 (April 26, 1971), pp. 1395–1397.

A direct and concise look at the present state of bibliography by a noted twentieth century bibliographer along with definitions and a defense of the enumerative bibliographer. [Chapters One and Four]

31. Borko, Harold, and Charles L. Bernier. *Indexing Concepts and Methods*. New York: Academic Press, 1978. 261p.

A general treatise on methods and concepts involved in indexing. Basic standards for evaluating indexes can be found in Chapter Fourteen. [Chapter Seven]

32. Bowers, Fredson Thayer. *Bibliography and Textual Criticism*. Oxford, Eng.: Clarendon Press, 1964. 207p.

A discussion of the evidence on which textual bibliography operates, the logical forms of its reasoning, the techniques it uses and the results it can achieve. The style in this work is definitely technical and meant for advanced literary students. [Chapter Five]

33. ________. *Essays in Bibliography, Text and Editing*. Charlottesville, VA: Published for the Bibliographical Society of the University of Virginia by the University Press of Virginia, 1975. 550p.

A collection of twenty six essays by this renowned analytical bibliographer. These essays in bibliography (analytical, descriptive, textual) demonstrate Bowers' perceptiveness in approach and the thoroughness of his method. [Chapter Five]

34. ________. "The Function of Bibliography," *Library Trends*, 7 (April 1959), pp. 497–510.

A general survey of the field (particularly analytical bibliography) that explores its relationship to librarians and other information specialists who serve the public, as well as to textual scholars. [Chapters One and Five]

35. ________. *Principles of Bibliographical Description*. Princeton, NJ: Princeton University Press, 1986, ©1949. 505p.

The most authoritative work on the subject of descriptive bibliography. Bowers makes a complete analysis of the descriptive principles that guide the bibliographer. From these principles he develops methods by which each part of a book is described, according to a standard system that can be widely understood. Each step in the description is explained in detail and illustrated by numerous examples, which cover both the usual and the special problems encountered by the bibliographer. [Chapter Five]

36. Brack, O. M., Jr., and Warner Barnes, eds. *Bibliography and Textual Criticism: English and American Literature, 1700 to the Present*. Chicago: University of Chicago Press, 1969. 345p.

The essays contained in this collection tend to be relatively cohesive and well balanced in their treatment of analytical bibliography and textual criticism of post-Renaissance literature. [Chapter Five]

37. Bradshaw, Henry. *Henry Bradshaw, 1831–1886*. By Roy Stokes. Metuchen, NJ: Scarecrow Press, 1978. 272p. (The Great Bibliographers Series, No. 6)

Bradshaw was Librarian of Cambridge University and contributed widely to the development of bibliographical studies in Great Britain in the 19th century. [Chapters One and Five]

38. Braswell, Laurel Nichols. *Western Manuscripts from Classical Antiquity to the Renaissance: A Handbook*. New York: Garland Publishers, 1981. 382p.

This work is basically an annotated bibliographic guide to manuscript materials from ancient times to the Renaissance. Extensive in its coverage of related works. [Chapter Three]

39. Brenni, Vito J. *Essays on Bibliography*. Metuchen, NJ: Scarecrow Press, 1975. 552p.

Selected to instruct students in the scope and basic nature of bibliography, these fifty essays are arranged under nine broad topics such as bibliographic theory and history, organization and control, analytical and subject bibliography, and the bibliographical functioning of librarianship. The essays are well-selected, representing a wide range of subject matter written by reputable scholars. [Chapter One]

40. Breslauer, Bernard H., and Roland Folter. *Bibliography: Its History and Development*. New York: Grolier Club, 1984. 223p.

Many of the significant works that were instrumental in the historical development of bibliography are included in this well designed catalog. Graduate students—especially library school graduate students—could come to a better understanding of libraries by studying these historical documents. [Chapter Two]

41. Brookes, B. C. "Jesse Shera and the Theory of Bibliography," *Journal of Librarianship*, 5 (October 1973), pp. 233–245, 258.

The author synthesizes Shera's concepts of macrobibliography or social epistemology and their implication for the field. [Chapter One]

42. Brown, James Duff. "Practical Bibliography," *The Library*, 4 (1903), pp. 144–151.

Bibliographers have wasted much time on such ephemeral matters as typography, physical description of books and the like, according to Brown, a preeminent English public librarian. He contends that analytical bibliographers should concentrate on more practical matters such as the compilation of useful bibliographies. [Chapter Six]

43. Brundage, Christina A. "Using Personal Computers to Access Bibliographic Databases." In: *Excellence in Education: A Conference on the Use of Personal Computers in Higher Education: Proceedings*. Northridge, CA: Association of California State University Professors, 1987, pp. A45–A53.

An excellent examination of user friendly online search systems available to users that are nontrained online searchers. [Chapter Eight]

44. Bruntjen, Scott. *Source Documents for American Bibliography: Three "McMurtrie Manuals."* Halifax, N.S.: Dalhousie University, University Libraries-School of Library Service, 1978. 80 leaves.
Presents the bibliographical record of early American printing and an analysis of three Douglas McMurtrie manuals dealing with the same subject. [Chapter Four]

45. Bryer, Jackson R. "From Second-Class Citizenship to Respectability: The Odyssey of An Enumerative Bibliographer," *Literary Research Newsletter*, 3 (Spring 1978), pp. 55–61.
The author's view of enumerative bibliography is a radical departure from that held by most of his colleagues who teach English or literature on the college or university level. He is convinced that enumerative bibliography has now become a respectable tool in the hands of the scholar. [Chapter Four]

46. Budd, John. "Publication in Library & Information Science," *Library Journal*, 113 (September 1, 1988), pp. 125–131.
The major focus here is on getting published in the library and information science literature; however, in the process, the quality of the literature is also discussed. [Chapter Twelve]

47. Burdett, Eric. *The Craft of Bookbinding: A Practical Handbook*. Newton Abbott, Eng.: David and Charles, 1975. 400p.
Intended as an introduction to bookbinding for both amateurs and practitioners, this handbook covers current trends and the designs of earlier periods. Burdett demonstrates how to do bookbinding and includes a glossary and list of suppliers which is now dated. [Chapter Three]

48. Butler, Pierce. "Bibliography and Scholarship," *Papers of the Bibliographical Society of America*, 16 (1923), pp. 53–63.
Butler (1886–1953), a well-known library educator and scholar, laments the lack of bibliographic interest of scholars in their work and problems that this presents. He offers some suggestions to help alleviate the situation. The general difficulties outlined in this article, unfortunately are still prevalent in modern scholarship. [Chapter One]

49. Cameron, Shelia H. M. "Compiling a National Bibliography," *SLA News, Official Journal of the Scottish Library Association*, No. 156 (March–April 1980), pp. 53–56.
Outlines the process involved in compiling the national bibliography of Scotland. This article is a good general statement of the problems encountered in compiling a national bibliography. [Chapter Four]

50. Cave, Roderick. "Historical Bibliographical Work: Its Role in Library Education," *Journal of Education for Librarianship*, 21 (Fall 1980), pp. 109–121.
Discusses "the traditional position of 'history of the book' courses in library education, the ambivalent attitudes of the library profession to the subject, and the question of value. Cave argues that a research course is superior to survey courses, and has significant educational value and relevance for third-world countries as well as for post-industrial nations." [Chapter Nine]

51. Chakraborti, Mukunda Lal. *Bibliography in Theory and Practice*. 3rd, rev. and enl. ed. Calcutta: World Press, 1987. 479p.
The author surveys the major branches of the field with emphasis on the Indian perspective. He presents a well-balanced discussion of bibliographic theory and practical application. [Chapter One]

52. Chen, Ching-chih, and Susanna Schweizer. *Online Bibliographic Searching: A Learning Manual*. New York: Neal-Schuman, 1981. 227p.
Designed as a beginners' guide to the skills necessary for the retrieval of information from computerized bibliographic files, with special emphasis on techniques of online interactive searching. [Chapter Eight]

53. Choldin, Mariana Tax. "A Nineteenth Century Russian View of Bibliography," *The Journal of Library History*, 10 (October 1975), pp. 311–322.
Demonstrates an extensive interest by nineteenth century Russian scholars in the subject of bibliography with a review of works and bibliographers. [Chapter Two]

54. Clapp, Clifford Blake. "Analytical Methods in Bibliography Applied to Daniel Webster's Speech at Worcester in 1832." In: *Bibliographical Essays: A Tribute to Wilberforce Eames*. New York: Burt Franklin, 1968, ©1924, pp. 213–220.
An excellent example of the practical application of analytical bibliographical methods to the conduct of research on a printed document's publication history and physical features. [Chapter Five]

55. Clapp, Verner W. "Bibliography," *Encyclopedia Americana*, 3 (1988), pp. 721–724.
An excellent general overview of the field with emphasis on enumerative or systematic bibliography. Clapp presents a clear and relatively neutral consensus definition of the two main branches of the discipline. He also provides illustrative works under each branch and a list of further references. [Chapters One and Four]

56. Cleveland, Donald B. and Ana D. *Introduction to Indexing and Abstracting*. Littleton, CO: Libraries Unlimited, 1983. 209p.
Presents an excellent introductory survey of indexing and abstracting written in an easy-to-understand style. Also provided is a brief discussion of employment opportunities in the field. [Chapter Nine]

57. Cohen, David A. "Understanding On-Line Literature Searching," *Teaching Political Science*, 14 (Winter 1987), pp. 69–73.
A very general survey of online literature searching and its applications to political science. [Chapter Eight]

58. Colainne, A. J. "The Aims and Methods of Annotated Bibliography," *Scholarly Publishing*, 11 (July 1980), pp. 321–331.
A brief but extremely valuable outline of annotation elements and practices in bibliographic preparation. [Chapter Six]

59. Cole, George Watson. "Compiling a Bibliography," *Library Journal*, 26 (November/December 1901), pp. 791–795; 859–863.

A discussion of both theoretical and practical issues involved in compiling a bibliography. [Chapter Six]

60. Collison, Robert L. *Bibliographies, Subject and National: A Guide to their Contents, Arrangement and Use*. 3rd ed. New York: Hafner, 1968. 203p.
A concise but thorough survey of the world's major bibliographies and catalogs supported with historical and critical notes. Now dated but still useful. [Chapter Four]

61. *Conceptual Frameworks for Bibliographic Education: Theory into Practice*. Edited by Mary Reichel and May Ann Ramey. Littleton, CO: Libraries Unlimited, 1987. 212p.
Essays in this volume relate to bibliographic instruction in the university library environment. Several deal with the use of bibliographies in specific subject areas. [Chapter Nine]

62. Condit, Lester. "Bibliography in Its Prenatal Existence," *Library Quarterly*, 7 (October 1937), pp. 564–576.
A survey of the beginnings of bibliography from the early library catalogs up to the sixteenth century. Condit discusses the contributions of various bibliographers and traces the development of the early union catalogs. [Chapter Two]

63. Conner, Martha. *Practical Bibliography Making with Problems and Examples*. Revised by Marion V. Higgins. New York: H. W. Wilson, 1938. 31p.
A practical manual designed primarily for students compiling bibliographies for various literary projects. [Chapter Six]

64. Coughlin, Ellen K. "Cameras, Computers Help to Decipher Ancient Texts," *The Chronicle of Higher Education*, 34 (November 11, 1987), pp. A6–A9.
Details the use of ultraviolet photography and computers to identify and decipher ancient biblical texts. [Chapter Five]

65. "Criteria for Evaluating a Bibliography," *RQ*, 11 (Summer 1972), pp. 359–360.
Perhaps the most authoritative statement of evaluating criteria available on outline form. These criteria were developed by the American Library Association's Bibliography Committee of the Reference Services Division Board. [Chapter Seven]

66. Croghan, Antony. *A Bibliographic System for Non-Book Media: A Description and List of Works*. 2nd ed. London: Coburgh Publications, 1979. 162p.
Describes the basic nature and uses of nonprint materials with pertinent examples and an extensive list of references. [Chapter Three]

67. Crossman, E. J., and Cheryl D. Goodchild. "A Way to Ease Preparation of Checklists and Bibliographies," *Scholarly Publishing*, 4 (April 1973), pp. 245–249.
Using tabbed strips, the authors describe an easy method for compilers of bibliographies in scholarly writing. [Chapter Six]

68. D'Aniello, Charles. "Bibliography and the Beginning Bibliographer," *Collection Building*, 6 (Summer 1984), pp. 11–19.
The activities of an academic librarian-bibliographer are defined and explained in terms of

collection development. This is an excellent survey article covering a wide spectrum of literature. [Chapter One]

69. Dafoe, Elizabeth. "Future of Bibliography and Documentation," *Canadian Library Association, Occasional Papers*, No. 7 (October 1955), pp. 1–6.
Discusses the main issues involved in bibliographic control and the need for more rigorous methods to meet changing demands for information. [Chapter Four]

70. Darley, Lionel S. *Introduction to Bookbinding*. London: Faber and Faber, 1978, ©1965. 118p.
Designed as a practical guide for the beginning bookbinder with illustrations and some plates. Emphasizes mostly the elementary aspects of the art. Includes a glossary, short bibliography, and index. [Chapter Three]

71. Davinson, Donald Edward. *Bibliographic Control*. 2nd ed. London: Bingley, 1981. 164p.
Discusses four approaches to universal bibliographic control: national library catalogs, national bibliographies, subject bibliographies, and special bibliographies. The problems inherent in the bibliographic control of various types of materials are explained in separate chapters: government publications, periodicals, theses, conference proceedings, nonprint media, etc. [Chapter Four]

72. Demas, Samuel. "Comparing BIG Bibliographies on CD ROM," *American Libraries*, 18 (May 1987), pp. 332–335.
The author, an expert in the field, evaluates two trade booklists on compact disc (BIP and AnyBook), and compares them with their print and fiche predecessors. [Chapter Eight]

73. Deuel, Leo. *Testaments of Time: The Search for Lost Manuscripts and Records*. New York: Knopf, 1965. 590p.
A description of the work being done to retrieve and restore ancient texts. This study is well written and thoroughly documented. [Chapter Three]

74. Devereux, E. J. "Analytical Bibliography and Literature: Printing and Textual Studies." In: *Annual Report of the American Rare, Antiquarian and Out-of-Print Book Trade, 1978/1979*. Edited by Denis Carbonneau. New York: BCAR Publications, 1979, pp. 189–191.
Surveys the role of printing and textual studies in the development of analytical bibliography. [Chapter Five]

75. Dewey, Barbara J. *Library Jobs: How to Fill Them, How to Find Them*. Phoenix, AZ: Oryx Press, 1987. 171p.
Examines knowledge, skills, and abilities needed for particular positions in a library. Also covered is the marketplace for librarian bibliographers and educational backgrounds needed by potential applicants. [Chapter Nine]

76. Dibdin, Thomas Frognall. *Thomas Frognall Dibdin: Selections*. Compiled by Victor E. Neuburg. Metuchen, NJ: Scarecrow Press, 1978. 245p. (The Great Bibliographers Series, No. 3)

Presents a general characterization of Dibdin's writings on bibliography, chronicles the major events of his life, and describes the state of bibliography and book collecting in England in his day. Also included are selections from Dibdin's writings. [Chapters One and Five]

77. Diehl, Edith. *Bookbinding: Its Background and Technique*. New York: Rinehart, 1946. 2 vols.

This is perhaps the most extensive and detailed history written on the subject. Volume One deals with primitive records and ancient book fairs; the book in the Middle Ages, Renaissance, and modern times; bookbinding styles; national styles of book decoration; and miscellaneous subjects. Volume Two examines bookbinding methods and techniques. Included are many illustrations and an extensive bibliography. [Chapter Three]

78. Diringer, David. *The Book Before Printing, Ancient, Medieval and Oriental*. New York: Dover, 1982, ©1953. 603p.

This work is a detailed history of early books and bookmaking materials enhanced with abundant illustrations. [Chapter Three]

69. Downs, Robert Bingham. "Problems of Bibliographical Control," *Library Trends*, 2 (April 1954), pp. 498–508.

A general discussion of the problems involved in the quest for complete bibliographical control. Downs emphasizes specific types of difficulties that seem to be unsolvable. [Chapter Four]

80. ________, and Frances B. Jenkins, eds. *Bibliography: Current State and Future Trends*. Urbana, IL: University of Illinois Press, 1967. 611p.

Contains thirty-seven articles by specialists who review in some detail the current status and future trends of bibliography, both in general and with respect to specific subject fields. The reader will find these subject bibliographic articles especially informative although now a little dated. [Chapter One]

81. Dunkin, Paul Shaner. *Bibliography, Tiger or Fat Cat?* Hamden, CT: Archon, 1975. 120p.

Contains the reflections and comments of this well-known librarian and classicist, who discusses for many areas of bibliography what has been done, how well it has been done, and whether it is useful or not. He draws upon the arguments and principles advanced by others, but he does not always agree with them. In an engagingly idiosyncratic style, Dunkin wends his way through the definitions of many terms particularly related to analytical bibliography. He will probably raise eyebrows many times as he entertains the reader. [Chapter Five]

82. ________. *How to Catalog a Rare Book*. 2nd ed. Revised. Chicago: American Library Association, 1973. 105p.

Written in a clear and refreshingly jargon-free style, this practical guide enables any cataloger to catalog rare books, using many of the conventions of descriptive bibliography. Dunkin tells how to examine a rare book in order to answer three key questions: Is it what it appears to be? What features are significant? Is it complete? The answers to these questions reveal how the copy in hand differs from other editions or printing of the same title. [Chapter Five]

83. Ebert, Frederick Adolf. *A General Bibliographical Dictionary*. From the German of Frederick Adolphus Ebert. Oxford: Oxford University Press, 1837; Detroit, MI: Gale, 1968.

A translation of *Allgemeines bibliographisches Lexikon*. Avowedly based on Jacques Charles Brunet's *Manual du libraire et de l'amateur de livres* (1810), Ebert's compilation was intended—unlike Brunet's—to assist both the bookseller and collector and the literary scholar. It is primarily an extensive bibliography with entries arranged in a single long author alphabet. Its chief value lies in the learned annotations provided by Ebert. [Chapter Four]

84. *Education for Professional Librarians*. Edited by Herbert S. White. White Plains, NY: Knowledge Industry Publications, 1986. 287p.

A useful collection of essays concerning current trends in professional education for librarian bibliographers. [Chapter Nine]

85. *Education of Library and Information Professionals: Present and Future Prospects*. Edited by Richard K. Gardner. Littleton, CO: Libraries Unlimited, Inc., 1987. 154p.

This collection of essays is dedicated to Martha Boaz, dean of the library school at the University of Southern California for many years. Some of these essays deal with the education of librarian bibliographers. [Chapter Nine]

86. Edwards, A. S. G. "Some Problems in Modern Enumerative Bibliography," *Text: Transactions of the Society for Textual Scholarship*, 1 (1981), pp. 327–336.

The author discusses the problems of location, identification, and recording of the significant forms of a writer's works in enumerative bibliography. [Chapter Four]

87. Eisenstein, Elizabeth L. *The Printing Revolution in Early Modern Europe*. Cambridge, Eng.: Cambridge University Press, 1983. 297p.

Essentially a general history of printing in Europe in two parts. The first focuses on the shift from script to print in Western Europe and the second deals with the transition from medieval to early modern times. [Chapter Three]

88. Esdaile, Arundell James Kennedy. *Esdaile's Manual of Bibliography*. 5th ed. Revised by Roy Stokes. Metuchen, NJ: Scarecrow Press, 1981. 397p.

Since 1931 this work has been considered by many as the best general treatment of the subject. It provides an overview of the history of book production and of the access to early books through bibliographies. Notes are updated and there are discussions of various aspects of the field. [Chapter One]

89. Evans, Martha M. "Bibliographic Control of Large Quantities of Research Material," *RQ*, 22 (Summer 1983), pp. 393–399.

Describes bibliographic methods for achieving high standards of quality while maintaining maximum efficiency in each step of bibliographic compilation. [Chapter Four]

90. Fayen, Emily Gallup. "Beyond Technology: Rethinking 'Librarian,' *American Libraries*, 17 (April 1986), pp. 240–242.

In discussing libraries of the future, Fayen assesses the bibliographic implications of CD-ROMs and online systems. [Chapter Eight]

91. Feather, John. "The Book in History and the History of the Book," *Information Reports and Bibliographies*, 16, No. 4 (1987), pp. 2–7.

A summary of the history of the book emphasizing its historical importance and social impact. [Chapter Three]

92. Fenichel, Carol H., and Thomas H. Hogan. *Online Searching: A Primer*. 2nd ed. Medford, NJ: Learned Information, 1984. 188p.

Intended as a basic introduction to all facets of online searching. Provides many examples and illustrations. [Chapter Eight]

93. Foskett, D. J. *Notes on Compiling Bibliographies for the Guidance of Students Preparing Reports and Theses in the Field of Education*. 2nd ed. London: University of London, Institute of Education, 1967. 22p.

Provides guidelines for preparing bibliographies in a specialized field. [Chapter Six]

94. Fothergill, Richard and Ian Butchart. *Non-Book Materials in Libraries: A Practical Guide*. London: Bingley; Hamden, CT: Linnet Books, 1978. 256p.

A general guide to the nature and uses of nonprint materials. It is also useful as a handbook for librarians dealing with the bibliographical aspects of nonprint materials. [Chapter Five]

95. Foxon, David F. *Thoughts on the History and Future of Bibliographical Description*. Los Angeles, CA: School of Library Service, University of California at Los Angeles; Berkeley, CA: School of Librarianship, University of California, 1970. 31p.

Foxon provides some interesting insights as he surveys the context of descriptive bibliography and its prospects for the future. [Chapter Five]

96. Francis, Sir Frank C. "Bibliography," *The New Encyclopaedia Britannica, Macropaedia*, 2 (1983), pp. 978–981.

A general survey article emphasizing critical or analytical bibliography but containing some suggestions for compilers. [Chapters One, Five, and Six]

97. Freer, Percy. *Bibliography and Modern Book Production*. Johannesburg: Witwatersrand University Press, 1954. 345p.

Written as an introductory guide for students to the literature of bibliography including essential bibliographies. Now somewhat dated it is still valuable especially for the enumeration of definitions contained in Chapter I. [Chapter One]

98. Friend, Linda. "Independence at the Terminal: Training End Users to do Online Literature Searching," *Journal of Academic Librarianship*, 11 (July 1985), pp. 136–141.

A discussion of BRS/After Dark and DIALOG's Knowledge Index as end user systems and training in using them. [Chapter Eight]

99. Fulton, John Farquhar. *The Great Medical Bibliographers: A Study in Humanism*. Philadelphia: University of Pennsylvania Press, 1951. 107p.

This work is a brief but excellent biographical survey of early bibliographers and their contribution to the development not only of medical bibliography but bibliography in general. [Chapter One]

100. Gallup, Donald. *On Contemporary Bibliography, with Particular Reference to Ezra Pound*. Austin, TX: Humanities Research Center, The University of Texas at Austin, 1970. 28p. (Bibliographical Monograph Series, No. 4)
Using Ezra Pound as an example, Gallup examines the tasks of bibliographers and the problems they encounter. [Chapter One]

101. Gaselee, Sir Stephen. "The Aims of Bibliography," *Transactions of the Bibliographical Society* (London), (1932–1933), pp. 225–258.
Outlines the history of enumerative bibliography and discusses the role of bibliographers in the bibliographic process. [Chapters One and Four]

102. Gaskell, Philip. *A New Introduction to Bibliography*. Reprinted with corrections. Oxford, Eng.: Clarendon Press, 1974. 438p.
Designed as a successor to McKerrow (item 175). This study covers the transmission of texts by explaining the process of book production, beginning with the hand-press period of 1500–1800. It is a new book, not a revision of McKerrow, incorporating the results of wide ranging bibliographical research over the past forty years. For example, an account of the printing practices and textual problems of the nineteenth century is presented. [Chapter Five]

103. Gilreath, Charles L. *Computerized Literature Searching: Research Strategies and Databases*. Boulder, CO: Westview Press, 1984. 177p.
The opening chapters provide the basics of computer literature search systems and how to set up primary search strategies. These are followed by an annotated classified list of databases. [Chapter Eight]

104. Gore, Daniel. *Bibliography for Beginners*. 2nd ed. New York: Appleton-Century-Crofts, 1973. 248p.
The second chapter gives a brief outline of descriptive bibliographic principles. Generally designed as an introduction to reference materials, this work is a good basic overview. [Chapter Five]

105. Gorman, Gary E., and J. J. Mills. *Guide to Current National Bibliographies in the Third World*. 2nd rev. ed. London: Zell, 1987. 372p.
Provides an extensive annotated list of third world national bibliographies. [Chapter Four]

106. Gratch, Bonnie. "Toward a Methodology for Evaluating Research Paper Bibliographies," *Research Strategies*, 3 (Fall 1985), pp. 170–177.
Using the examples of four research studies which evaluated student bibliographies, this article identifies and discusses the specific criteria and processes employed. Also developed is a set of criteria and procedures for rating the bibliographies. [Chapter Seven]

107. Gration, Selby, and Arthur P. Young. "Reference Bibliographies in the College Library," *College and Research Libraries*, 35 (January 1974), pp. 28–34.
The authors define the function of a reference bibliographer as a book selector and a compiler of bibliographies within the college library framework. [Chapter One]

108. Greg, Sir Walter Wilson. "Bibliography—A Retrospect." In: *Bibliographical Society, 1892–1942; Studies in Retrospect*. Cambridge, Eng.: Cambridge University Press, 1945, pp. 23–31.
Traces the history of analytical bibliography and provides insights into the activities of major bibliographers in the process. [Chapter Five]

109. ________. "Bibliography—An Apologia," *The Library*, 4th Ser. 13 (September 1932), pp. 113–143. (Also in his *Collected Papers*, pp. 239–260)
Bibliography, according to Greg, is not merely the enumeration and description of books but also the study of the transmission of literary documents. In defending his views, Greg goes to considerable lengths to produce supporting evidence of his thesis. [Chapter Five]

110. ________. *Collected Papers*. Edited by J. C. Maxwell. Oxford, Eng.: Clarendon Press, 1966. 449p.
Greg was influential in the development of analytical bibliography and this collection of his papers documents his contributions to the field. [Chapters One and Five]

111. ________. "The Present Position of Bibliography," *The Library*, 4th Ser., 11 (December 1930), pp. 241–262.
From the perspective of the early 1930s, Greg provides a status report indicating, among other things, that bibliography has come to be recognized as something important to literary scholarship. [Chapter Five]

112. ________. "What Is Bibliography?" *Transactions of the Bibliographical Society* (London), 12 (1914), pp. 39–53. (Also in his *Collected Papers*, pp. 75–88)
Greg clarifies his definition of bibliography: the transmission of all symbolic representation of speech or other ordered sound or even logical thought. He proceeds to examine the broad methods bibliographers employ in studying the transmission of texts. [Chapter Five]

113. Grove, Pearce S. *Nonprint Media in Academic Libraries*. Chicago: American Library Association, 1975. 239p.
Presents a general overview of the history and use of nonprint materials and examines their bibliographic organization and standards. [Chapter Three]

114. *Guide for Writing a Bibliographer's Manual*. The Collection Management and Development Committee, Resources and Technical Services Division. Chicago: American Library Association, 1987. 24p.
"This guide is intended to help write a bibliographer's manual that can serve as an informational, administrative, and training document for their library's collection development and management program." [Chapter One]

115. "Guidelines for the Preparation of a Bibliography," *RQ*, 22 (Fall 1982), pp. 31–32.
This is actually a restatement with a different purpose of the criteria for evaluating bibliogra-

phies published in *RQ*, Vol. 11 (Summer 1972), pp. 359–360. These guidelines are a good practical format to follow in compiling any enumerative bibliography. [Chapter Six]

116. Hackman, Martha L. *The Practical Bibliographer*. Englewood Cliffs, NJ: Prentice-Hall, 1970. 118p.

The author provides some excellent in-depth discussions, with illustrations, on most types of enumerative bibliographies. [Chapter Four]

117. Hagler, Ronald, and Peter Simmons. *The Bibliographic Record and Information Technology*. Chicago: American Library Association, 1982. 346p.

This work is a lucid treatment of everything from the purposes and methods of bibliography to the context and format of bibliographic files and the creating of bibliographic records and networks. [Chapter Six]

118. Hale, Barbara M. *The Subject Bibliography of the Social Sciences and Humanities*. Oxford: Pergamon, 1970. 149p.

Hale describes the various types of subject bibliographies that have been developed since the advent of printing. The hope is to control not only the ever-increasing amount of knowledge and information but also the great variety of forms in which it appears. An analysis is made of the types of bibliographic arrangement, with examples of specific tools drawn from the social sciences and humanities. These are related to a survey carried out among the teaching staff of five university departments. [Chapter Four]

119. Harlow, Neal R. "Bibliographers in an Age of Scientists," *Revue de l'Université d'Ottawa*, 23 (January/March 1953), pp. 37–49.

Examines the effects of some of the early electronic devices on the activities of bibliographers. [Chapter One]

120. ________. "The Well-Tempered Bibliographer," *Papers of the Bibliographical Society of America*, 50 (1956), pp. 28–39.

Presents an excellent overview of bibliography as it has developed discipline status over the centuries. Harlow provides some interesting insights into the nature of bibliography along with movements that gave rise to its importance. He does not discuss individual works as much as some other writers have, but this article is valuable for obtaining a concise picture of bibliographical study. [Chapters One and Two]

121. Herron, Nancy L. "The Paperless Society," *Encyclopedia of Library and Information Science*, 41, Supplement 6 (1986), pp. 277–289.

A survey article exploring the famous prediction of F. W. Lancaster and assessing its impact upon the library and information science fields. [Chapter Ten]

122. Hewitt-Bates, James Samuel. *Bookbinding*. 8th ed., rev. Leicester, Eng.: Dryad, 1967. 127p.

An introductory work emphasizing the practical aspects of the art. Also covers the history of bookbinding, includes numerous illustrations and a short bibliography. [Chapter Three]

123. Higgins, Marion Villers. *Bibliography: A Beginner's Guide to the Making, Evaluation and Use of Bibliographies*. New York: H. W. Wilson, 1941. 43p.

Actually, this brief work is an elaboration of an earlier manual by Martha Conner. It is a practical guide to compiling enumerative bibliographies. [Chapter Six]

124. Hinman, Charlton. *The Printing and Proof-Reading of the First Folio of Shakespeare*. Oxford, Eng.: Clarendon Press, 1963. 2v.
This work is a landmark study in the field of analytical bibliography. [Chapter Five]

125. "Hinman Collator," *Bulletin of the New York Public Library*, 75 (January 1971), pp. 5–6.
A brief description of the Hinman Collator and a discussion of its uses in identifying texts. [Chapter Five]

126. Holley, Edward G. "Does Library Education Have a Future?" *American Libraries*, 17 (October 1986), pp. 702–704, 706.
A noted library educator examines new trends in the training of librarians and concludes that it will develop to meet future needs, including bibliographic training. [Chapter Nine]

127. Horne, Herbert Percy. *The Binding of Books, An Essay in the History of Gold-Tooled Bindings*. 2nd ed. London: K. Paul, Trench, Trubner & Co., 1915. 232p.
Up to the time of its publication, this work was the most authoritative and thorough study of the subject. The author believes that bookbinding is a living and growing art, capable of new motives and new forms of expression. [Chapter Three]

128. Horne, Thomas Hartwell. *Introduction to the Study of Bibliography, To which Is Prefixed a Memoir on the Public Libraries of the Ancients*. Dobbs Ferry, NY: Glanville Publishers, 1981, ©1814. 2v.
Also reprinted by Gale in 1967. When originally published, this work was the best available survey of general bibliography, libraries, bookselling, etc. Although outdated and full of misconceptions which over a century and a half of scholarship have corrected, this work still contains some useful information. [Chapter Two]

129. Howard-Hill, Trevor Howard. *British Bibliography and Textual Criticism: A Bibliography*. Oxford: Clarendon Press; New York: Oxford University Press, 1979. 2v.
An extensive bibliography mainly for textual problems in printed books published after 1475. Information contained in these two volumes will be of immeasurable value to textual critics, bibliographers, and bibliophiles. There are some references to standard works on editing with a useful section on bookbinding and another on libraries. [Chapter Five]

130. ———. "Computer and Mechanical Aids to Editing." In: *Proof: The Yearbook of American Bibliographical and Textual Studies*. Edited by Joseph Katz. Columbia, SC: J. Faust & Co., 1977, Vol. 5, pp. 217–235.
Discusses textual editing with attention to specific devices, programs, and literature related thereto. [Chapter Five]

131. ———. "A Practical Scheme for Editing Critical Texts with the Aid of a Computer." In: *Proof: The Yearbook of American Bibliographical and Textual Studies*. Edited by Joseph Katz. Columbia, SC: University of South Carolina Press, 1973, Vol. 3, pp. 335–356.

Discusses the hardware etc. that allows critical editions to be prepared almost completely with the aid of computers. [Chapter Five]

132. Hunter, Dard. *Papermaking: The History and Technique of an Ancient Craft*. 2nd ed., rev. and enl. New York: Knopf, 1947. 611p. (Reprinted, New York: Dover, 1978)
This work is considered by most experts to be the definitive study of its kind. It is a "comprehensive history of papermaking from its invention in other Oriental countries and its introduction into Europe and development there." Hunter also covers the development of papermaking by hand and machine. He provides a chronology of papermaking and its uses along with a map illustrating the spread of the craft. Contains many illustrations, a bibliography, and notes. [Chapter Three]

133. ________. *Papermaking in Pioneer America*. Philadelphia: University of Pennsylvania Press, 1952. 178p.
Covered here is the early development of papermaking in more than eight states. Hunter treats not only the beginnings of papermaking in each of these states but examines equipment and the operation of early paper mills. There are few illustrations and a checklist, alphabetically arranged by papermaker of a particular firm, which serves as an index. [Chapter Three]

134. ________. *Papermaking Through Eighteen Centuries*. New York: William Edwin Rudge, 1930. 358p. (Reprinted, New York: Burt Franklin, 1970)
Covers much the same territory as his more extensive work and emphasizes the early methods of paper fabricating. Contains many illustrations. [Chapter Three]

135. Hutchinson, Geoffrey H. "Developments in the Technology and Applications of Offset Lithographic Printing Inks," *Chemistry and Industry*, No. 22 (November 17, 1986), pp. 764–769.
Covers inks used for offset lithography emphasizing vehicle technology, progress, and prospects. Trends in ink materials are covered along with a comprehensive treatise dealing with inks for all the established presses. [Chapter Three]

136. Johnson, Alfred Forbes. *Type Designs: Their History and Development*. 3rd ed., rev. London: Deutsch, 1966. 184p.
An introductory survey of type design up to the nineteenth century. [Chapter Three]

137. Johnson, Elmer D. *Communication: An Introduction to the History of Writing, Printing, Books and Libraries*. 4th ed. Metuchen, NJ: Scarecrow Press, 1973. 152p.
Provides an excellent historical survey of libraries, books, and printing. This work includes much important background material on the development of bibliographical study. [Chapter Two]

138. Johnson, Pauline. *Creative Bookbinding*. Seattle, WA: University of Washington Press, 1963. 263p.
A discussion of bookbinding "as an educative medium as well as an amateur pursuit." Deals less with the technical aspects of the craft than with its artistic values and possibilities. Contains many illustrations, a list of supply sources, and a bibliography. [Chapter Three]

139. Jones, John Bush, ed. *Readings in Descriptive Bibliography*. Kent, OH: Kent State University Press, 1974. 208p.
An outstanding collection of thirteen essays to update the work of Fredson Bowers. With emphasis on method, except where a particular book or problem is used to demonstrate method, the treatments range from general and introductory to quite detailed and relate to various periods in the history of books. [Chapter Five]

140. Kapr, Albert. *The Art of Lettering: The History, Anatomy, and Aesthetics of the Roman Letter Forms*. Translated from the German by Ida Kimber. München: Saur, 1983. 470p.
Contains a history of writing and printing with an aesthetic investigation of the 26 characters in the Roman alphabet. The concluding chapter is a selection of several hundred of the best typefaces available. [Chapter Three]

141. Katz, William A. *Introduction to Reference Work: Vol. 1. Basic Information Sources*. 5th ed. New York: McGraw-Hill, 1987. 397p.
Includes an excellent discussion of bibliographic types along with examples and functions. [Chapter Four]

142. Keresztesi, Michael. "The Science of Bibliography: Theoretical Implications for Bibliographic Instruction." In: *Theories of Bibliographic Education: Designs for Teaching*. Edited by Cerise Oberman and Katina Strauen. New York: Bowker, 1982, pp. 1–26.
Within the framework of bibliographic instruction, Keresztesi focuses on the cooperation between librarians and scholars in elevating bibliography from its custodial function to that of research, communication, and the dissemination of knowledge. [Chapter Nine]

143. Kingery, Robert E. "Bibliography," *Collier's Encyclopedia*, 4 (1982), pp. 141–142.
Briefly discusses bibliography, its various branches and uses. [Chapter One]

144. Kinney, Mary Ramon. *The Abbreviated Citation: A Bibliographical Problem*. Chicago: American Library Association, 1967. 57p. (ACRL Monographs, No. 28)
Illustrates various problems encountered when citing references for bibliographies. [Chapter Six]

145. ________. *Bibliographical Style Manuals: A Guide to Their Use in Documentation and Research*. Chicago: American Library Association, 1953. 21p. (ACRL Monographs, No. 8)
Now out of date but still useful for its evaluation of basic guides. [Chapter Six]

146. Kohl, David F. and Charles H. Davis. "Ratings of Journals by ARL Library Directors and Deans of Library and Information Science Schools," *College and Research Libraries*, 46 (January 1985), pp. 4–47.
This study covered the prestige factor in a core group of library journals. A rebuttal by William E. McGrath and a response by Kohl and Davis can be found in *College and Research Libraries*, 48 (March 1987), pp. 169–173. [Chapter Twelve]

147. Krummel, Donald William. *Bibliographies: Their Aims and Methods*. London: Mansell, 1984. 192p.

Intended as a practical handbook for compilers of bibliographies, Krummel carefully describes ideal practices and features that characterize the most respected bibliographies. Written in a clear concise style and accompanied by copious references, this work is an essential guide for the aspiring bibliographer. [Chapter Six]

148. ________. "The Dialectics of Enumerative Bibliography: Observations on the Historical Study of the Practices of Citation and Compilation," *Library Quarterly*, 58 (July 1988) pp. 238–257.

Through the study of the history of enumerative bibliography, Krummel analyses the methods and concepts used by bibliographers as they contributed to the development of scholarly inquiry in different historical periods. Discusses the specific uses of bibliographical models. [Chapter Six]

149. ________, and John Bruce Howell. "Bibliographical Standard and Style," *Scholarly Publishing*, 10 (April 1979), pp. 223–240.

A thorough discussion of the problems involved in bibliographic standardization evolving out of the American National Standard for Bibliographical References (1977). [Chapter Six]

150. Kumar, Girja and Krishan Kumar. *Bibliography*. New Delhi: Vikas Publishing House, 1976. 257p.

Provides an overview of bibliography as a field of study. The authors take into consideration contributions made by Western and Indian writers, with special emphasis on describing problems faced by bibliographers in developing countries like India. [Chapter One]

151. Lancaster, F. W. "The Paperless Society Revisited," *American Libraries*, 16 (September 1985), pp. 553–555.

The leading exponent of The Paperless Society, ten years after his famous prophecy, takes stock of changes and concludes that his predicted revolution is proceeding more rapidly than he expected. [Chapter Ten]

152. ________. *Toward Paperless Information Systems*. New York: Academic Press, 1978. 179p.

Lancaster summarizes achievements in the application of computers to information retrieval since 1963, reviews the status of the application of paperless systems within the intelligence community, discusses the reliability of paperless systems for scientific and technical communication, presents a scenario for a possible system of the year 2000, and concludes with the identification of problems that need to be solved before the paperless systems of the future can be fully realized. [Chapter Ten]

153. Landon, Richard G. "Education for Descriptive Bibliography," *Papers of the Bibliographical Society of Canada*, 18 (1979), pp. 27–29.

Landon outlines what he considers is important in training a descriptive bibliographer within the context of Canadian higher education. [Chapter Nine]

154. Lang, Jovian. "Evaluation of Reference Sources Published or to Be Published," *The Reference Librarian*, No. 15 (Fall 1986), pp. 55–64.

Provides a useful list of criteria for evaluating reference sources including bibliographies. [Chapter Seven]

155. Larsen, Knud. *On the Teaching of Bibliography with a Survey of Its Aims and Methods*. Copenhagen: The Royal School of Librarianship, 1961. 27p.
A general survey of bibliography emphasizing its nature and applications within the library environment. There is a particular focus upon bibliographic forms and functions. [Chapter One]

156. Larsen, Wayne A., Alvin C. Rencher, and Tim Layton. "Who Wrote the *Book of Mormon*? An Analysis of Wordprints," *Brigham Young University Studies*, 20 (Spring 1980), pp. 225–251.
An interesting use of wordprints to identify the authors of ancient texts. [Chapter Five]

157. Laurence, Dan H. "A Portrait of the Author as a Bibliographer," *The Book Collector*, 35 (Summer 1986), pp. 165–177.
An eloquent discourse on the value of author bibliographies and the plight of the author-bibliographer by one who has great expertise in this area. [Chapters One and Four]

158. Lawson, Alexander. *Printing Types, An Introduction*. Boston: Beacon, 1972. 120p.
Intended to help beginners become familiar with the wide variety of printer's typefaces. The author outlines how to recognize and identify them, discusses their history, and provides a nomenclature for their classification. [Chapter Three]

159. Levarie, Norma. *The Art and History of Books*. New York: James H. Heineman, 1968. 315p.
A well-written and illustrated history of books from the earliest times to the present. Contains many black and white illustrations, bibliography and, index. [Chapter Three]

160. Lewis, Naphtali. *Papyrus in Classical Antiquity*. Oxford, Eng.: Clarendon Press, 1974. 152p.
A very detailed and sometimes technical study of papyrus and its uses during the period. Lewis discusses not only the uses of papyrus but its manufacture and sale as well, providing an analysis of the papyrus industry. Includes an index of passages cited and subjects. [Chapter Three]

161. Lewis, Roy Harley. *Fine Bookbinding in the Twentieth Century*. New York: Arco Publishers, 1985, ©1984. 151p.
Presents a history of modern bookbinding since the beginning of the current century accompanied by both black and white and some colored illustrations. [Chapter Three]

162. Lieberman, J. Ben. *Type and Typefaces*. 2nd ed. New Rochelle, NY: The Myriade Press, 1978. 142p.
Discussing many varieties of type, this work is directed toward those who know nothing about typefaces or printing in general. It is clearly written, very thorough and includes many illustrations. Useful for those expert in the field as well as for the novice. [Chapter Three]

163. Liebert, Herman W. *Bibliography, Old & New*. Austin, TX: Humanities Research

Center, The University of Texas at Austin, 1974. 25p. (Bibliographical Monograph Series, No. 6)
A brief introspective look into the historical development of bibliography and those bibliographers and their works that have shaped the discipline. [Chapters One and Five]

164. Lopez, Manuel D. "A Guide for Beginning Bibliographers," *Library Resources and Technical Services*, 13 (Fall 1969), pp. 462–470.
Contends that intense subject training, periods of internship, and qualifying examinations, which are required of European librarian-bibliographers, should be adopted in the United States. [Chapters One and Nine]

165. Madan, Falconer. *Books in Manuscript, a Short Introduction*. 2nd ed., rev. New York: Empire State Book Co., 1927. 208p.
Chronicles the history of manuscripts from the earliest times. Includes discussions of manuscript use, treatment, organization, etc. [Chapter Three]

166. ________. "On Method in Bibliography," *Transactions of the Bibliographical Society*, 1 (1893), pp. 91–102.
Discusses the basic weaknesses of bibliographic practice including inaccuracy, lack of enough information for identification, etc. He also describes a method for citation. [Chapter Six]

167. Maddox, Harry Alfred. *Paper: Its History, Sources, and Manufacture*. 6th ed. London: Pitman, 1947. 180p.
A popular treatment of paper and its manufacture. Although it is written for the general reader, it tends to be a little technical. Maddox does provide a brief history of papermaking, its materials and processes. [Chapter Three]

168. Magalhaes, Rodrigo. "The Impact of the Micro-electronics Revolution in Library and Information Work: An Analysis of Future Trends," *UNESCO Journal of Information Science, Librarianship-Archives Administration*, 5 (January–March 1983), pp. 2–11.
Some bibliographic implications of the computer revolution are discussed in this article. [Chapter Six]

169. Malclès, Louise Noëlle. *Bibliography*. Translated by Theodore Christian Hines. Metuchen, NJ: Scarecrow Reprint, 1973, ©1961. 152p.
This work is perhaps the most detailed history of bibliography yet published. It is arranged chronologically. Within each division are included general, summary comments about the contemporary state of the art of bibliography, and separate sections on specialized, universal, national, and other bibliographies of the period. Each division is devoted almost entirely to brief but pertinent remarks upon the character and quality of specific bibliographies and their compilers. The emphasis is on European contributors to the field, although American accomplishments are briefly mentioned. [Chapter Two]

170. Mallaber, Kenneth Aldridge. *A Primer of Bibliography*. London: Association of Assistant Librarians, 1954. 192p.
Intended as an introductory textbook for library school students. The primary focus is on the origin and production of the book and its physical characteristics. [Chapter One]

171. Mangouni, Norman. "An International Style for Bibliographic References," *Scholarly Publishing*, 5 (April 1974), pp. 239–254.

Drawing upon cataloging models, Mangouni offers suggestions for standardization of bibliographic citations. [Chapter Six]

172. McCrank, Lawrence J. "Analytical and Historical Bibliography: A State of the Art Review." In: *Annual Report of the American Rare, Antiquarian and Out-of-Print Book Trade, 1978/1979*. Edited by Denis Carbonneau. New York: BCAR Publications, 1979, pp. 175–185.

With discussions of the nature and functions of analytical bibliography and its branches, McCrank surveys recent developments in the field, including codicology and its relation to analytical bibliography, collation techniques in textual studies, computer applications (such as "wordprints"), conservation techniques, the analysis of book materials, and the development of microform collections. [Chapter Five]

173. McKenzie, Donald F. *Bibliography and the Sociology of Texts*. London: British Library, 1986; Wolfeboro, NH: Longwood, 1987. 70p.

Presented in this work are three lectures delivered by McKenzie as the first in a series concerning bibliographic subjects dedicated to Sir Anthony Panizzi (1797–1879), a famous British librarian and scholar. The lectures contained in this work concentrate on what bibliography is and how it relates to other disciplines. The major subjects treated here include the nature of the book, non-book texts, and the role of bibliography now. Emphasis is on analytical bibliography and its uses. [Chapter Five]

174. ————. "Printers of the Mind: Some Notes on Bibliographical Theories and Printing-House Practices," *Studies in Bibliography*, 22 (1969), pp. 1–75.

A commentary on bibliographical theories and printing-house practices that is a landmark in bibliographical scholarship. On the basis of rigorous examination of the records of two 18th century printing houses, McKenzie proves that many accepted assumptions about the printing of books were rooted in attitudes only valid for our own industrial age. [Chapter Five]

175. McKerrow, Ronald Brunlees. *An Introduction to Bibliography for Literary Students*. Oxford, Eng.: Clarendon Press, 1927. 358p.

One of the classics in the field of analytical bibliography. McKerrow gives a complete view of the process of bookmaking in England up to 1800, focusing on the Shakespearian period. The first part considers book production from the perspective of the producers, the compositor, and the pressman. The second part compares the book as it appeared in print with the original manuscript of the author. [Chapter Five]

176. ————. *Ronald Brunlees McKerrow: A Selection of His Essays*. Compiled by John Phillip Immroth. Metuchen, NJ: Scarecrow Press, 1974. 240p. (The Great Bibliographers Series, no. 1)

Considered by many as the father of twentieth century descriptive bibliography, McKerrow was the author of numerous bibliographical studies, essays on printing, printers, booksellers, and Shakespearian studies. This collection is a clear reflection of the bibliographic contributions of this outstanding bibliographer. [Chapters One and Five]

177. McKitterick, David. "Author Bibliographies," *The Book Collector,* 32 (Winter 1983), pp. 391–393, 395–396, 399–402, 405–406, 409–410.

An extremely valuable survey of what makes author bibliographies important along with the problems involved in the enterprise. [Chapter Three]

178. ———. "The Limits of Library History," *Information Reports and Bibliographies,* 16, No. 4 (1987), pp. 8–13.

McKitterick attempts to emphasize the connection between an understanding of library history and bibliographical investigation by discussing the questions surrounding particular books. [Chapter Five]

179. McMullin, B. J. "Indexing the Periodical Literature of Anglo-American Bibliography," *Studies in Bibliography,* 33 (1980), pp. 1–17.

The author provides a series of linked observations on the indexing of bibliographical periodicals designed to show how much is being indexed and how appropriately the indexing is being accomplished. [Chapter Twelve]

180. McMurtrie, Douglas C. *The Book: The Story of Printing and Bookmaking*. 3rd ed., rev. New York: Oxford University Press, 1943. 676p. (Many reprints)

McMurtrie is acknowledged as perhaps the leading authority on the history of the book. This work, widely used as a text in books and printing courses, is a clear and detailed chronological treatment of the subject. Included are a number of black-and-white illustrations, and each chapter has an extensive bibliography appended. [Chapter Three]

181. ———. *Douglas C. McMurtrie: Bibliographer and Historian of Printing*. Compiled by Scott Bruntjen and Melissa L. Young. Metuchen, NJ: Scarecrow Press, 1979. 206p. (The Great Bibliographers Series, No. 4)

Portrays through selections of his published writings, a cross section of McMurtrie's thought and activity. Included are two biographical sketches along with selections from his writings with an extensive bibliography. [Chapters One and Five]

182. *Medieval Scribes, Manuscripts & Libraries: Essays Presented to N. R. Ker*. Edited by Malcolm Beckwith Parkes and Andrew G. Watson. London: Scolar Press, 1978. 395p.

A collection of essays dealing with Medieval manuscripts and their care in libraries. Each essay is written by a scholar and is well documented. [Chapter Three]

183. Menapace, John. "Some Approaches to Annotation," *Scholarly Publishing,* 1 (January 1970), pp. 194–205.

Examines the problem of annotating bibliographic references in the context of scholarly publishing. Provides numerous examples with a variety of formats. [Chapter Six]

184. Menédez y Pelayo, Marcelino. "Of Bibliographical Matters," *The American Book Collector,* 7 (January 1957), pp. 15–21.

A brief statement of bibliographic usefulness in book collecting and libraries by the late librarian of Spain's Biblioteca Nacional and one of Spain's most outstanding literary critics. [Chapter One]

185. Middleton, John Henry. *Illuminated Manuscripts in Classical and Mediaeval Times, Their Art and Their Technique*. Cambridge, Eng.: Cambridge University Press, 1892. 270p.

Provides an historical overview of the illuminated manuscript from antiquity through the Middle Ages. Well illustrated. [Chapter Three]

186. Moran, James. *Printing Presses: History and Development from the Fifteenth Century to Modern Times*. Berkeley, CA: University of California Press, 1978, ©1973. 263p.

A concise survey of the development of the relief printing press that assesses the social impact of continuous technical breakthroughs in the dissemination of information through the printed word. [Chapter Three]

187. Morrill, J. S. "Microfilm and the Historian," *Microform Review*, 16 (Summer 1987), pp. 204–212.

A discussion of the value of microfilming historical documents which makes them available to textual researchers as well as historians. [Chapter Five]

188. Moxon, Joseph. *Mechanick Exercises on the Whole Art of Printing (1683–4)*. Edited by Herbert Davis and Harry Carter. 2nd ed. New York: Dover Publications, 1978, ©1962. 550p.

Reprinted from the Oxford University Press editions, this early work is a compendium of everything known about printing at the latter part of the 17th century, and the first complete book written about typography (1683–4). Contains full descriptions of methods, tools and equipment. [Chapter Three]

189. Mudge, Isadore Gilbert. *Bibliography*. Chicago: American Library Association, 1915. 25p.

A brief and now dated statement on kinds of bibliographies, and their standard use in libraries. [Chapter One]

190. Muir, Percival Horace. *Book-Collecting: More Letters to Everyman*. London: Cassell, 1949. 156p.

Some discussions of bibliographic descriptions appear in related but unusual places. Muir's chapter on how to use a bibliography contains an interesting overview of descriptive bibliography as applied to book collecting. [Chapter Five]

191. Myerson, Joel. "The Bibliographer and His Public(s)," *Literary Research Newsletter*, 5 (Fall 1980), pp. 163–170.

Bibliographers seem only to talk and compile for themselves, so claims Joel Myerson. He urges bibliographers to realize that they create bibliographies for a wider audience and they should alert them to the many things bibliographies do and what they can provide. These uses include: insight to an author's professional career, how an author is perceived by contemporaries, scholarly research, assistance for booksellers, etc. [Chapter One]

192. Nash, N. Frederick. "Enumerative Bibliography from Gesner to James," *Library History*, 7 (1985), pp. 10–20.

Nash surveys the contributions of bibliographers from around 1545 through 1605. He covers the development of enumerative bibliography emphasizing inclusions and omissions. [Chapter Four]

193. Needham, Chris. "If Bibliography is Out, What is In?" In: *Bibliography and Reading: A Festschrift in Honour of Ronald Staveley*. Edited by Ia McIlwaine, John McIlwaine and Peter G. New. Metuchen, NJ: Scarecrow Press, 1983, pp. 106–117.

Needham explores the reasons for the elimination of the term bibliography from library school curricula and the new directions currently being followed. [Chapter Nine]

194. Needham, Christopher Donald, ed., assisted by Esther Herman. *The Study of Subject Bibliography with Special Reference to the Social Sciences*. College Park, MD: School of Library and Information Services, University of Maryland, 1970. 221p.

This work is an important contribution to the study of subject bibliography. Basically, its importance lies in the scope and direction of the book rather than in the student contributions which tend to be somewhat uneven. As a whole, however, this approach to teaching bibliography is an excellent illustration of applications and outcomes. [Chapter Four]

195. Needham, Paul. *Twelve Centuries of Bookbindings, 400–1600*. New York: Pierpont Morgan Library and Oxford University Press, 1979. 338p.

This work is an exhibit catalog of 100 bindings housed in the Pierpont Morgan Library. Featured are specimens from Coptic Egypt, gilded and bejeweled monastic treasure bindings from the early Middle Ages, and masterpieces of leather ornamentation from royal libraries of the 16th century. The binding styles are discussed along with additional related material. [Chapter Three]

196. Neufeld, M. Lynne and Martha Cornog. *Abstracting and Indexing Career Guide*. 2nd ed. Philadelphia, PA: National Federation of Abstracting and Information Services, 1986. 63p.

Provides an overview of the field including background information and training guidelines and an evaluation of growth areas. [Chapter Nine]

197. *The New Professionals*. Proceedings of the Singapore-Malaysia Congress of Librarians and Information Scientists. Singapore 4–6, September 1986. Edited by Ajita Thuraisingham. Aldershot, Eng.: Gower, 1987. 356p.

Some of these essays contain useful information related to training librarian-bibliographers. [Chapter Nine]

198. Oakman, Robert L. "The Present State of Computerized Collation: A Review Article." In: *Proof: The Yearbook of American Bibliographical and Textual Studies*. Edited by Joseph Katz. Columbia, SC: University of South Carolina Press, 1972. Vol. 2. pp. 333–348.

Although large strides have been made toward computerization of textual collation, the literature up to this date indicates that there is still much left to do. [Chapter Five]

199. Ojala, Marydee. "End User Searching and Its Implications for Librarians," *Special Libraries*, 76 (Spring 1985), pp. 93–99.

Contends that the trend in online searching is toward end user access of online systems. [Chapter Eight]

200. Olmstead, Marcia. "The End User and the Librarian: Perspectives from a DIALOG Trainer," *Canadian Library Journal*, 43 (February 1986), pp. 49–53.
Olmstead concludes that end users are a growth population and the role of the information intermediary changes to meet this growth. [Chapter Eight]

201. Padwick, Eric William. *Bibliographical Method: An Introductory Survey*. Cambridge, Eng.: James Clarke, 1969. 250p.
This work is a clear and concise survey of the methods used in analytical and descriptive bibliography. Includes a digest of methods employed in bibliographical description formulated by Greg and Bowers. [Chapters Two and Five]

202. *Paper—Art & Technology*. Paulette Long, Editor. San Francisco, CA: World Print Council, 1979. 118p.
A collection of essays based on an international conference covering the history and techniques of papermaking (both European and Japanese), scientific explanations about the chemistry, texting, and care and conservation of papers, and the artistic uses of paper. [Chapter Three]

203. *Paper Structure and Properties*. Edited by Anthony Bristow and Peter Kolseth. New York: Dekker, 1986. 390p.
In this work paper is presented as a material with a structure which can be described at different levels. It also describes the characterization of different aspects of its structure and indicates their importance. [Chapter Three]

204. Pearce, M. J. *A Workbook on Analytical & Descriptive Bibliography*. London: Bingley; Hamden, CT: Linnet, 1970. 110p.
A combination of workbook and manual. Pearce gives instruction, examples, and exercises for the student of descriptive bibliography. This is an excellent companion volume to Bowers and Gaskell. [Chapter Five]

205. Piercy, Esther J. "Is Bibliographic Standardization Possible?" *Library Resources and Technical Services*, 4 (Winter 1960), pp. 67–70.
From a cataloging perspective, Piercy examines the issues involved in the standardization of bibliographic citations. [Chapter Six]

206. Pollard, Alfred William. *Alfred William Pollard: A Selection of His Essays*. Compiled by Fred W. Roper. Metuchen, NJ: Scarecrow Press, 1976. 244p. (The Great Bibliographers Series, No. 2)
A collection of essays that provides some insight into the life and works of this accomplished British bibliographer and author. [Chapters One and Five]

207. ________. "The Arrangement of Bibliographies," *The Library*, New series, 10 (1909), pp. 168–187.
In this landmark article, Pollard delineates various arrangements of entries for bibliographies, e.g., alphabetical, classified, and chronological. [Chapter Six]

208. ________. "Practical Bibliography," *The Library*, 4 (1903), pp. 151–162.
This is a reply to J. D. Brown's article by the same title. Pollard, of the British Museum,

deplores Brown's narrowness of mind and defends scholarly studies of books and their production. [Chapter One]

209. *Printing and Society in Early America*. Edited by William L. Joyce and others. Worcester, MA: American Antiquarian Society, 1983. 322p.
A collection of essays by scholars attempting to unite bibliographical study with the history of the book, and presenting approaches to the impact of printing and the early book trade in the United States. These studies are thoroughly documented and abound with both facts and insights. [Chapter Three]

210. Proctor, Robert George Collier. *Bibliographical Essays*. New York: Burt Franklin, 1969, ©1905. 243p.
In the tradition of the great British bibliographers, Proctor (1865–1903), was instrumental in the formulation of ideas that influenced those who developed the new bibliography—Greg, Pollard and others. [Chapters One and Five]

211. *Prospects for Change in Bibliographic Control*. Edited by Abraham Bookstein, Herman H. Fussler, and Helen F. Schmierer. Chicago: University of Chicago Press, 1977. 138p.
Provides an analysis of current studies of bibliographic control. Includes papers presented at the thirty-eighth annual conference of the Graduate Library School of the University of Chicago. [Chapter Four]

212. Reichmann, Felix. "Acquisitions Librarians as Bibliographers," *College and Research Libraries*, 10 (July 1949), pp. 203–207.
Indicates that acquisitions work, by its nature, is an excellent training ground for bibliographers. [Chapter One]

213. Richmond, Phyllis A. "Document Description and Representation," *Annual Review of Information Science and Technology*, 7 (1972), pp. 73–102.
Discusses basic principles related to bibliographic citation practices and critically evaluates codes and policies. [Chapter Six]

214. Robinson, Anthony Meredith Lewin. *Systematic Bibliography: A Practical Guide to the Work of Compilation*. 4th ed. With an additional chapter by Margaret Lodder. New York: Saur, 1979. 135p.
An excellent formulation of basic principles involved in the practical work of compiling enumerative bibliographies. This work is intended for the nonlibrarian who is obliged to undertake bibliographical work as well as for the student of librarianship. [Chapters Four and Six]

215. Robinson, Ivor. *Introducing Bookbinding*. New York: Watson-Guptill, 1968. 112p.
An "introduction to tools, equipment, and materials of the craft together with sequential demonstration of basic bookbinding skills likely to be within the scope of the average school, college or similar miscellaneous hand bindery." Includes many illustrations and a list of suppliers. [Chapter Three]

216. Rota, Anthony. "Points at Issue: A Bookseller Looks at Bibliography," *Information Reports and Bibliographies,* 15, No. 2 (1986), pp. 16–21.

Booksellers provide much of the raw material for bibliography according to Rota. He builds a case for greater cooperation between bibliographers and booksellers in the standardization of bibliographic organization, accuracy in presentation and adequate updating of standard descriptive bibliographies. [Chapter Three]

217. Rothman, Irving N. "The Houston Editing Desk and Editing Frame," *Papers of the Bibliographical Society of America,* 72 (1978), pp. 130–136.

Rothman discusses his device which is designed to facilitate the organization of flat copy during the process of editing and proofreading. [Chapter Five]

218. Sable, Martin H. "Systematic Bibliography as the Reflection of Reality," *International Library Review,* 13 (January 1981), pp. 17–24.

Sable is concerned about bibliographies accurately reflecting what they purport to represent. He appeals for better bibliographic organization. [Chapter Four]

219. Sadleir, Michael. *Michael Sadleir, 1888–1957*. By Roy Stokes. Metuchen, NJ: Scarecrow Press, 1980. 154p. (The Great Bibliographers Series, No. 5)

A publisher and novelist as well as bibliographer, Sadleir's bibliographical works covered the full spectrum of Victorian life. This biographical study provides insights into Sadleir's contributions to analytical bibliography. [Chapters One and Five]

220. Saltman, David. *Paper Basics: Forestry, Manufacture, Selection, Purchasing, Mathematics, Metrics, and Recycling*. New York: Van Nostrand Reinhold Co., 1978. 223p.

Presents a well designed survey covering background material and information on the paper market. Particularly useful in its treatment of how modern paper is made. [Chapter Three]

221. Savage, Ernest A. "Casual Amateur in Bibliography," *The Library Association Record,* 65 (October 1963), pp. 361–365.

The author recounts his experiences as a bibliographer and assesses his development. [Chapter One]

222. Schlosser, Leonard B. "A History of Paper." In: *Paper—Art & Technology*. San Francisco, CA: World Print Council, 1979, pp. 2–19.

A well-written and informative brief survey of papermaking from its beginnings to the present day. Includes a number of illustrations and a bibliography. [Chapter Three]

223. Schneider, Georg. *Theory and History of Bibliography*. Translated by Ralph Robert Shaw. New York: Columbia University Press, 1934. 306p.

Schneider covers the development of bibliographic study in Part 5 (pp. 271–293) of this work. Although decidedly nationalistic, especially in the treatment of Conrad Gesner, this work does provide a good discussion of historical movements in the field. [Chapter Two]

224. Shapiro, Fred R. "Earlier Uses of Bibliography and Related Terms," *Notes and Queries,* n.s., 31 (March 1984), p. 30.

The author briefly surveys the persons and sources responsible for early definitions of "bibliography" and related terms. [Chapter One]

225. Shaw, Ralph Robert. "Integrated Bibliography," *Library Journal*, 90 (February 15, 1965), pp. 819–822.

A plea for a systematic approach to the bibliographic description of cited materials. [Chapter Six]

226. ________. "Mechanical and Electronic Aids for Bibliography," *Library Trends*, 2 (April 1954), pp. 522–531.

Includes an excellent outline for preparing enumerative bibliographies. The information on mechanical and electronic aids is quite out of date now, but it provides insights into the beginnings of our modern electronic devices for storing and retrieving bibliographic data. [Chapter Six]

227. Shera, Jesse Hauk. "Bibliographic Organization," *Wilson Library Bulletin*, 40 (April 1966), pp. 703–705.

Shera examines the major problem of effectively organizing the records of human communication and concludes there is a long way to go. [Chapter Four]

228. ________. "Bibliographic Management," *American Documentation*," 2 (January 1951), pp. 47–54.

Shera asserts that bibliographic organization is made up of organization plus effective management. Management is the ordering of those operations that are designed to bring about, as efficiently as possible, the planning, development, execution, and evaluation of those services for which the enterprise is established, which, in this case, is information transfer through effective bibliographic organization and management. [Chapter Four]

229. ________. *Documentation and the Organization of Knowledge*. Edited with an introduction by D. J. Foskett. Hamden, CT: Archon, 1966. 185p.

This collection of Shera's essays on the relationship of documentation and librarianship deals specifically with the history of classification systems and of documentation, information gathering, habit studies, coordinate indexes (including machine-searched coordinate indexes), automation of library operations, education for librarianship, recruiting of technical-information specialists, and the role of the library in society. [Chapter Four]

230. ________, with Margaret E. Egan, eds. *Bibliographic Organization*. Chicago: University of Chicago Press, 1951. 275p.

This work contains the papers presented at a symposium of bibliographers and documentalists at the fifteenth annual conference of the Graduate Library School of the University of Chicago. It was the first book in the English language to treat systematically all aspects of the problem of recording, organizing, locating, and transmitting the published and unpublished records essential to scholarship. [Chapter Four]

231. Shoemaker, Richard H. "Bibliography (General)," *Library Trends*, 15 (January 1967), pp. 340–346.

Provides one of the best and most concise discussions on the structure and purpose of bibliography. Accompanying his general survey of the two branches of the field are many examples. This article is a good starting place for the beginner. [Chapter One]

232. Shores, Louis. *Basic Reference Sources: An Introduction to Materials and Methods*. Chicago: American Library Association, 1954. 378p.
Although out of print and largely out of date, this work is still valuable for retrospective sources. Shores also provides an excellent discussion of types, methods, and uses of reference materials including bibliographies. [Chapters One and Eleven]

233. Silva, Georgette and Harold Love. "The Identification of Text Variants by Computer," *Information Storage and Retrieval*, 5 (October 1969), pp. 89–108.
An extensive description of a working program for collating texts. The procedure identifies text variants ranging from minute differences in punctuation and spelling to additions and deletions of larger portions of text. [Chapter Five]

234. Simon, H. R. "Introduction: Why Analyze Bibliographies?" *Library Trends*, 22 (July 1973), pp. 3–8.
The introduction to an issue of *Library Trends* in which the essays deal with the paths along which scholarly information is being transmitted. Bibliographies are worth investigating under carefully and ethically defined conditions. [Chapter Seven]

235. Simon, Oliver. *Introduction to Typography*. 2nd ed. Edited by David Bland. London: Faber and Faber, 1963. 164p.
Attempts to "describe as briefly as possible . . . some of the many fundamentals of book production," A good place to find information on type in the production of the printed page. [Chapter Three]

236. Sinks, Perry Wayland. *The Reign of the Manuscript*. Boston: R. G. Badger, 1917. 176p.
Traces the development of the manuscript from ancient times to the modern age. Emphasizes different types of writing materials and problems associated with their preservation. [Chapter Three]

237. Small, Christopher. *The Printed Word, An Instrument of Popularity*. Aberdeen, Scot.: Aberdeen University Press, 1982. 176p.
A very general historical survey of printing from Gutenberg to the twentieth century. [Chapter Three]

238. Smith, F. Seymour. *Bibliography in the Bookshop*. 2nd ed.; rev. London: Deutsch, 1972. 193p.
Deals with the function of the bookseller in the community and the techniques of search, from the use of bibliographies, trade bibliographies, and terminology, to daily practice. [Chapters One and Three]

239. Staveley, Ronald. *Notes on Subject Study*. London: Deutsch, 1962. 144p.
Provides a basic overview of subject bibliography and analysis of problems encountered in this area. [Chapter Four]

240. ________, with Ia C. McIlwaine and John H. St. J. McIlwaine. *Introduction to Subject Study*. London: Deutsch, 1967. 288p.
An in-depth discussion of the problems and functions of subject bibliography as well as subject study generally. [Chapter Four]

241. Steinberg, Sigfrid Henry. *Five Hundred Years of Printing*. 3rd ed. Baltimore, MD: Penguin, 1974. 400p.
A standard historical survey that traces the close interrelation between printing and culture. It covers not only a long time-span but also particular topics like censorship, best-sellers, popular series, and the connection between printing and education, language, and literature. [Chapter Three]

242. Stevens, Norman. "Evaluating Reference Books in Theory and Practice," *The Reference Librarian*, No. 15 (Fall 1986), pp. 9–19.
Examines the importance of the reviewing experience, the definition of a reference book and the distinction between theory and practice. Relates to the evaluation of bibliographies as reference sources. [Chapter Seven]

243. Stokes, Roy. *Bibliographical Control and Service*. New York: London House and Maxwell, 1965. 125p.
Asserts that bibliographical control is essential to the advancement of knowledge and research. The author devotes considerable space to notes on bibliographies and reference books, starting with universal bibliographies and concluding with research materials. The notes themselves are succinct and well phrased. [Chapter Four]

244. ________. "Bibliography," *Encyclopedia of Library and Information Science*, 1 (1969), pp. 407–419.
Although Stokes outlines the various aspects of bibliography as a study, he emphasizes the role of critical bibliography and its major contributors. [Chapters One and Five]

245. ________. "Critical Bibliography," *Encyclopedia of Library and Information Science*, 6 (1971), pp. 276–286.
A good general summary of critical or analytical bibliography accompanied by pertinent examples. [Chapter Five]

246. ________. *The Function of Bibliography*. 2nd ed. Aldershot, Eng.: Gower, 1982. 201p.
Presents a guide to all aspects of bibliography. In the process, Stokes describes a revolution in the study of literary texts. Reference is also made to the work of great bibliographers of the past as well as to that of several who are still living. [Chapters One and Five]

247. ________. "Historical Bibliography," *Encyclopedia of Library and Information Science*, 36, Suppl. 1, (1983), pp. 219–229.
Along with summarizing the various elements in historical bibliography, Stokes explores its impact upon historical studies in general. [Chapter Five]

248. ________. "Textual Bibliography," *Encyclopedia of Library and Information Science*, 30 (1980), pp. 392–401.

The primary aspects of textual bibliography are explored accompanied by examples and applications. [Chapter Five]

249. *The Structure and Physical Properties of Paper*. Edited by H. F. Rance. Amsterdam: Elsevier Scientific, 1982. 288p.
Modern papermaking focusing on structure and properties are treated in this study. [Chapter Three]

250. Stueart, Robert D. *The Area Specialist Bibliographer: An Inquiry into His Role*. Metuchen, NJ: Scarecrow Press, 1972. 152p.
This is an excellent study that explores the ways in which area specialists in libraries function as bibliographers. [Chapter One]

251. Subramanyam, K. "Information Technology and Library Education," *Encyclopedia of Library and Information Science*, Vol. 41, Supplement 6 (1986), pp. 161–193.
The effect of new technology on library education especially online systems are explored in this informative article. There is an extensive bibliography provided. [Chapter Nine]

252. Summers, Montague. *Montague Summers: A Bibliographical Portrait*. By Frederick S. Frank. Metuchen, NJ: Scarecrow Press, 1988. 277p. (The Great Bibliographers Series, No. 7)
Reveals the bibliographic prowess of this rather controversial writer and bibliographer. Included are some essays on Summers' career, selections from his writings, a chronology, and an extensive bibliography. [Chapters One and Five]

253. Tanselle, G. Thomas. "The Bibliography and Textual Study of American Books," *American Antiquarian Society*. *Proceedings*, 95, pt. 1 (1985), pp. 113–151.
Tanselle offers suggestions for strengthening research on the history of the book in America and introduces general criticisms about procedures or methods in the use of sources for historical study. In general, this essay is a cogent and eloquent plea for the use of bibliographical analysis to study the physical characteristics of books. [Chapter Five]

254. ________. "Bibliographers and the Library," *Library Trends*, 25 (April 1977), pp. 745–762.
Examines the problems that arise between librarian-bibliographers and those in other subject disciplines. Also included is a discussion of other areas of tension related to libraries and their bibliographic functions. [Chapter One]

255. ________. "Bibliography and Science," *Studies in Bibliography*, 27 (1974), pp. 55–89.
A discussion of bibliographers and the scientific aspects of their practices and procedures. [Chapter One]

256. ________. *The History of Books as a Field of Study*. Chapel Hill, NC: Hanes Foundation, Rare Book Collection/Academic Affairs Library, The University of North Carolina at Chapel Hill, 1981. 16p.
A carefully developed, thoughtful rationale of the vital role that the analysis and description

of the physical book play in the study of the transmission of texts and in wider studies of publishing history and the spread of ideas. [Chapter Five]

257. ________. "The Periodical Literature of English and American Bibliography," *Studies in Bibliography*, 26 (1973), pp. 167–191.
An extensive treatment of English language periodicals related to the study of bibliography with a discussion of their value and limitations. Tanselle also provides insights into the problem of access and bibliographic control by comparing, historically, attempts to index the literature. [Chapter Twelve]

258. ________. "A Proposal for Recording Additions to Bibliographies,"*Papers of the Bibliographical Society of America*, 62 (1968), pp. 227–236.
Proposes the creation of a clearing-house that would assist in the correcting and updating of standard bibliographies. [Chapter Six]

259. ________. *Selected Studies in Bibliography*. Charlottesville, VA: Published for the Bibliographical Society of the University of Virginia by the University Press of Virginia, 1979. 506p.
A collection of eleven essays by Tanselle previously published in *Studies in Bibliography*. They deal with various issues in analytical bibliography and show Tanselle's extraordinary thoroughness and expertise. [Chapter Five]

260. ________. "The State of Bibliography Today," *Papers of the Bibliographical Society of America*, 73 (1979), pp. 289–304.
Tanselle surveys the state of analytical bibliography and explores such problem areas as the hostility of literary critics to analytical bibliography and the need for rigorous historical study of bibliographical elements. [Chapter Five]

261. ________. *Textual Criticism Since Greg: A Chronicle, 1950–1985*. Charlottesville, VA: The University Press of Virginia, 1988. 176p.
The three essays contained in this collection provide a comprehensive history of modern textual editing. [Chapter Five]

262. Taylor, Archer. "The History of Bibliography." In: *Essays in History and Literature*. Edited by Heinz Bluhm. Chicago: Newberry Library, 1965, pp. 193–199.
This essay is not a chronological treatment of the subject, as the title might suggest. Taylor discusses bibliographical achievements in general, drawing upon the works of several noted bibliographers. The author is a well-known bibliographer himself, and this article is valuable for its view of the discipline. [Chapter Two]

263. *Theories of Bibliographic Education: Designs for Teaching*. Edited by Cerise Oberman and Katina Strauch. New York: Bowker, 1982. 233p.
Contains a collection of outstanding essays on library orientation and bibliographic searching. The uses of bibliographies in information seeking is well documented. [Chapter Nine]

264. Thompson, Anthony Hugh. "Knowledge or Format—Which Comes First?" *Audiovisual Librarian*, 12 (November 1986), pp. 184–188.
Libraries that put books (printed formats) before audiovisual materials (nonprint formats)

and try to segregate the two, put format before knowledge according to Thompson. He makes a case for audiovisual materials being more effective in the learning process. [Chapter Three]

265. Thompson, Lawrence S. "The Humanist Bibliographer," *American Book Collector*, 6 (October 1955), p. 11.
Indicates that anyone can bring together a collection of books and list them, but to make bibliography meaningful is the task of the scholar. Whatever the task may be, the humanist bibliographer must combine all the critical skills at his or her command and bring them to bear on the subject. [Chapter One]

266. ________. *Who Killed Bibliography?* Berkeley, CA: Peacock Press, 1965. 15p.
This brief polemical essay provides an interesting examination of certain elements such as inaccuracy, indifference to detail and inconsistency and their detrimental effect upon the study of bibliography. [Chapters One and Nine]

267. Thorpe, James Ernest. *The Use of Manuscripts in Literary Research: Problems of Access and Literary Property*. New York: Modern Language Association of America, 1974. 40p.
Valuable as a guide to the use of manuscript materials in research and the problems related to access and use. [Chapter Three]

268. Tracy, Walter. *Letters of Credit: A View of Type Design*. Boston: Godine, 1986. 219p.
Covers the history of type and type-founding in the 20th century. Well presented with many illustrations. Discusses both type design and major type designers. [Chapter Three]

269. Turner, Robert K., Jr. "Analytical Bibliography and Shakespeare's Text," *Modern Philology*, 62 (August 1964), pp. 51–58.
Turner examines analytical bibliographical methods and Shakespearian texts focusing on the use of the Hinman Collator. [Chapter Five]

270. UNESCO/Library of Congress Bibliographical Survey. *Bibliographical Services, Their Present State and Possibilities of Improvement*. Washington, DC: Library of Congress and Paris: UNESCO, 1950. 2v. and Appendix.
This report by Verner W. Clapp was prepared as a working paper for an international conference on bibliography. Volume One analyzes the state of bibliographic services at that time and projects their future role. Volume Two is a survey of national bibliographies and proposals for their development. Volume Three is an appendix by Kathrine Oliver Murra, containing notes on the development of the concept of current complete national bibliography. [Chapter Four]

271. U.S. Library of Congress. *Papermaking: Art and Craft*. Washington, DC: Library of Congress, 1968. 96p.
A guide to an exhibition held at the Library of Congress. It gives a brief historical survey of papermaking and includes many illustrations and a bibliography. [Chapter Three]

272. U.S. Library of Congress. General Reference and Bibliography Division. *Bibliographical Procedures and Style: A Manual for Bibliographers in the Library of Congress*. By

Blanche Prichare McCrum and Helen Dudenbostel Jones. Washington, DC: Library of Congress, 1954. (Reprinted in 1966) 133p.

This work is a very thorough and systematic manual for compiling bibliographies. The format is that which the Library of Congress used prior to the adoption of the Anglo-American Cataloging Rules 2 in 1978. [Chapter Six]

273. ________. *Current National Bibliography*. Compiled by Helen F. Conover. Washington, DC: Library of Congress, 1955. (Reprinted by Greenwood Press, 1968) 132p.

Contains an annotated listing of the records of publishing in sixty-seven countries. In addition, it lists periodicals and newspapers. Although this work is dated, it is still useful for retrospective study. [Chapter Four]

274. Updike, Daniel Berkeley. *Printing Types: Their History, Forms and Use—A Study in Survivals*. 3rd ed. Cambridge, MA: Belknap Press of Harvard University, 1967. 2v.

This is one of the more authoritative studies on typography. Its intent "is to supply a basis for the intelligent appreciation of the best printing types through the study of their history, forms, and use." [Chapter Three]

275. Van Hoesen, Henry Bartlett, with the collaboration of Frank Keller Walter. *Bibliography, Practical, Enumerative, Historical: An Introductory Manual*. New York: Burt Franklin, 1971, ©1928. 519p.

A thorough discussion of types of enumerative bibliographies. Although somewhat dated, this work is must reading for the bibliographer who wants to develop an understanding of basic bibliographical methods. [Chapters Four and Six]

276. Vigil, Peter J. *Online Retrieval Analysis and Strategy*. New York: Wiley, 1988. 242p.

Presents in a clear and useful style the concepts and principles of online interactive searching applicable for both searching and creating a database. [Chapter Eight]

277. Voet, Andries. *Ink and Paper in the Printing Process*. New York: Interscience, 1952. 213p.

"This book is intended as an introduction to the physics and chemistry of ink and its interaction with paper in the printing process. It is written for the more experienced graphic arts specialist with a basic understanding of science." Although it is somewhat technical, this book does offer some information on the development of printing ink that can be understood by the layperson. [Chapter Three]

278. Walford, Albert John. "Plight of the Subject Bibliographer," *Library Review*, 14, No. 134 (Summer 1960), pp. 403–408.

Walford is concerned with subject bibliographers not being able to do their job effectively because of constraints of time and resources. [Chapter One]

279. Wali, Moti Lal. "Study of Bibliography and its Role in the Academic World," *Herald of Library Science*, 22 (July–October 1983), pp. 204–215.

The author defines bibliography and discusses the various branches. Stresses the need of bibliography, prescribes a method for compiling and analyses its role in scholarly writing. [Chapter One]

280. Wall, Thomas B. "Nonprint Materials: A Definition and Some Practical Considerations on Their Maintenance," *Library Trends*, 34 (Summer 1985), pp. 129–140.
Examines the nature and scope of nonprint materials and suggests various preservation practices and techniques. [Chapter Three]

281. Watson, Aldren A. *Hand Bookbinding: A Manual of Instruction*. New York: Bell, 1963. 95p.
One of the better introductory manuals on the subject. Includes a good historical overview of the development of bookbinding from ancient China to the present day. Contains many helpful illustrations. [Chapter Three]

282. Weatherford, Richard M. "Computers in the Antiquarian Book Trade," *AB Bookman's Weekly*, 77 (January 6, 1986), pp. 14, 16–18.
This is one of a series of articles by Weatherford examining the various computer applications to the antiquarian book trade including bibliographical practices. [Chapter One]

283. Weber, David C. "Bibliographical Blessings," *Papers of the Bibliographical Society of America*, 61 (1967), pp. 307–314.
Lamented is the fact that few students training to become librarians enter the field of cataloging or other types of direct bibliographic activity. Weber makes a solid case for the virtues of bibliographic work as rewarding and exciting. [Chapter Nine]

284. Whittaker, Kenneth. *Systematic Evaluation: Methods and Sources for Assessing Books*. London: Bingley, 1982. 154p.
Although the subject matter of this small study is directed toward book selection in the library, it does offer excellent guidelines for evaluating bibliographies. [Chapter Seven]

285. Whouley, Mary. "Guide for the Analysis and Evaluation of Bibliographical Instruments." (Unpublished paper prepared for Course L230, Bibliographical Organization, School of Librarianship, University of California, Berkeley, July 15, 1969), 27p.
An excellent study of the process of bibliographical evaluation. Whouley analyzes the elements of bibliographical instruments and develops a set of standards by which they can be evaluated in terms of their potential usefulness. [Chapter Seven]

286. Wilborg, Frank Bestow. *Printing Ink: A History with a Treatise on Modern Methods of Manufacture and Use*. New York: Harper, 1926. 299p.
A well-written, nontechnical study of the development of printing ink through the first part of the twentieth century. Wilborg includes a number of plates and illustrations, a bibliography of sources, and an excellent index. [Chapter Three]

287. Williams, W. P., and C. S. Abbot. *An Introduction to Bibliographical and Textual Studies*. New York: The Modern Language Association of America, 1985. 106p.
Designed as an introduction to the intricacies of analytical bibliography, describing modern bibliographical and textual investigation. The reference bibliography is especially useful, well organized, solid in coverage, and with commentary that is economical and informative. [Chapter Five]

288. Williamson, Derek. *Historical Bibliography*. Hamden, CT: Archon Books, 1967. 129p.

An introduction to the history of books and book forms, and to the scope and purpose of analytical bibliography. [Chapter Five]

289. Williamson, William L. "Thomas Bennet and the Origins of Analytical Bibliography," *The Journal of Library History*, 16 (Winter 1981), pp. 177–186.

An historical study of Bennet's contributions to analytical bibliography previous to Greg, Pollard and others who have been credited for developing the discipline. [Chapter Five]

290. Willoughby, Edwin Elliott. *The Uses of Bibliography to the Students of Literature and History*. Hamden, CT: Shoe String Press, 1957. 105p.

Written primarily for students of literature and printing history, Willoughby provides a basic discussion of both major aspects of the field focusing mainly on analytical bibliography. [Chapter Five]

291. Wilson, Patrick. *Two Kinds of Power; An Essay on Bibliographical Control*. Berkeley, CA: University of California Press, 1978, ©1968. 155p.

Provides a powerful, rigorous, and detailed study of bibliographical control. Because of its highly abstract and theoretical nature, this work is not for beginning students. It is, however, an important contribution to information theory. [Chapters One and Three]

292. Winans, Robert B. "The Beginnings of Systematic Bibliography in America up to 1800: Further Explorations," *Papers of the Bibliographical Society of America*, 72 (1978), pp. 15–35.

This is an authoritative examination of early systematic bibliographies in America and is an expansion of Jesse Shera's article published in 1951. Includes a chronological list at the end. [Chapter Four]

293. Winckler, Paul A., ed. *Reader in the History of Books and Printing*. Englewood, CO: Information Handling Services, 1978. 406p.

This collection of readings is designed to provide the reader with introductory material on the evolutionary history of graphic communication emphasizing the role of books and printing in recording, preserving, and disseminating ideas and their impact on society. Contains a number of illustrations along with a bibliography appended to each chapter. [Chapter Three]

294. Winterich, John T. *Early American Books & Printing*. New York: Dover Publications, 1981, ©1935. 252p.

A general survey of books and printers of pre- and post-colonial America, up to the time and works of Washington Irving. There are chapters on early American newspapers and periodicals, printshops and their tools, and a final word on bibliography and book collecting. [Chapter Three]

295. Wolf, Edwin, 2nd. "Historical Grist for the Bibliographical Mill," *Studies in Bibliography*, 25 (1972), pp. 29–40.

An excellent discussion on American historical bibliography and what is needed for further investigation. [Chapter Five]

296. Wyer, James Ingersol. "Practical Bibliography," *Bulletin of Bibliography*, 3 (July 1902), pp. 21–23.

Practical bibliography, as defined by Wyer, is the ability to find promptly and to record as completely as possible, all the data and information concerning the literature of any subject. He then makes a case for the development of adequate bibliographic instruments and the need for well trained bibliographers. Included is a brief but important discussion on annotated bibliographies and their importance to scholarly research. [Chapter Four]

297. Wynar, Bohdan S. *Introduction to Bibliography and Reference Work; A Guide to Materials and Sources*. 4th ed. Littleton, CO: Libraries Unlimited, 1967. 310p.

The historical development of bibliography as a discipline is treated on pages 44–46. Wynar's historical overview is a clear and concise, although brief, discussion. What is valuable here is his analysis of the current status of the discipline. He also defines the areas within the study of bibliography and includes a list of references. [Chapters One, Two, and Three]

NAME INDEX

The Name Index below is limited to personal names only. Corporate entries or institutions are included in the Subject Index. Page numbers preceded by "(b)" indicate that the name is included in a bibliographic citation. Page numbers preceded by a "(n)" indicate that the name appears in a note.

SUBJECT INDEX

TITLE INDEX

In the index entries below article titles are enclosed within quotation marks. Titles of book or monograph material are in italics. The surnames of authors or editors are contained within parentheses.